THE HEROIC IMAGE IN FIVE
SHAKESPEAREAN TRAGEDIES

THE HEROIC IMAGE
IN FIVE
SHAKESPEAREAN
TRAGEDIES

BY MATTHEW N. PROSER

PRINCETON, NEW JERSEY

PRINCETON UNIVERSITY PRESS · 1965

Publication of this book has been
aided by the Ford Foundation program
to support publication, through
university presses, of works in the
humanities and social sciences

Printed in the United States of America
by Princeton University Press, Princeton, New Jersey

ACKNOWLEDGMENTS

All quotations from the texts of Shakespeare's plays are taken from Neilson and Hill's *The Complete Plays and Poems of William Shakespeare*, Cambridge, Mass.: The Riverside Press of Houghton Mifflin Co., 1942. The section on *Coriolanus* appeared in an earlier form under the title "Coriolanus: The Constant Warrior and the State" in *College English*, XXIV (April 1963), 507-512.

I would like to express my sincere thanks to Professor Brents Stirling of the University of Washington for his advice and criticism of my work and to note my indebtedness as well to Professors Arnold Stein and William Irmscher of the same university. I would like to thank Professor Robert Frank of The Pennsylvania State University for reading this book when it was still in manuscript form and for giving much needed encouragement. My thanks also to Professor J. Mitchell Morse for advice on the *Macbeth* chapter and to Professors Leonard F. Dean of the University of Connecticut and C. L. Barber of Indiana University for commentary and suggestions. My gratitude also to Mrs. James Holly Hanford of Princeton University Press for her help in preparing this book for the press; to Miss Karen McGuire, a student at the University of Connecticut, for her help in proofreading; and to Miss Carol Babcock, also a student at the University of Connecticut, for her help in preparing the index. To my wife, who has read, typed, reread and proofread, my debt is infinite.

CONTENTS

CONTENTS

THE HEROIC IMAGE IN FIVE
SHAKESPEAREAN TRAGEDIES

BIBLIOGRAPHICAL ABBREVIATIONS

APSR	*American Political Science Review*
AR	*Antioch Review*
CE	*College English*
ELH	*Journal of English Literary History*
EIC	*Essays in Criticism*
HR	*Hudson Review*
JEGP	*Journal of English and German Philology*
KR	*Kenyon Review*
MLQ	*Modern Language Quarterly*
MLR	*Modern Language Review*
MP	*Modern Philology*
N&Q	*Notes & Queries*
PMLA	*Publications of the Modern Language Association of America*
RES	*Review of English Studies*
SAB	*Shakespeare Association Bulletin*
SR	*Sewanee Review*
SNL	*Shakespeare Newsletter*
SQ	*Shakespeare Quarterly*
SS	*Shakespeare Survey*
TSLL	*Texas Studies in Literature and Language*
UTQ	*University of Toronto Quarterly*
WVUB	*West Virginia University Bulletin*

INTRODUCTION

I am interested in the symbolic aspects of the Shakespearean tragic hero's mind and conduct and in the relationship between his thoughts and actions. In these essays I have centered my attention upon five plays: *Julius Caesar, Macbeth, Othello, Coriolanus,* and *Antony and Cleopatra.*

For me the tragedy in each of these plays partly ensues because of the discrepancy between the main character's self-conception and his full humanity as it is displayed in action. Briefly my idea is this: although in each tragedy we find a major character who is confronted by a critical situation, the action the hero takes is as much determined by his conception of himself, his "heroic image," as by exterior circumstances. This heroic self-image is often implied in various key speeches the character makes. It has both public and private aspects. On the one hand, the image suggests a certain public role, a *persona* the hero takes for the sake of action; on the other, it captures what the hero feels are vital aspects of his most personal self. The image is gauge to the hero's hopes, wishes, aspirations—his impulse to play the heroic part. But insofar as the image is a symbolic reality, in its very nature it must fail to capture the entire human reality of the man. The image, in short, is a kind of metaphoric simplification. Or to put the matter another way, the protagonist fails to see or suppresses the ambiguity cast upon the image by the total reality of his situation, and in neglecting this ambiguity he simplifies that situation disastrously.

The image itself intimates the sort of action the main character must take if he is to fulfill his conception of his heroic identity. But since the image is emotional, not rational, action becomes an emotional matter as much as a practical one. Since the crisis in the dramatic situation places the hero's self-conception in jeopardy, the protagonist is forced to prove to himself that he is the man he believes he is, or at least, hopes he is. From this standpoint, conduct becomes in part a series of symbolic acts, poses, stances, and gestures which seek to define the heroic image in action. The image conveyed to the audience by the protagonist's language becomes, let us say, an enacted image, an enacted "word."

In attempting to enact the image, be it that of the Roman patriot, as in Brutus' case, or that of the constant warrior, as in Coriolanus', the hero sacrifices his humanity and others' as well for the sake of a mental illusion, a heroic conception, which his own human nature ultimately defeats. Thus if the heroic image embodies the man's aspirations and dreams, and his sense of his own capacities, it also embodies the illusory quality of the nobility in the image. Only the hero's death allows us to abstract the nobility that was in the man and to see whether and how much he has made the image a "true" image. For the hero's death converts the living man into an image of himself, and therefore he can, despite his failure in action, become a symbol of the nobility he sought to represent—provided his death is sufficiently heroic in proportion. More broadly speaking, however, the image itself, its reality, to our eyes at least, remains Janus-faced, an index to the hero's triumph and his defeat: to the complete tragedy.

The result of the protagonists' self-dramatizing endeavors, their attempts to enact an image, is a series of tragedies which exposes the discrepancy between man's self-conception and himself, between his aspirations and limitations, between his words and deeds. But it is also a series of tragedies in which the human animal is limited by the context in which he finds himself, or which he makes for himself. The kind of context is different in each play, and it is this difference, aside from the distinguishable natures of the heroes, which allows latitude for the variety of approaches I have taken in the respective chapters. Because of the differences in the situations surrounding the protagonists, it is necessary to recognize those special thematic factors complicating my informing idea and to give them their just due. For instance, *Julius Caesar* is a tragedy in which politics and history serve as limitations for the major character. They are the chief contexts, among others, within which Brutus must act. It is important, therefore, to establish the meaning of the contexts while showing how they relate to Brutus and how Brutus relates to them. Intensive study of the self-image arises after we have come to understand the relationship between politics and history implied by the play and their importance as reflections of both Brutus' personal and universal limitations as a man. In order to do this we must investigate other important characters who surround Brutus and, in addition, various constellations of imagery which evoke important historical and political concepts. From these elements and Brutus' connection with them emerges the principal thematic issue: the quandary of the moral man forced into political action, the kind of action which places not merely the man's morality, but all human morality, in doubt.

In *Othello* the situation is quite different. Our context

is neither political nor historical. Rather, it is intensely personal. The tragedy's suggestiveness is less social than that of *Julius Caesar,* and more "psychological." Therefore we may feel free to investigate intensely "psychological" matters, while we remain aware that an investigation of Othello's psychology is an investigation of universal human nature (just as we must remain aware that an investigation of Brutus' "social" reality is nevertheless also an investigation of his personality as well as of human nature in general). Since we are immediately confronted with personal issues from the outset of *Othello,* the Moor's self-image is a matter of consequence from his very first entrance. With this entrance, Othello presents the domestic and personal problem which is to form the heart of the play: his marriage to Desdemona. The part Othello's self-image plays in the destruction of this marriage, in the destruction of Othello and Desdemona themselves, is one of the principal questions to be resolved in the chapter.

It can be seen that the thematic problems I am dealing with in both *Julius Caesar* and *Othello* are principally moral and psychological, although there is some variation in emphasis on these matters in each discussion. The same generalization can be made about my analyses of *Macbeth* and *Coriolanus.* In the former I have attempted to show the moral implications of Macbeth's self-image while examining his psychological deterioration as a human being. But I might have made this statement in just the opposite way. Clearly morality and psychology are not distinct issues in *Macbeth,* but are two aspects of the same human problem. (This is true, of course, for the other plays as well.) *Coriolanus,* once again, like

Julius Caesar, is complicated by politics. In fact, so paramount are the political issues in their moral importance, so inextricably are the various classes in the Roman state entangled in the tragedy of *Coriolanus,* that we have in this play Shakespeare's most complete tragedy of state. *Antony and Cleopatra,* however, offers new issues and additional complications. Here the moral and psychological questions, though of much importance, are intertwined with another thematic element, one which makes itself increasingly apparent as we move on to the tragi-comedies.

If in plays like *Julius Caesar* or *Macbeth* Shakespeare evokes the awful discrepancy between personal ambitions and public aims and reveals an almost anguished concern over this discrepancy, in *Antony and Cleopatra* we receive the impression that Shakespeare has come to recognize that political order, organization, and empire cannot be separated from the personal ambitions of world leaders. The political leader in making order makes his own order. Thus with "stability" necessarily come the calculating strategies and distasteful frigidity of an Octavius Caesar. Equally, Shakespeare recognizes the anarchic quality in the sensual life Cleopatra represents, but he pays homage to the force of Cleopatra's magical power and delineates the claims of the human heart and the imaginative mind. These claims are recognized most fully in Cleopatra's poetry, which magnifies Antony's self-image and her own, even as her more satirical remarks deflate Antony's heroic posture. In the end, Cleopatra's poetic empire stands because of its power to capture our imaginations. Caesar, that most prosaic and practical of men, conquers Egypt; but Cleopatra, although we acknowledge her failings, and Antony's, captures us. Her language, gestures, and theatrics—her "artistry"—immortalize her and her lover before our very eyes. Therefore the nature of her artistry becomes a thematic question of some importance in *Antony and Cleopatra*.

It should be evident by this time that in these discussions I am not concerned with the problem of defining tragedy or tragic character except as such definitions are implied by what I more concretely state in the pages to follow. To all intents and purposes I accept those traditional definitions of tragedy which see in its "form" the pitiful and awe-provoking fall of a prince because of fortune, fate, and character. I subscribe as well to those definitions which see in tragedy's "content" an intensified engagement with those high moral and spiritual dilemmas arising out of the universal human predicament. But for me, the whole issue of "heroics" is held up by Shakespeare to the closest scrutiny. In the heroic image each central character chooses can be found the measure of his aspiring nature and the index to the self-deception and even egotism which allows such a man to mistake an image for reality, and to act upon the image. Each man, nevertheless, must be examined in his own right; for in each tragedy our evaluation of the man and his tragedy cannot be separated from our evaluation of the circumstances in which he finds himself. The part the heroic image plays in each chapter is determined by the breadth and quality of the thematic material each drama offers. What I have tried to provide is a certain fullness of interpretation which will not make the plays conform to any single preconception of my own. Instead

I have tried to show how the preconception plays its role in each of the tragedies; how it is a significant thread tying in any number of other thematic features encompassed in the action and imagery; how it is a force worth investigating in its own right; and how it is used by Shakespeare in conjunction with the other themes and problems which make each play a distinguishable work of art.

I

BRUTUS:

THE IMAGE OF THE PATRIOT

At the heart of *Julius Caesar* lies the issue of freedom—
freedom not merely in its political sense, but in its philosophical meaning as well. The conspirators' cries for
"liberty," however, are not a call to which *we* should
react with the simple emotionalism of the masses; nor
should we fail, on the other hand, to admit a certain
justice in these cries. Rather, our purpose, and Shakespeare sets it for us, is to hear the cries in a context of
limitations which attempt in action to define and expose
the term itself. These limitations are, at their narrowest,
personal: they stem from important traits of the chief
characters themselves. At their broadest, they are universal, presenting as they do an insight into the nature
of man. In between come politics and history. These,
however, though we must discuss them, are not the real
subject of our story. Brutus is. Politics and history are
the contexts in which Brutus finds himself, and loses
himself.

We begin with history because it is the first limitation
Shakespeare evokes in *Julius Caesar*. Caesar, who came
"in triumph over Pompey's blood" initiates the typical
Elizabethan cycle of divine vengeance. Caesar kills Pompey and disrupts the state; Brutus kills Caesar and
disrupts the state; Antony conquers Brutus and temporarily restores the state. In this light both Brutus and
Antony become agents of the divine will, even though
acting by means of their own will. They are seen as
subject to the very roles they choose; indeed, looking

at their position from this historical standpoint, we might say their roles choose them.

Shakespeare uses the figure of the dead Pompey to confirm history's cyclical quality in *Julius Caesar*. During the first half of the play our eyes are continually directed back to his image and his image is continually associated with blood, blood which is answered by that of the other characters. The play has scarcely started before Pompey becomes an object of our attention:

> O you hard hearts, you cruel men of Rome,
> Knew you not Pompey? Many a time and oft
> Have you climb'd up to walls and battlements,
> To tow'rs and windows, yea, to chimney-tops,
> Your infants in your arms, and there have sat
> The live-long day, with patient expectation,
> To see great Pompey pass the streets of Rome;
> And when you saw his chariot but appear
> Have you not made an universal shout,
> That Tiber trembled underneath her banks
> To hear the replication of your sounds
> Made in her concave shores?   (I.i. 41-52)

In a few lines comes the reference to Caesar's triumphant march over Pompey's blood. A little later, when the conspirators are about to seek out Brutus, we find they must first repair to "Pompey's porch." The term is mentioned twice along with a somewhat more interesting one: "Pompey's Theatre." Here the idea of acting out roles, indeed, of acting out historical roles, suggests itself. Finally, when Caesar is murdered he dies at the foot of Pompey's statue, his blood besmearing its base. The death scene is a kind of fulfillment of Calpurnia's dream. In the dream Calpurnia saw Caesar's statue "like a fountain with an hundred spouts" running "pure blood." Now Pompey's statue runs with Caesar's blood. By reawakening us to the historical referent, Pompey, in this climactic scene, Shakespeare ties together the deaths of the two leaders. That Shakespeare is consciously linking the two deaths with an artistic device of his own can be demonstrated by reference to Plutarch. In Plutarch Calpurnia's dream mentions neither statue nor blood: "For she dreamed that Caesar was slain, and that she had him in her arms." Plutarch also speaks of another version, that given by Titus Livius. In it, once again, no blood or statue is mentioned: ". . . the Senate having set upon the top of Caesar's house, for an ornament . . . a certain pinnacle, Calpurnia dreamed that she saw it broken down, and that she thought she lamented and wept for it." But the blood is described by Plutarch in the assassination scene, and in conjunction with the idea of Pompey's "revenge" on Caesar. Plutarch pictures Caesar as driven ". . . against the base whereupon Pompey's image stood, which ran all of a gore-blood till he was slain. Thus it seemed that the image took just revenge of Pompey's enemy, being thrown down on the ground at his feet, and yielding up the ghost there. . . ." We have evidence, therefore, that Shakespeare, although he may have derived the idea for the cyclical "arrangement" of his play from Plutarch, nevertheless conceived the appropriate artistic method by which this arrangement could be symbolically suggested. The blood "connection" between Pompey's statue and the statue in Calpurnia's dream appears to be Shakespeare's inspiration.

But Shakespeare links the deaths of Pompey and Caesar in two other ways as well. Before Caesar actually dies he allows us to see him as a piece of "living statuary." This is in the scene leading up to his assassination, the scene during which he is "immovable" in his "constancy." Shakespeare's third method lies in a word. By having Cassius refer to Caesar earlier as a "colossus," Shakespeare provides us with an image that will be useful for establishing irony in the death scene and one which also relates to the other "statue" images. However, the link between Pompey and Caesar lies not only in the idea that the two men are visualized as statues or that Caesar tends to build verbal monuments to himself (just as Marullus in the play's opening scene builds a verbal monument to Pompey). The link is also the blood spilled in the respective deaths of the two men—blood concretely visualized for us on the stage during Caesar's assassination at the base of Pompey's statue. At this point in the action, if it has not done so before, blood takes on a certain historical significance in addition to the moral significance which first meets the eye. It becomes a river to past and future, and a means to an end.

In view of this historical limitation, Brutus' "error" in murdering Caesar may be understood as a kind of violation of history itself. He becomes isolated in the major action with which he is involved. If he sees himself as the possible "savior" of Rome at moments, he does not seem to realize, or at least, realize adequately, that Caesar also probably thinks of himself as the "savior" of Rome; witness Caesar's ready acceptance of Decius Brutus' interpretation of Calpurnia's dream. Decius says the dream "signifies that from you great Rome shall suck/Reviving blood. . . ." Indeed, Brutus fails to realize that Caesar very likely thought he was saving Rome when he triumphed over Pompey, and that Pompey, when he was in power, undoubtedly also saw himself as the state's savior. A recognition of this sort might have suggested that "saving Rome" by means of killing a "tyrant" can produce a kind of tyranny in itself, perhaps the very sort of tyranny from which someone else is going to have to "save Rome." Where Brutus is concerned, this of course proves to be the case. Antony and Octavius are to be the new "liberators."

But the recognition mentioned, significantly, is one that Brutus never makes at the point where he could most use it. Quite to the contrary, he feels it morally incumbent upon himself to act in order to avert the tyranny he fears will come from Caesar. He believes, and most humanly, that he dare not wait to see what the future brings. It is in this sense that he isolates himself in one climactic event and in what he envisions as the necessity for that climactic event. The sign of this historical isolation is that in having accepted the role of assassin (which by the very nature of the "liberating" deed he must take on at the same time he assumes the role of "savior") he makes the mistake of not following through and killing Antony. He fails, that is, to provide adequately against future opposition. This, however, might be interpreted as a purely political mistake. On the other hand, it is symptomatic of his ultimate failure to plan any future course of action at all. It is as if he expected Caesar's death to settle everything—to bring about liberty through the magic of the "sacrifice" itself. He attempts to make one act *the* critical act, but a critical act without possible adverse historical repercussions. His error, politically speaking, may be that having decided to take no chances with Caesar he does not follow through and decide to take no chances with Antony. His error, historically speaking, is his not having looked over his shoulder at

Pompey's statue at the crucial moment to examine it in its broadest historical light. Instead of facing the doubt-ful qualities in his act, he suppresses them. He cannot concede history's complexity. He simplifies it, shall we say, in order to give himself the "freedom" to act.

The idea of freedom returns us once again to our start-ing point and to the second limitation we must deal with, that of "politics." Where this subject is concerned in *Julius Caesar* the general critical tendency has been to choose political sides. Thus the questions "Is Shakespeare for republicanism and against Caesarism, or vice versa?" or "Is Shakespeare for democracy and against monarchy?" have seemed to some students of the play extremely im-portant ones.[1] The answers, of course, depend upon our definitions of republicanism and Caesarism, of democracy and monarchy, and upon our corresponding attitudes toward these forms of government. However, since the government of Rome was not a democracy in a strictly contemporary sense and since the term "Caesarism" is not Shakespeare's, it becomes difficult to draw any firm

---

[1] See introduction to "Julius Caesar," *The Works of Shakespeare*, ed. Dover Wilson (Cambridge, 1949). Wilson finds Caesar represen-tative of tyrannical "Caesarism" and Brutus heroic in the cause of freedom. See also the following: introduction to *Julius Caesar*, New Arden edition, ed. T. S. Dorsch (London, 1955). According to Dorsch we are really supposed to be sympathetic toward Caesar despite his shortcomings. His ambition is an "essential accompaniment of greatness." Brutus, on the other hand, is not to be trusted. His "ineffectual" idealism involves him in a "senseless" and dreadful murder (pp. xxxix-xl); Virgil K. Whitaker, *Shakespeare's Use of Learning* (San Marino, Calif., 1953), pp. 224-250. Whitaker finds Shakespeare not a republican, but a supporter of the Renaissance dicta against rebellion. Caesar is the symbol of monarchy and Shakespeare does more to ameliorate Plutarch's case for Caesar than to denigrate it; James E. Phillips Jr., *The State in Shakespeare's Greek and Roman Plays* (New York, 1940). Phillips suggests that the whole purpose of the play is to point out the virtues of absolute monarchy.

conclusions on the subject. If, for instance, we focus our attention upon Caesar's conduct during the scene in which his death occurs, we may be able to build up a case against Caesar the Tyrant. This would be true even though we are aware the conspirators' appeal for Publius Cimber is very possibly a put-up job. Caesar's attempts at self-glorification are distasteful whatever the reason;[2] they are even threatening. But the question is, do they make him a complete tyrant? The answer must be "no" if we are considering real acts of tyranny prior to the scene of the assassination.[3] We may condemn him for his pompous manner, but pomposity alone does not make a tyrant. The fairest attitude to take toward Caesar when considering him next to Brutus and when considering the parties they represent is that suggested by Adrien Bonjour: ". . . we are emotionally attracted, and repulsed, by both sides; our sympathies are made to oscillate from one hero, and one party, to the other, according to the side of the Roman medal we are shown, obverse and then reverse, until the swing of the pendulum eventually ceases, suspended as it were between two equal forces, and then the sympathies are perfectly divided between

[2] The issue of the "braggart" or "thrasonical" Caesar is one of the most discussed in the criticism of this play. To consider the spread of interpretation and its background, see: M. W. MacCallum, *Shakespeare's Roman Plays and Their Backgrounds* (London, 1925), pp. 179-180; Wilson's introduction to *Julius Caesar*, p. xxiii; Harry Morgan Ayres, "Shakespeare's *Julius Caesar*," *PMLA*, XXV (June 1910), 183-227; Ernest Schanzer, "The Problem of *Julius Caesar*," *SQ*, VI (Summer 1955), 297-308; and Joan Rees, " 'Julius Caesar'—An Earlier Play, and an Interpretation," *MLR*, L (April 1955), 135-141.

[3] The same question might also be asked of the disappearance of Flavius and Marullus, "put to silence" for disrobing Caesar's images. The expression, which seems patently ominous when first considered, after further thought takes on a disturbing ambiguity.

the victim of the crime and the victim of the punishment."[4]

Again, looking more closely at Caesar, who in a sense is practicing for the role of king throughout the play, we might ask ourselves if it is not, after all, merely the commanding pose he strikes, the image he presents, which frightens and alienates the conspirators and convinces them he already *is* a tyrant; in short, we might ask ourselves if it is not this very pose which ironically brings about his death, rather than his deeds themselves. Thought of in this light, Cassius' dialogue with Casca in Act I, scene iii is particularly rewarding. Cassius, in sounding out his friend, works himself up to a high pitch of "oratory" during which he and Casca list some of Caesar's offensive "deeds." A careful look at these "deeds" is revealing. And we ought to note that this scene occurs before Caesar tries to play god at the capitol. *That* offense has not occurred yet and hence can play no part in Cassius' argument. Cassius says:

> Now could I, Casca, name to thee a man
> Most like this dreadful night,
> That thunders, lightens, opens graves, and roars
> As doth the lion in the Capitol,—
> A man no mightier than thyself or me
> In personal action, yet prodigious grown
> And fearful, as these strange eruptions are.
>
> (I.iii.72-78)

A few lines later Casca says:

> Indeed, they say the senators to-morrow
> Mean to establish Caesar as a king;

4 Adrien Bonjour, *The Structure of Julius Caesar* (Liverpool, 1958), p. 24.

And he shall wear his crown by sea and land
In every place, save here in Italy.   (I.iii.85-88)

By line 103, Cassius is saying:

And why should Caesar be a tyrant then?

The speech in which this line occurs is followed by an important response by Casca:

Hold,—my hand.
Be factious for redress of all these griefs,
And I will set this foot of mine as far
As who goes farthest.   (I.iii.117-120)

However, we might react to Casca's statement concerning "all these griefs" by simply asking "what griefs?" since Cassius and Casca have presented not one concrete deed by which Caesar may be condemned. Instead Cassius constructs a frightening analogy which substitutes for concrete detail. Caesar has grown as "prodigious" and "fearful" as "this dreadful night" of prodigies, which "thunders, lightens, opens graves, and roars." Moreover, though attempting to prove that Caesar is a "man no mightier than thyself or me," he apparently misses the deeper implications of Caesar's common humanity even as he points it out. It is as if he actually took the image of the "prodigious" Caesar for the real thing. Cassius and Casca respond, so to speak, to a picture of Caesar they have in their minds, the picture, strangely enough, Caesar himself at moments tries to present.[5] But they, like Caesar, do not seem to realize that the picture is not

[5] Schanzer takes a similar position in "The Problem of *Julius Caesar*," pp. 305-306. For him Caesar remains nothing but an image in the eyes of the various other characters throughout the play; indeed, Caesar himself is constantly constructing an image of himself for his own and others' benefit.

necessarily the man, that the very hollowness they see in Caesar's pose, the very weaknesses Cassius remarks in his character, weaknesses he has pointed out to Brutus in the previous scene, indicate the degree to which he is incapable of power unless, in their fear of his outward pose, they give it to him. And in a sense this is precisely what they do by murdering him. Caesar's "spirit" is never stronger than after his death.

Thus does Cassius ask why Caesar should be a tyrant, and thus do Cassius and Casca see Caesar as a tyrant before he has become one. For the fact is that, barring the scenes of Caesar's entrance to and exit from the festival games, we see the "tyrant" always through the eyes of the conspirators, eyes which can and do perceive some truth, but which are perhaps less objective than our own. It is not until Act II, scene ii, the scene with Calpurnia, that we really get a direct view of Caesar, and there we see a man whose posturings may strike us more as absurd than threatening. It will be observed, however, that we have come back to the issue of "freedom" once again. Cassius' statement,"Why should Caesar be a tyrant then?" is set in a discussion of free will. Cassius says he can free himself of political bondage by killing himself if he so chooses; therefore Caesar should not be a tyrant since, according to Cassius, men are intrinsically free by nature and tyranny is futile since men need not be bound by it. Nevertheless, Cassius' conception of Caesar, and the way in which he plans to act in reference to that conception, suggests that Cassius is not free, but constrained by the limitation of his own way of seeing things and by the fear this way of seeing things engenders.[6] Thus a strong

[6] Thus, perhaps, the heavy concentration on the word "fear" where all the main characters are concerned, particularly in the

irony plays around Cassius' words on freedom, an irony
of which he is totally unaware. This irony at the same
time reveals how choosing political sides in *Julius Caesar*
fails to bring out the play's deepest significance.[7] To the
conspirators the issues at stake may appear to be republicanism and monarchy (which here means tyranny); but
the virtues and failings of these forms of government are
never really demonstrated in the play. In a very real way
they are beside the point, for the terms do not reflect
concrete actuality; they reflect the attitudes of the conspirators to Caesar, a man in power whom the conspirators subjectively associate with an abstraction called
"tyranny"; they reflect the attitudes of the conspirators to
themselves, men apparently out of power who subjectively
associate themselves with an abstraction called "republicanism" or "liberty." But the men and the abstractions
subjectively associated with them never quite get together.
At the center is the chaos of worlds yet unrealized.

Politics in *Julius Caesar*, then, may be looked upon
more profitably as a kind of limitation rather than as an
"explanation" of the play. The conspirator's political use
of language greatly influences their attitudes. In saying
this, however, we ought to realize immediately that if the
limitation lies in an accepted usage of inadequately de-

---

first act. See I.ii.79-80; I.ii.196; I.ii.198; I.ii.211-212; I.iii.54; and
I.iii.70.

[7] As examples of such interpretations see H. B. Charlton's *Shakespearean Tragedy* (Cambridge, 1952), pp. 69-82; J. E. Uhler's "*Julius
Caesar*—A Morality of Respublica," *Studies in Shakespeare*, ed. Arthur D. Matthews and Clark M. Emery (Coral Gables, Fla., 1953),
p. 106; Hazelton Spencer's *The Art and Life of William Shakespeare*
(New York, 1940), p. 227; Phillips' *The State in Shakespeare's Greek
and Roman Plays*, p. 179; Bernard R. Breyer's "A New Look at
Julius Caesar," *Essays in Honor of Walter Clyde Curry* (Nashville,
Tenn., 1954), pp. 161-180; and Dover Wilson's introduction to his
edition of *Julius Caesar*.

fined words (*liberty, tyranny, republican, freedom,* etc.)
and if this accepted usage limits the conspirators' com-
prehension of the situation and themselves, it is, at the
same time, the conspirators themselves who use the words
in a perverted and self-deceptive manner. In this light,
the political limitation may be understood as a personal
limitation, for the defining force can be said to lie in the
way the conspirators conceive of the various political abstractions they employ, and in the way they "see" Caesar
and "see" themselves. The same thing may be said of
their "historical" limitation. From the standpoint we have
just taken, it is the conspirators' failure to view history
from the right perspective that causes their "historical"
difficulty. At the root of the problem lies a defect of vision.
In *Julius Caesar* the kind of personal limitation we have
been discussing is most fully demonstrated in the figure
of Brutus.

In speaking of Brutus we might best begin with Marc
Antony's terminal assessment of him:

> This was the noblest Roman of them all.
> All the conspirators, save only he,
> Did that they did in envy of great Caesar;
> He only, in a general honest thought
> And common good to all, made one of them.
> His life was gentle, and the elements
> So mix'd in him that Nature might stand up
> And say to all the world, "This was a man!"
>
> (V.v.68-75)

We will take the point of view that Antony's words are
just. Brutus *was* the noblest of all the conspirators. He
did not kill Caesar because he envied him and there is
nothing in the play which indicates that he feared Cae-

sar's power because he wanted it for himself. When thinking over the dangers of Caesar as king, Brutus is as much concerned about Rome in general as he is about himself —perhaps even more. He is clearly depicted as having the quality of true gentleness in various famous scenes in the play. Of all the conspirators, of all the play's characters, including Caesar, whose grandiloquence is almost humorous at times, and Antony, who may well strike us as an opportunist who is a bit too quick to let "mischief" do its work, Brutus remains the most honorable, the most morally conscious.

Yet despite these high qualities Brutus is not a god. Though he does not envy Caesar, his fear of him ultimately puts Brutus into the position of a Caesar. Though he is concerned with the well-being of Rome, he succeeds in sacrificing Rome in order to live up to a preconception of himself. Though he reveals a gentleness both moving and admirable, he is cruel enough to kill his friend. These are the indictments we can make against Brutus, and they are valid indictments. Though he is the noblest of the Romans, he is not noble enough to prevent what he perhaps inadvisedly conceives of as liberty from turning into political and moral chaos.

However, before going on to Brutus' personal limitations we ought to say a few more words about his historical and political ones, moving, as it were, from his outer world to his inner as we do so, indeed sometimes inadvertently mixing the two, since they are by nature parts of the same world. In order to do this a review of one or two matters may be helpful.

We have stated that Julius Caesar is somewhat adept at erecting verbal monuments to himself. This capacity is displayed most fully, of course, in the scene of his murder.

We noted too some of the significance of these "verbal monuments" in relation to Cassius' description of Caesar as a "colossus" and in relation to the statue of Caesar as it appears in Calpurnia's dream. The dream, we recall, was connected with Caesar's death at the base of Pompey's statue, Pompey's blood being the historical connection between the two Roman leaders.

This "historical connection" in the end engages Brutus; his blood becomes a tributary to the river of blood which flows from past to future. When we observe the setting of "statuary" about which this "blood-dimmed tide" rises, it becomes appropriate that one of the notes by which Cassius hopes to further Brutus' involvement in the conspiracy (notes supposedly from the populace) is "set . . . up with wax/Upon old Brutus' statue." Cassius' maneuver is obvious. By having the note placed on the statue of Brutus' patriotic ancestor, he seeks to bring Brutus into the plot by playing upon his historical awareness of his family's traditional "republicanism."[8] And we can see from Brutus' reactions to this sort of appeal that Cassius' technique works, at least to a degree. At such points in the play where like appeals are made, Brutus' conception of history becomes limited by the role his ancestors played in liberating the Rome of Tarquin. This might appear a rather perverse statement, considering that the liberation of Rome from Tarquin seems to have been a good thing. Yet it might be argued that a perspective which focuses

[8] R. W. Foakes, "An Approach to *Julius Caesar*," *SQ*, V (Fall 1954), 259-270. According to this interpretation, Caesar stands for power and royalty, Brutus for honor. But both men's actions show how they do not "live up to" their names and reveal the conflict between their public names and themselves. Foakes points out that the name of Rome and the words "Roman" and "liberty" are also important in this sense. None of the men live up to the name of Roman except in their very deaths (p. 270).

on this act of liberation as a guidepost to action dismisses a broader historical perspective, a perspective which sees the shedding of blood as the beginning of a long series of violent deaths, a cosmically directed "eye for an eye." From this angle, Brutus fails to take into consideration at certain key moments a broader limitation, but one of considerable moral force (especially where Elizabethans were concerned). Thus it might be said that Brutus, like Cassius and Casca, reacts to an idea—the idea of liberty as it is imaged forth in his conception of his ancestors. This idea, as mentioned earlier, is isolated in time to the extent that Brutus does not fully plan for what is to take place after "liberty" is achieved and to the extent that he does not relate the projected murder to the death of Pompey. The symbol that represents to Brutus the idea of liberty, the statue of old Brutus, is lifted out of circumstances somewhat different from those existing under Caesar, and is transported to the present. At the same time Shakespeare inserts the statue into the system of statue imagery he has established in regard to Caesar and Pompey.

As to politics (in its contemporary, somewhat derogatory sense)—this is a reality which Brutus cannot openly accept. Cassius is capable of doing things for strictly political reasons, whatever he may say about "liberty" and "tyranny." Moreover, he does not feel self-conscious about this ability. He can, for instance, ask Marc Antony directly after the murder: "Will you be prick'd in number of our friends;/Or shall we on, and not depend on you?" —this after Cassius has spent some time trying to convince Brutus that Antony should be slain. Brutus, on the other hand, could never make such a concession with equanimity. Often by will power alone, or so it would seem, he sustains himself upon idealistic heights of abstraction even in the face of political necessity. During the great quarrel scene in Act IV Brutus is capable of condemning Cassius at once for the means by which he had obtained gold to pay his soldiers and for not sending Brutus financial assistance. Moreover, he flies out of Cassius' reach with remarks such as:

> Remember March, the ides of March remember:
> Did not great Julius bleed for justice' sake?
> What villain touch'd his body, that did stab
> And not for justice?   (IV.iii.18-21)

His position, of course, is unassailable. We are even justified in admiring it. Yet we ought to realize that in his purely idealistic conception of politics, he willfully refuses to acknowledge a part of reality with which he is nevertheless very much involved. He seeks to keep the issues abstract even when his actions or language, as in the gold business, tell us he is acting in his own way as politically as Cassius. The hard necessity of politics, then, is something Brutus will not fully recognize as a limitation, and we might commend him for this. Conversely, it becomes clear that the refusal of acknowledgment, the willful sustaining of politics on an abstract level, is the means, and a somewhat self-deceptive means, for getting himself to act.

This brings us round again to the idea that Brutus' limitation is in part a personal one—the way in which he envisions the issues with which he is concerned. The limitation is particularly well demonstrated in his soliloquy of "decision" in Act II. Reducing matters to their simplest, Brutus' primary error seems to be that he ap-

plies his distrust of monarchy in general to Caesar specifi-
cally, while still aware that Caesar has not yet become a
tyrant.[9] Here his own argument is of importance:

> Crown him? That—
> And then, I grant, we put a sting in him
> That at his will he may do danger with.
> Th' abuse of greatness is when it disjoins
> Remorse from power; and to speak truth of Caesar,
> I have not known when his affections sway'd
> More than his reason.   (II.i.15-21)

Brutus' evaluation of "greatness" which disjoins remorse
from power is a valid one, but his admission that in his
experience he has not known Caesar's passions to "sway"
his reason partially undercuts his argument. Perhaps
feeling this to be true, Brutus begins to argue himself
out of a position which would lead *him* to "remorse":

> But 'tis a common proof
> That lowliness is young Ambition's ladder,
> Whereto the climber-upward turns his face;
> But when he once attains the upmost round,
> He then unto the ladder turns his back,
> Looks in the clouds, scorning the base degrees
> By which he did ascend. So Caesar may;
> Then lest he may, prevent.   (II.i.21-28)

"So Caesar may!" This is the point of "decision" or
"rationalization," depending upon the perspective taken.
With the statement Brutus reaches the outposts of tem-

[9] See MacCallum, p. 204 and John Palmer, *Political Characters of
Shakespeare* (London, 1945), p. 7. Palmer believes that Caesar already is a tyrant, but that Brutus is ". . . obsessed by a pedantic
horror of kingship, by the republican traditions of his family and
by hypothetical evils which may follow upon a preconceived theory
of government."

poral reality. It is also the point to which we ought refer Caesar's conduct directly preceding his assassination. There the issue is the appeal for Publius Cimber, and we will recall that during the scene Caesar demonstrates the very kind of arrogance Brutus fears. But we must realize that Caesar's conduct in this scene may be somewhat predetermined by the conspirators themselves. First of all, Caesar, having been informed earlier by Decius Brutus that the senate plans to give him a crown, may feel it necessary to prove to the senate that he deserves the honor by showing precisely how "kingly" he can be. Secondly, judging by the quality of Caesar's response to the appeal for Publius Cimber (it reaches belligerence at points) we might conclude that the conspirators have purposely chosen an especially sensitive issue to present so that Caesar will "prove" himself stubborn and arrogant and hence "justify" the coming assassination. If this is the case, the conspirators have to a degree forced Caesar into a highly charged situation, a crisis situation, in which all parties instead of acting rationally are trying to prove things they already believe to be true. (But the irony is that the impulse to prove something to oneself indicates there is actually some unconscious doubt about it. The act of "proof" is used to corroborate preconceptions instead of to reveal objective truth.) Hence the importance of the preceding scene, the one during which Caesar invites the conspirators to wine and acts courteously and ingratiatingly toward them. The contrast of Caesars in each of the scenes mentioned may reveal that the great man has possibilities, at least, in the more personal areas of his life, and that to characterize him as a tyrant and act on that characterization does not do justice to the whole man.[10]

[10] On the other hand, it ought to be acknowledged that Caesar's

This difficulty of acting on a preconceived characterization is what stands out in the last part of Brutus' soliloquy of "decision." We noted before that Brutus' main argument against Caesar was his feeling that monarchy (a corruptive force according to Brutus) is bound to corrupt Caesar although Caesar is not corrupted yet: "He would be crown'd:/How that might change his nature, there's the question." The "question" is precisely to the point. According to Brutus' conception of monarchy, the answer must be: the change will be for the worse.[11] However, without Brutus' preconception, it would be possible to argue in just the opposite manner. Of course, we must not draw the conclusion that an Elizabethan audience would condemn the forthcoming murder because of their reluctance to kill kings *per se*. As Irving Ribner points out, Shakespeare's Caesar, derived as he is from Plutarch's, remains ". . . an adventurer, who, by force has replaced another adventurer, Pompey, and is now reaping the civil acclaim which had been Pompey's. . . ."[12] Ribner notes

---

gracious and amenable frame of mind at this point may be attributable to the promising interpretation Decius Brutus has just given Calpurnia's dream, and to his learning from the same source that the senators intend to confer a crown upon him.

[11] Ernest Schanzer, in "The Tragedy of Shakespeare's Brutus," *ELH*, XXII (March 1955), 9, argues that Brutus' "opposition to kingship rests on his fears of the corrupting effect of power, not on the nature of its office."

[12] Irving Ribner, "Political Issues in *Julius Caesar*," *JEGP*, LVI (January 1957), 11. Ribner notes that as an ordinary man, Caesar, in Elizabethan eyes, could not "aspire to kingship" (p. 3). He adds later that the Elizabethans admired the Roman political organization and accepted the republican form of government as one of the three classic forms. The great fear for Elizabethans was change of government once one of these forms had been long established. For Ribner, Brutus' dilemma is that of a good man who uses evil means to achieve worthy ends. Ribner's ideas on Brutus and Caesar appear in a readapted form in *Patterns in Shakespearian Tragedy* (London, 1960), pp. 53-64.

that Caesar could not appeal to Elizabethans as a king who rules with the sanction of divine right, and who therefore is a minister of God on earth. But Ribner goes on to say that Shakespeare's Caesar, like Plutarch's, and like Muret's, Grevin's, and Garnier's as well, is a would-be tyrant; and he claims for the speech of "decision" in the orchard complete logic. Yet Ribner quotes only lines 21-28 of this speech, neglecting those lines in which Brutus says he has not known when Caesar's "affections sway'd more than his reason." Nor does he quote the last lines of the speech, which are equally ambiguous in their own way, lines we shall deal with momentarily. Ribner is correct, however, when he suggests that *Julius Caesar* is not a play about "an actual king or a symbol of kingship who is murdered by rebellious citizens";[13] he is correct, that is, if he means the play is not one which treats material identical to that in *Gorboduc*. He is inaccurate, however, in not recognizing that Caesar, although he is not a king, functions as a symbol of kingship in Brutus' mind (not in the Elizabethans'). Brutus responds to Caesar's symbolical suggestiveness as well as to his "ambition."

In this light, Brutus makes his "decision" at least partly out of a preconception about monarchy, a preconception probably abstracted from Rome's experience with such tyrants as Tarquin. But were Brutus able to see the possibility of such a thing as a good king, he might draw quite a different conclusion about the necessity for Caesar's murder, a conclusion built on Caesar's past conduct, which Brutus admits has consisted of reason unswayed by passion. Brutus' subsequent reference to Tarquin in this very scene (when he finds the note planted

13 *Ibid.*, p. 12.

by Cassius) reveals Cassius' success in appealing to Brutus on an emotional level, not a deliberative one. Brutus' response to the note is: "Shall Rome stand under one man's awe? What Rome?/My ancestors did from the streets of Rome/The Tarquin drive when he was call'd king" (II.i.52-54). But Brutus' vision is limited by Rome's experience with Tarquin—a kind of political experience. He uses Tarquin's reign to characterize what Caesar must necessarily become and creates an image of potential tyranny which moves him to action:[14]

> And, since the quarrel
> Will bear no colour for the thing he is,
> Fashion it thus: that what he is, augmented,
> Would run to these and these extremities;
> And therefore think him as a serpent's egg
> Which, hatch'd, would, as his kind, grow
> mischievous,
> And kill him in the shell.   (II.i.28-34)

The idea of "fashioning" is paramount in this speech. The word itself is important because it is repeated several times in the play. Cassius, for instance, says Casca will tell of the offering of the crown to Caesar "after his sour fashion" (I.ii.180). Cicero describes the night before the murder as a "strange-disposed time" and adds, "But men may construe things after their fashion/Clean from the purpose of the things themselves" (I.iii.33-35). Brutus says he will "fashion" Caius Ligarius for the conspiracy (II.i.

---

[14] L. C. Knights, "Shakespeare and Political Wisdom," *SR*, LXI (Winter 1953), 43-55. See especially p. 53. Knights pinpoints the Shakespearean view of "politics" in this clear and well-written discussion of *Julius Caesar* and *Coriolanus*. He further points out that Brutus makes of Caesar a political abstraction of a king or tyrant and neglects Caesar's humanity.

220). At the end of the play Brutus notes that "slaying is the word,/It is a deed in fashion" (V.v.4-5). The ambiguity of "fashion" is especially arresting when we connect the word with the use of such terms as "construe," "mend," and "seems" at various points in the play. "Fashioning" more and more takes on the possible supplementary meaning of "creating" issues without sufficient grounds, that is, of "misconstruing everything."

As used in the context of lines 28-34 of the "orchard speech," the simplest meaning of "fashion" is: "Let us look at the situation this way." But in so looking Brutus "fashions" an image which in fact forms the substance of the last portion of his argument. Instead of looking at Caesar as man and friend, he verbally transforms him into a "serpent's egg," the snake within being mortally dangerous. In a sense we might say that Brutus concludes his argument and "convinces" himself he is right by reacting to the very image he has created instead of reacting to Caesar in all his complexity. He frightens himself through his own strong powers of imagination (much as Macbeth does) and, as Adrien Bonjour suggests, decides to kill Caesar "For fear of what might fall, so to prevent/The time of life."[15]

Brutus' ability to create vivid metaphors is a trait revealed at various points throughout *Julius Caesar*. It is notable, too, that whenever he does create these metaphors, they tend to be cosmetic, to hide the dreadful physical reality of the act under consideration. Even the "egg" metaphor is cosmetic to the degree that it blackens Caesar, thus making the assassination appear more justifiable, more an act of "liberty." By the same token, he tends to "whiten" himself and the conspirators. When

[15] Bonjour, pp. 49-50.

plotting the assassination with this group of men, he chooses to see himself as a kind of sacrificial high priest rather than as a "butcher":[16]

> And, gentle friends,
> Let's kill him boldly, but not wrathfully;
> Let's carve him as a dish fit for the gods,
> Not hew him as a carcass fit for hounds.
>
> (II.i.171-174)

And later, after the assassination, we find Brutus admonishing the conspirators:

> Stoop, Romans, stoop,
> And let us bathe our hands in Caesar's blood
> Up to the elbows, and besmear our swords;
>
> (III.i.105-107)

But the murder scene itself and the episode of the "blood bath," rather than supporting Brutus' sonorous metaphor (with its suggestiveness of sacrifice and purification) destroy it. For in the murder scene what strikes us most is Caesar's "Et tu Brute"; and in the following episode, as Leo Kirschbaum points out, far from being taken in by the incantatory tone, the ritualizing protectiveness of the language which accompanies the action, we are instead repelled by what we see before us and by Brutus' words themselves.[17] Moreover, we are meant to be repelled. For at the conspirators' feet lies the one indisputable truth: Caesar's hacked and bloody corpse, hewed "as

---

[16] Brents Stirling finds that the conflict in Brutus "has taken outward form in his attempt to purify the assassination through ceremony" (*Unity in Shakespearean Tragedy* [New York, 1956], pp. 51-52). See also Maurice Charney, *Shakespeare's Roman Plays* (Cambridge, Mass., 1961), p. 49.

[17] Leo Kirschbaum, "Shakespeare's Stage Blood," *PMLA*, LXIV (June 1949), 522.

a carcass fit for hounds." It is this very same corpse that Marc Antony displays to the populace during his long oration, an oration which further peels away the rich coat of Brutus' figurative language and more clearly reveals the bloody wounds.

This tendency of Brutus to visualize himself as a sacrificial priest, thus masking part of reality, is clearly related to the more general role he assumes for the play's action —that of "savior" or "liberator" of Rome. Where this more general role is concerned, what strikes us is the process by which the image gains power, how it becomes more defined for Brutus in increasingly emotional terms. Thus at the beginning of the process—that is, when Cassius presents his case against Caesar to Brutus—it is rather difficult to tell whether Cassius "convinces" Brutus into seeing himself as the natural inheritor of the Brutus family's patriotically republican image or whether Brutus, who seems self-possessed enough, in his silence is really allowing Cassius to display *himself.* Cassius, of course, believes he has "tricked" Brutus. When he is alone he says:

> Well, Brutus, thou art noble; yet, I see,
> Thy honourable metal may be wrought
> From that it is dispos'd. . . .   (I.ii.312-314)

Nevertheless, Brutus' last words of importance on the subject in this scene reveal admirable restraint, even a sort of refusal to fall into, at least without careful consideration, Cassius' "trap."

> That you do love me, I am nothing jealous;
> What you would work me to, I have some aim.
> How I have thought of this and of these times,
> I shall recount hereafter; for this present,
> I would not, so with love I might entreat you,

Be any further mov'd. What you have said
I will consider; what you have to say
I will with patience hear, and find a time
Both meet to hear and answer such high things.

(I.ii.162-170)

The quality of the speech, its careful phrasing and balanced rhythms, reveals certainly a character who declines
to be hoodwinked into commitments by means of an emotional appeal, but who at the same time recognizes a
modicum of justice in the implications which have been
presented to him. After having been treated to Cassius'
high rhetorical style, replete with inflated apostrophes
("Age, thou art sham'd! Rome, thou hast lost the breed of
noble bloods!") and after having witnessed Cassius' petty
backbiting of Caesar[18] (which brings out some fairly human weaknesses of Caesar rather than any concrete instances of the great man's tyranny), we can only praise
Brutus for his refusal to let emotions get the better of
him. Yet he does show Cassius where his sensitive spot is.
Cassius' remark at lines 58-62, which presents by implication the patriotic republican image for Brutus to consider,
draws a revealing response. This occurs at the end of the
sanely cautious speech mentioned above. Cassius has said:

I have heard

Where many of the best respect in Rome,
Except immortal Caesar, speaking of Brutus
And groaning underneath this age's yoke,
Have wish'd that noble Brutus had his eyes.

---

[18] Cassius' account of the swimming contest in the Tiber, when
Caesar cried "Help me, Cassius or I sink!" (I.ii.111) and Caesar's
illness in Spain, when he called for drink "as a sick girl" (I.ii.127-
128). Charney (*Shakespeare's Roman Plays*, p. 72) calls the accounts
"specious arguments."

Brutus, in concluding his response to Cassius' appeal, says:

> Till then, my noble friend, chew upon this:
> Brutus had rather be a villager
> Than repute himself a son of Rome
> Under these hard conditions as this time
> Is apt to lay upon us. (I.ii.171-175)

Brutus' implied statement that in case Caesar becomes a tyrant he would be willing to take up the patriotic role gives Cassius something to "chew upon" indeed. The remark helps to confirm Cassius' course. His part must be to make Brutus feel that Caesar's tyranny is the immediate threat he feels it is; he must exacerbate the situation and upset Brutus' moral equilibrium while at the same time delineating as reductively as possible Brutus' role. The presentation of the crown to Caesar three times during their conversation has, to be sure, helped things tremendously. If Cassius can build on this lucky moment, he can perhaps frighten Brutus sufficiently into more rapid commitment. If he can appeal to Brutus' patriotism while making him feel that the sanction of Brutus' own honorable self confers justification upon the conspiracy, he will have won his man. Cassius determines upon the following plan:

> I will this night,
> In several hands, in at his windows throw,
> As if they came from several citizens,
> Writings all tending to the great opinion
> That Rome holds of his name; wherein obscurely
> Caesar's ambition shall be glanced at. . . .
>
> (I.ii.319-324)

Cassius' plan is, of course, a success. There are several notes, but Brutus' reaction is caught for us principally in his response to the message found by Lucius on the night before the assassination. Cassius' note and Brutus' reaction to it confirm the conclusion Brutus has "intellectually" formulated. However, it is interesting to see at this point how his language begins to fall into an emotional pattern vaguely suggestive of Cassius' during their earlier conversation. Observe Brutus reading the note:

> "Brutus, thou sleep'st; awake, and see thyself!
> Shall Rome, etc. Speak, strike, redress!"
> "Brutus, thou sleep'st; awake!"
> Such instigations have been often dropp'd
> Where I have took them up.
> "Shall Rome, etc." Thus must I piece it out:
> Shall Rome stand under one man's awe? What,
>   Rome?
> My ancestors did from the streets of Rome
> The Tarquin drive when he was call'd a king.
> "Speak, strike, redress!" Am I entreated
> To speak and strike? O Rome, I make thee promise,
> If the redress will follow, thou receivest
> Thy full petition at the hand of Brutus!

(II.i.46-58)

The note, then, marks a kind of modified "deterioration" of Brutus, a new willingness to be moved by outside forces. This willingness is reflected in the increased rhetoric of his language some lines later. Brutus is about to admit the conspirators to his house. Lucius has just told him of the group of men waiting outside with "their faces buried in their cloaks." The servant's description makes Brutus suddenly aware of the doubtfulness of an endeavor which forces men to hide themselves even from darkness. Yet having recognized himself as a potential savior of his country, he manages to squelch his reservations. He has concluded that "all the populace" evidently wish him to lead the revolution because they think of him as the most noble of the Romans. The language of his speech is, barring its high metaphorical content, curiously unlike him. Note the rhetorical flourish which characterizes his diction and the new "politic" frame of mind: they may be looked upon as an indication of how much Cassius' "political" attitude has begun, at least temporarily, to infiltrate Brutus' thinking:

> O Conspiracy,
> Sham'st thou to show thy dangerous brow by night,
> When evils are most free? Oh, then by day
> Where wilt thou find a cavern dark enough
> To mask thy monstrous visage? Seek none, Con-
> spiracy!
> Hide it in smiles and affability;
> For if thou path, thy native semblance on,
> Not Erebus itself were dim enough
> To hide thee from prevention.   (II.i.77-85)

At the same time, this Machiavellian speech is informed by a tone of moral reservation, of self-disgust, or at least a sense of being trapped, of being forced from the outside into a situation which will not relinquish him. Indeed, are not the conspirators waiting at the door?

Yet Brutus' loss of mental independence does not mean that Brutus fails to have his own ideas on how a conspiracy should be run, but that he has involved himself in Cassius' brand of "politics" whether he realizes it or not. For now, apparently having forgotten his own reason

for killing Caesar—to prevent tyranny—he begins to envision his friend as a tyrant already. An example of this
new perspective occurs during his discussion of why
oaths should not be required to hold the conspirators
together:

> If these be motives weak, break off betimes,
> And every man hence to his idle bed;
> So let high-sighted tyranny range on,
> Till each man drop by lottery.   (II.i.116-119)

At this point Brutus speaks of "tyranny" as if it had been
"ranging" for a considerable length of time, when earlier
he had admitted Caesar's acts were not yet of a tyrannical
nature. His new political role has modified the clarity of
his vision, even as it has already covered his face in
shadow.

The interior modification within Brutus is, of course,
suggested in his language, and it is therefore significant
that we learn from *his* words, with their rhetorical "disguise," that the situation requires not oaths, but masks.
The conspirators, we find, must bear their parts "as our
Roman actors do," and looks must not show purposes to
the outside world. The Roman stage and the Roman
political platform blend in what sounds like the advice
of a seasoned politician. Moreover, we find that if looks
must not show purposes to the outside world, neither
must they to the inner world. For Brutus, in order to
live with himself, must strip the word "assassin" of its
habitual suggestive force, indeed must suppress the word
altogether in order to continue to visualize himself as the
patriotic savior of his country. That "savior" and "assassin" are presently part of the same reality—the same
act (in both senses of the word) cannot be consciously

admitted and felt if action is to be taken. Thus it is in his own mind that Brutus finds "a cavern dark enough to mask" his "monstrous visage."

We may observe in Brutus, then, two tendencies which help contribute to his ultimate tragedy. The first is an ability to use language at various crucial moments as a vehicle not for "reason," but for his own fears and preconceptions and to misconstrue these as "reason." He projects these fears and preconceptions into a language which magnifies the issues but at the same time blurs their complexity. The language takes on a reality in its own right, a vivid metaphorical reality which in some way disguises the less appetizing features of his chosen action; and it is to this very language that Brutus responds. This is one important reason he is capable of seeing Caesar as a serpent in the shell and himself as a patriotic sacrificial priest and then of acting upon what he "sees" rather than what Caesar most fully "is." Connected with this ability is Brutus' tendency to believe what he "sees" because he himself has "fashioned" it, because he is, we might say, Rome's acknowledged artist of the good and he knows it.[19]

This confidence in his point of view, even at the expense of other perspectives and even when other perspectives, like that of Cassius, inform his own, is revealed, for instance, in his instinctive assumption of the conspiracy's leadership and in his insistence that the plot be run according to his stipulations. However, in order to be fair to Brutus, we should point out that this capacity bears

[19] Gordon R. Smith ("Brutus, Virtue, and Will," *SQ*, X [Summer 1959], 367-379) finds at least fourteen occasions during which Brutus tends to "dominate or domineer over his fellows" (p. 368). According to Smith, Brutus is self-righteous and has a need to run everything himself. As I try to show in my text, things seem perhaps more complicated than this. But see Charney, *Shakespeare's Roman Plays*, p. 56.

an alternative interpretation. His "hard-headedness" may also reveal something of a sense of insecurity. Thus we notice that the way he wants things run (the whole impulse to sacrificial ritualizing) can be understood as a means for mollifying conscience. Mollifying conscience, nevertheless, does not necessarily imply here a strictly negative value. It can mean that Brutus at least wishes to do things for the "right" reasons (rather than for purely political ones) even if his sense of what the right reasons are is not entirely accurate. To a degree then, Brutus, though self-deceptive, reveals himself as not conscienceless but actually as in a more sympathetic position than Cassius, who for all his political "forthrightness" is still an envious man acting in a conscienceless manner.

Finally, we ought not blame Brutus' assumption of the conspiracy's leadership completely on him. For the conspirators have accentuated the point that Brutus is necessary to their plan, and when they are at last assured of his participation, they are willing enough to give him sway when he suggests, for example, that Cicero might hinder the conspiracy more than help it because "he will never follow anything/That other men begin" or when he implores the group to let Antony live. In the first case, an ironical one in that Brutus at the moment he is speaking illustrates the very trait he attributes to Cicero, no one objects to Brutus' reasoning. In the second, only Cassius objects, but the rest of the group in their silence apparently take Trebonius' position:

> There is no fear in him [Antony]; let him not die;
> For he will live, and laugh at this hereafter.

> (II.i.190-191)

Hence we might conclude that Brutus is given the

leadership for the very reason he takes it. In this scene his moral force is felt so strongly that the conspirators almost automatically and without direct verbal acknowledgment accept him as their leader. We do not sense they are merely playing up to him or "flattering" him so that he will not back out. After all, he has made his position quite clear during the speech on "oaths." There he implied his motives were strong enough not to require verbal bonds, even if theirs were not. His speech on oaths gives them the freedom to speak their minds, and we can assume they do, those of them that contribute verbally to the scene. We can say, then, that Brutus, on his part, finds himself in the position of leadership not because he demands this position, but because of the moral force of the words he speaks. For in spite of his "purifying" the assassination by presenting it in sacrificial terms, and in spite of his unconscious self-deception, it is evident that he wishes to act in a disinterested manner. What Brutus wants in this scene is not the leadership of the conspiracy, but an acknowledgment of his position. That he receives the leadership with this acknowledgment cannot justify our accusing him of "ambition." If he becomes leader of the conspirators because he believes his reasons for killing Caesar are the right reasons and because he wishes to make sure the deed itself reflects these right reasons, this is not the same as wanting power for power's sake alone—that is, out of ambition in the conventional sense of the word. Brutus, we should remember, acts because of certain beliefs, because of the way he "sees" things, not because he wishes to be king.

Thus it is fair to say, all parties contributing to his "election" as they do, that Brutus, rather than "taking" the conspiracy's leadership, suddenly finds he has it. The

act of taking is not a declaration, but a scene—the whole
scene; at its conclusion Brutus is "leader" because everyone has inadvertently helped him act the role of leader,
and he has acted this role not in any premeditated fashion
but spontaneously, indeed according to what he felt to be
his most honest self.

The scene in which Brutus assumes the role of leader
is important in its own right, but it provides an additional usefulness when compared with another important
scene: that in which Brutus gives his funeral oration to
the populace. Here the situation is intensified, and the
issue of leadership now concerns not the conspiracy, but
all Rome. As in the earlier scene, Brutus makes a speech
(in the first he makes two in fact) and it is full of con-
viction and disinterest. What he wants, once again, is an
acknowledgment and acceptance of his position. However,
this time acknowledgment, when it comes, is not "silent,"
and it brings with it an unexpected conferral of leadership, a kind of leadership Brutus could never acknowledge and certainly does not want. It brings him the offer
of a crown:

> *All.* Live, Brutus! live, live!
> *1. Pleb.* Bring him with triumph home unto his house.
> *2. Pleb.* Give him a statue with his ancestors.
> *3. Pleb.* Let him be Caesar.
> *4. Pleb.*   Caesar's better parts
> Shall be crown'd in Brutus.   (III.ii.53-57)

The irony here is intense. Brutus, who has killed to prevent the establishment of a monarchy now finds himself
in the very position Caesar was in: the crowd about him
clamoring for his own enthronement. His sense of himself, so strongly connected with the republican principles

of his ancestors, with the statue of old Brutus, has brought him his own statue, the very statue he would wish for himself, but one, to speak metaphorically, disfigured by the crown Caesar desired. Somehow the self-image he constructed has betrayed him, and in a world which possibly for the first time he finds he has not understood at all. As we observe Brutus listening to the shouting mob, his profound silence is indeed eloquent. What he feels at this moment is hard to guess, but surely aside from any satisfaction he might have received from "convincing" the mob (another instance where language and the image it casts move men), there is at least the possibility he might be sensing that vast disillusionment which comes with the inward recognition that one's best self was not really quite good enough to achieve even its most explicit purposes. The crowd, like Cassius in his death scene, like Brutus throughout, has "misconstrued everything."

This interpretation may help to clarify Brutus' point of view on the ensuing battle with Antony and Octavius. Faced with the reality that Rome wants a king, yet feeling as strongly as he does about monarchy, Brutus is defending his country against its own worse judgment and hoping to prevent the establishment of one of his new enemies as monarch. Yet if this is true, the conditions of war bring him into even greater power. The life or death choice he has made concerning Caesar is augmented into a life or death choice where a whole army is concerned, and we sense that both his physical and mental capacities have been strained by his new responsibilities. Portia's death, of course, has aggravated nerves worn from lack of sleep and a spirit heavy with a past he would rather forget. His tone with Cassius during their meeting in Brutus' tent is symptomatic of his condition. The impatience, the new aggressiveness in argument reflect a temper hardening under mental duress and reveal that kind of defensiveness which cannot acknowledge another view of things for fear one's authority will somehow be impaired. We might even go so far as to say that Brutus in his own way and in his own peculiar circumstances is beginning to feel the kind of pressures a Caesar customarily experiences. Life and death choices have become the rule of the day. In this light several of the remarks Brutus makes to Cassius become especially interesting; for Shakespeare draws several parallels in language at this point which are perhaps meant to indicate exactly what we have been suggesting: that Brutus in obtaining something of a Caesar's power (indeed of Caesar's power) becomes, despite himself, something like Caesar. These parallels may be seen if we compare certain speeches in the scene we have been discussing (IV.iii.) with several of Caesar's more distasteful ones. Caesar's speeches are drawn from the scene with Calpurnia (II.ii.) and the scene of his assassination (III.i.). The first parallel is one of tone, the second of content, and the third of an important word:

Caesar

    Danger knows full well
That Caesar is more dangerous than he.
We [are] two lions litter'd in one day,
And I the elder and more terrible;
And Caesar shall go forth. (II.ii.44-48)

Brutus

There is no terror, Cassius, in your threats,
For I am arm'd so strong in honesty

That they pass by me as the idle wind
Which I respect not.   (IV.iii.66-69)

Caesar

I could well be mov'd, if I were as you;
If I could pray to move, prayers would move me;
But I am constant as the northern star . . . .

(III.i.58-60)

Brutus

Must I budge?
Must I observe you? Must I stand and crouch
Under your testy humour? (IV.iii.44-46)

Caesar

Hence! wilt thou lift up Olympus?   (III.i.74)

Brutus

Cas. You love me not.
Bru.   I do not like your faults.
Cas. A friendly eye could never see such faults.
Bru. A flatterer's would not, though they do appear
        As huge as high Olympus.   (IV.iii.89-92)

We ought to note, of course, that Brutus' remarks (as
well as Caesar's) should be qualified by the situations in
which they occur. On the other hand, this use of parallels
is a typical Shakespearean technique for creating irony.
Brutus' tone of pride, his display of "immovability" in
these quotations does not quite measure up to the scope
of Caesar's, but surely it is a new tone for him and something more like Caesar than his former way of speaking.
Then, too, the parallel of the word "Olympus" in the last
speech of Brutus helps cast our minds back to the earlier
scene in which the word appears so that a comparison can

be made. The term also makes us think of the "heights" of power and the "godly" position in which the men at these two points find themselves, while simultaneously premonishing, by means of the action which followed in Caesar's case (his death), Brutus' ultimate fall. And finally the word helps us to note that like Caesar, when he used it, Brutus is in fact not on the moral "heights," but in a somewhat doubtful position.[20]

The defining irony in the scene with Cassius, then, is that Brutus, who kills Caesar in order to prevent power from corrupting Caesar, in doing so places himself in a powerful position which corrupts his own judgment. For both Brutus and Caesar, "Olympus" turns out to be not the home of the gods but a place of moral isolation, the metaphysical border to the territory of death. Brutus' ultimate suicide, at least for us, is a kind of unconscious recognition of the "blood-connection" he had with Caesar, the connection the hero failed to take sufficiently into consideration during the act of murder and which is in a sense revealed to us by means of the parallels we have just discussed. According to this analysis, then, the release of Brutus' blood, strangely enough, brings him, as it brought Caesar, back into the human family, and we are justified in saying with Antony, "This was a man."

We have been speaking of Brutus' personal limitations and it is not difficult to see that they are in fact universal ones, that the "metaphorical style" in which the hero thinks and even comes to act is in fact to some degree the style in which Cassius, Casca, and Caesar think, in which we all think and act in situations of crisis when we do not know and cannot possibly know all the "facts." Moreover,

---

20 Charney (*Shakespeare's Roman Plays*, p. 76) recognizes echoes of Caesar's typical language in speeches of Octavius during the last two acts of the play.

it is evident that this propensity to reason by means of emotionally charged generalizations continues to have political ramifications. But the problem at its root is philosophical, not political. If Brutus fashions his fears into images and acts on these images rather than on "reality," it is because there are areas of reality unperceivable to the human eye. This statement refers not only to the future, but to the truism that it is impossible to really know what is going on inside another human being and to guess how this internal life will be affected by new circumstances. One must take chances and hope for the best. When a decision has to be made, as in Brutus' case, there is little one can do but project what one thinks one knows into the future and to "fashion" (using the word to mean *suppose* here) the outcome so that a decision can be formulated.

Therefore we can see that what is an individual limitation universally shared in fact implies a world with a defect in it. If we glance back at Brutus from *our* Olympian position, we cannot help seeing him in a new moral light, and one somewhat different from that hitherto revealed throughout most of this chapter. Now we may recognize that the world (made up, as it is, of imperfect men) cannot see itself or Brutus very clearly, and because of this inability, limits the kind of action he can choose, just as his own personal defect limits the world. In the words of Arthur Sewell: "External events cast an ironical shadow over the honesty of Brutus, and we marvel that in such good could be mixed such evil. . . . It is not merely failure that deepens that vision with the recognition that the attachment to honesty may be attachment to my honesty, and that it is not only Brutus's honesty, that is impugned but all moral honesty whatsoever. To find a flaw in this honesty is something particular to the act, [*sic*] making it dishonest, is to destroy the meaning of the play. For the study of Brutus is a study in that evil original in our flesh which brings in a little corruption—and often more than a little—whenever man, in decision and action, addresses himself, as he must, to his world."[21]

According to this interpretation, it is not simply an error of judgment that Brutus makes, but "an error inherent in the decision itself, in all decisions, even in their 'honesty.' "[22] It is the circumstance to which Brutus addresses himself that brings out his evil because that circumstance (and *he* is part of his own circumstance) already contains evil. Brutus, from this position, is flawed not because he is "dishonest"—he is as honest as he can be—he is flawed because he is human. His dishonesty or self-deception, to pursue Sewell, is not the disease but the symptom. Surrounded by a self-deceiving Caesar, an envious Cassius, a fickle and deluded populace, an opportunistic Antony, and an oversimplified "republican" self-image, the political materials which force him to make a decision are bound to betray him, are bound to force him to betray them and himself if he is to act at all. Because of this, the limitations we mentioned earlier, the historical and political ones, may also be understood as reflections of his human predicament. Politics is the perverse world of human interaction, and history compulsively chains all the major characters to its wheel.

From our new moral perspective, we might conclude that Brutus' greatest "error," philosophically speaking, is to have hoped for "freedom" in a life of tyrannical circumstance, a life, indeed, in which part of one's circumstance

21 Arthur Sewell, *Character and Society in Shakespeare* (Oxford, 1951), p. 56.
22 *Ibid.*, p. 53.

is the self one is "forced" to choose. For bound as he is to history's wheel, circumscribed as he is by a willful and intractable world, and limited as he is by an inherent imperfection of vision, how can he hope for liberty when circumstance has determined the very fact that he must make a decision and act? His statement immediately after the murder of Caesar implies the contradiction with an irony that punctures the rhetoric of the language itself:[23]

> Then walk we forth, even to the market-place,
> And, waving our red weapons o'er our heads,
> Let's all cry, "Peace, freedom, and liberty!"
>
> (III.i.108-110)

There can be no peace and freedom while red weapons are raised aloft; there could be no peace or freedom while there was any necessity for red weapons. These ideals could not exist because the Roman world is flawed, divided against itself, racked by conflicting desires, unpurged of its own blood, even as Brutus is. Rather than being realities, Roman freedom and Roman republicanism become the nonexistent political generalizations for which Brutus sacrifices his own life, his friend's, and Rome's. Liberty becomes, in fact, the generalization which can only be fulfilled in death: in the death act—in the act of death.

> *Mes.* Strato, where is thy master?
> *Stra.* Free from the bondage you are in, Messala;
> The conquerors can but make a fire of him,
> For Brutus only overcame himself,
> And no man else hath honour by his death.
>
> (V.v.53-57)

[23] See Knights, "Shakespeare and Political Wisdom," pp. 45-48.

The Roman ideal finds the means for its enactment in the Roman end, and Brutus' greatest moment turns out to be a kind of unconscious insight into the role he has played in history and in Shakespeare's drama:

> Farewell, good Strato. [Runs on his
>   sword] Caesar, now be still;
> I kill'd not thee with half so good a will.   [Dies]
>
> (V.v.49-51)

Fulfilling once again the role of sacrificer, the role he himself chose, he becomes the willing victim that completes Rome's long purge. Thus he satisfies his own conscience, political necessity, history (at least for a while), and that inscrutable power whose name is Fate.

In death Brutus achieves pure freedom—at the cost of himself. That this is true is a commentary not only upon politics but upon life even at its most personal. "It is a terrible thought but a true one: the statesman is never right, but to choose the right, he must continually endeavour. And this is true of every man, in all moral activity."[24] For civilized man, at the heart of action is the chosen self which reflects the chosen ideal, and even the necessity of choice is a form of tyranny. Beyond this is only a paradox: the complete fulfillment of the chosen self is always an act of self-destruction, and freedom seems to lie at some uncharted point in the human soul.

[24] Sewell, p. 56.

II

M A C B E T H :

THE MANLY IMAGE

Julius Caesar and *Macbeth* are related in several obvious ways. Both deal with the murder of a head of state; both employ Nemesis in the typical Elizabethan sense; both portray tragic heroes who suffer inner moral conflict over the murders they plan. In each case the hero's "single state of man"[1] is shaken and the resulting division of soul is reflected in the division of the state. In *Julius Caesar,* however, a kind of delicate balance restrains and complicates our judgments: it is difficult to assess the moral reality of both Brutus and Caesar because that reality is compounded with the political issues in their play and the relationship of the characters to these issues. In *Macbeth,* the political issues, such as they are, remain cut and dried. There is no conflict between "republicanism" and "monarchy," either of which, depending upon one's perspective, can evoke sympathy. Nor can we debate whether Macbeth is or could be a tyrant. He is one, and thus can be condemned in both Elizabethan and contemporary terms. In *Macbeth* Shakespeare makes his moral identification of characters clear. His strokes are broad and black, while in *Julius Caesar* the defining lines are harder to discern. We see in each of the main characters intimations of both good and evil and our impression of Brutus and Caesar is informed by doubt.

Macbeth, therefore, is in some respects a much simpler

[1] See H. B. Charlton, *Shakespearean Tragedy,* p. 160.

play than *Julius Caesar*. It is more like a medieval moral-ity.[2] From the moment we see the witches on the heath and immediately afterward, the Scottish battlefield, we know we are to witness the battle for one man's soul. These hags, so demonstrably representative of the powers of evil, have one aim—"to meet with Macbeth," and the exclusiveness of their interest sets the pattern for our own. Macbeth's soul, its terrible and wonderful workings, is to be our focus of attention. The play's complexity does not lie in the relationship of assassin and victim. In *Macbeth* the moral relationship of king and murderer is taken for granted. Macbeth has no morally valid reason for kill-ing Duncan and he knows it; the blame for the crime is his own and fate's. Duncan remains throughout his short stage-life a figure loaded with Christian graces. Brutus at least *believes* he has good reason for killing Caesar, and some critics, both in the play and outside of it, are prone to agree with him.

The suggestion that Macbeth himself is *Macbeth*'s cen-ter of complexity allows us to devote our entire attention to him. Barring Lady Macbeth, the other characters, de-spite their development as personalities, are subordinated by their symbolical roles. These become their chief func-tion. Banquo, Macduff, and Malcolm, whatever their per-sonal failings, are meant to represent first and foremost the powers of good, just as the three witches are meant to portray the powers of evil. Hence, to become involved in the subtleties of their conduct, as Bradley, Knight, and Muir do, is to distract ourselves from the complicated functioning of Macbeth's soul, and to do this is to destroy the play's extremely tight unity and its powerfully ob-

[2] Willard Farnham, *Shakespeare's Tragic Frontier* (Berkeley, 1950), p. 79.

sessive quality—in short, the play's effect.[3] Macbeth's
tremendous self-absorption should be reflected in our
absorption with his character. Just as the witches are primarily concerned with Macbeth's soul, so should we be.
Just as Shakespeare deals simply and directly with plot,
action, and the symbolical function of subordinate characters, we should also.

The landscape of Macbeth's moral reality may be depicted with reference to three major "scenic" locations in
the play. The first location of importance is that of Macbeth's castle itself, especially as it appears to Banquo's
eyes as he approaches with Duncan:

> This guest of summer,
> The temple-haunting [martlet] does approve,
> By his loved [mansionry], that the heaven's breath
> Smells wooingly here; no jutty, frieze,
> Buttress, nor coign of vantage, but this bird
> Hath made his pendent bed and procreant cradle.
> Where they [most] breed and haunt, I have observ'd
> The air is delicate.   (I.vi.3-10)

Here we see Macbeth's home, feudal in proportions and
surrounded by procreant nature. It is a seat of medieval
order, or should be, that order suggesting the nourishing
feudal bond between king and subject, lord and servant,
host and guest, kinsman and kinsman: the relationship of
Macbeth to Duncan in all its significant aspects. More

---

[3] See A. C. Bradley, *Shakespearean Tragedy* (London, 1932), pp.
383-385; G. Wilson Knight, *The Wheel of Fire* (London, 1949), pp.
151-153; and Kenneth Muir in the introduction to the New Arden
edition of *Macbeth* (London, 1957), p. lxviii—who find Banquo
guilty of acquiescing to Macbeth's enthronement, or of keeping the
secret of the prediction of the witches, or of not fighting Macbeth
after Duncan's murder. By the same token, Knight finds Macduff
guilty of cruelly deserting his family.

broadly this feudal order may be understood as a basic sense of decency or humanity. Ironically, the castle is surrounded by a wood containing a cavern—the witches' home. In Act IV, scene i, when Macbeth meets the witches in their cave, they are concocting a magic potion in a great cauldron. The brew contains a number of "unnatural" ingredients, or natural ingredients perverted to evil uses:

> Eye of newt and toe of frog,
> Wool of bat and tongue of dog,
> Adder's fork and blind-worm's sting,
> Lizard's leg and howlet's wing.
>
> (IV.i.14-17)

Space prevents our savoring a more complete list. The cavern is the second important scenic location. It is here, let us say, that the charms of evil work upon the desires men hide from the world at large. Since the witches are unnatural creatures, their power is anarchic. Their appeal is to desire alone; and for those, like Macbeth, who submit themselves to their power, desire alone becomes a standard of action. According to the "ethic" of the cavern (as opposed to the feudal ethic the exterior of the castle suggests), one acts upon one's wishes, and justice and humanity are irrelevant. What's right is what one wants. The third important location is "the battlefield": the heath at the play's beginning, the "castle" at the end. Here the first two "ethics" conflict. Here desire, in winning the battle with conscience, actually uses conscience in furthering the claims of desire. Reason becomes the traitor within the gates. But it is here, too, that the forces of Nemesis finally achieve victory, or at least they do in green Birnam wood, which surrounds the castle—the same wood which surrounds the witches' cavern. For the battle is the entire play, and as it turns out, the battleground is all of Macbeth, all of Scotland.

It is the proposed violation of moral order, feudal obligation, and human decency that calls forth Macbeth's feelings of guilt and, more importantly for the moment, those speeches of his which make it eminently clear that he is totally aware, unlike Brutus, of the heinousness of the crime he plans. Thus at the end of Act I he says of Duncan's projected murder:

> But in these cases
> We still have judgement here, that we but teach
> Bloody instructions, which, being taught, return
> To plague th' inventor. This even-handed justice
> Commends th' ingredients of our poison'd chalice
> To our own lips. He's here in double trust:
> First, as I am his kinsman and his subject,
> Strong both against the deed; then, as his host,
> Who should against his murderer shut the door,
> Not bear the knife myself. Besides, this Duncan
> Hath borne his faculties so meek, hath been
> So clear in his great office, that his virtues
> Will plead like angels, trumpet-tongu'd, against
> The deep damnation of his taking-off. . . .
>
> (I.vii.7-20)

This portion of the soliloquy, whatever interesting interpretations Bradley may have given to explain it,[4] in-

---

[4] Bradley (*Shakespearean Tragedy*, pp. 355-356) suggests that Macbeth's talk of consequences is in fact a kind of "cover-up" for the real pain of conscience in him. Bradley derives, of course, from Coleridge, who said: "Macbeth mistranslates the recoilings and ominous whispers of conscience into prudential and selfish reasonings, and after the deed, the terrors of remorse into fear from ex-

forms us that Macbeth fully understands the moral issues involved in murdering Duncan. The clarity of the language itself, its balanced argumentative rhythms, suggests the kind of mental control that makes for clear thinking. Indeed, as the speech resolves itself into the brilliant and evocative image of pity "like a naked newborn babe/Striding the blast," and its proper result, the tears "in every eye" which shall "drown the wind," we sense Macbeth is not only capable of recognizing the moral arguments against his act, but is also capable of metaphorically expressing their awesome power.[5]

This speech, with its trumpet-tongu'd angels and hors'd cherubin, unites Macbeth momentarily with the system of Christian values he is bound to violate by fulfilling his "vaulting ambition." That he can visualize God's angels so vividly may suggest that, ironically, he is close to them even as he contemplates murder, that he feels they are watching him. Christianity appears an actual force in his life which might make a positive difference were there not other forces acting upon him more powerful in effect because his soul is already divided.

The values of Christian humanity, acknowledged and understood by Macbeth, are pitted, as we have said, against the more primitive code of the "cavern." It is a

ternal dangers. . . ." *Coleridge's Shakespearean Criticism*, ed. Thomas M. Raysor (Cambridge, Mass., 1930), I, 80.

[5] Arnold Stein, "Macbeth and Word-Magic," *SR*, LIX (Spring 1951), 271-284. Stein suggests that Macbeth's morality (perverted though it becomes) is displayed in the speeches directly after the hero sees the witches for the first time and in his arguments for not killing Duncan; in these speeches moral force asserts itself through language, making itself real by means of a kind of magical evocation: white magic—as contrasted to the "verbal charms" (black magic) he uses to get himself to act. See also Irving Ribner, *Patterns in Shakespearian Tragedy*, p. 165.

code of desire, but something more as well. Lady Macbeth exemplifies its system of simple and clearly defined "non-ethics." She is, in another way, the fourth "witch," and her arguments "bewitch" Macbeth. To her, virtue is limited to "manliness," and action is dissociated from everything but the murder of Duncan. Eugene M. Waith believes that Macbeth's "mental torment grows out of the conflict between the narrow concept of man as the courageous male and the more inclusive concept of man as a being whose moral nature distinguishes him from the beasts."[6] Brutus stands as an illustration of the more inclusive virtue, which combines soldierly qualities with gentleness. Of him Marc Antony says, "This was a man."[7] But, according to Lady Macbeth's argument, it is physical daring alone, the *act* of murder, which can prove Macbeth a man. By means of force he can take what he wishes:

> Art thou afeard
> To be the same in thine own act and valour
> As thou art in desire?   (I.vii.39-41)

Lady Macbeth asks this question of her husband only a few lines after the soliloquy in which Macbeth voices the argument against murder. Her jibe is aimed directly at Macbeth's most important sense of himself: that derived from those soldierly characteristics which gained him Cawdor's title. But in the case of the battle against Macdonwald and Cawdor, Macbeth's valor and fearlessness

---

[6] Eugene M. Waith, "Manhood and Valor in Two Shakespearean Tragedies," *ELH*, XVII (December 1950), 266. Waith supports his conclusions with material from two Jacobean sources: Thomas Beard's *The French Academy*, 1602, translated from the French of Pierre de la Primaudaye and Thomas Milles' *The Treasurie of Auncient and Modern Times*, 1613. See Waith's thorough and convincing argument.

[7] *Ibid.*, p. 264.

were associated with Duncan's just cause. These traits were demonstrated in the name of nature, order, and humanity, and hence take the color of heroism:

> For brave Macbeth—well he deserves that name—
> Disdaining Fortune, with his brandish'd steel,
> Which smok'd with bloody execution,
> Like Valour's minion carv'd out his passage
> Till he fac'd the slave;
> Which ne'er shook hands, nor bade farewell to him,
> Till he unseam'd him from the nave to th' chaps,
> And fix'd his head upon our battlements.
>
> (I.ii.16-23)

Here "justice" is "with valour arm'd" and the imagery as it is further developed, although horrifying in its grisly extremity, sets up a vision of the hero meant to be admired. As Wilson Knight has it, "The value of warriorship may not be dissociated from allegiance: it is one with the ideal of kingship and imperial power. . . . Only in terms of this allegiance is courage an honorable ideal."[8] Thus in the case of the murder of Duncan, where valor and fearlessness are separated from "allegiance" and indeed from every moral justification, these traits imply instead of heroism a kind of inbred bestiality. It is for this reason that Macbeth recoils from his wife's attack upon

[8] G. Wilson Knight, *The Imperial Theme* (London, 1939), p. 126. By this Knight means allegiance to the family-state, i.e. those bonds with clan and nation conceived in "peace, concord, life." Absolute courage is not necessarily honorable: honor "must be a service, or it is worthless. Macbeth knows this." See I.iv.22. On the other hand, John Holloway (*The Story of the Night* [London, 1961], p. 58), finds the bloody image of Macbeth disdaining fortune "ambivalent." He is not merely a "destroyer of revolt; but himself an image of revolt." This is true, but I would say the image, as such, serves to premonish future action.

his courage and pleads for a more humane image of manliness:

> I dare do all that may become a man;
> Who dares [do] more is none.
>
> (I.vii.46-47)

He is aware that Lady Macbeth's provocation is directed toward something primitive enough within him to
be denied the name of man; but her irony and her inverted logic[9] cut short his more humane impulses:

> What beast was't, then,
> That made you break this enterprise to me?
> When you durst do it, then you were a man;
> And to be more than what you were, you would
> Be so much more the man.   (I.vii.47-51)

Lady Macbeth succeeds in separating valor from "justice"
and establishing the former as a virtue in its own right.
Her attempt to brand Macbeth's reticence as cowardice
scorches the living center of his reality—his conception of
himself as valorous soldier. In self-defense he falls back
upon her point of view. In fact, so emotional is his response that he continues to see himself, even when planning the crime, as Duncan and the other lords saw him
after the battle with the treacherous Macdonwald and
Cawdor. He envisions himself as a kind of hero. The
murder becomes a "terrible feat," a great enterprise which
can prove his manhood, now placed in doubt by Lady
Macbeth—and it can gain the crown at the same time.[10]
Moreover, he finds in his wife's further comments an

---

[9] See Theodore Spencer, *Shakespeare and the Nature of Man*
(New York, 1942), p. 156.
[10] Bradley, *Shakespearean Tragedy*, p. 367.

example of the audacity and resolution he might well
emulate if he is to attain his ends:

> I have given suck, and know
> How tender 'tis to love the babe that milks me;
> I would, while it was smiling in my face,
> Have pluck'd my nipple from his boneless gums
> And dash'd the brains out, had I so sworn as you
> Have done to this.   (I.vii.54-59)

On its most obvious level this speech gives us a picture of nature completely inverted. Motherhood, instead
of nursing the babe, destroys it. Womanliness, normally
tender, apprehensive, and compassionate, transforms itself into a cruelty that denies its usual characteristics.
Here "the milk of human kindness" is turned to gall.
However, of equal importance to Shakespeare's implied
moral commentary is the inflection of the speech itself.
Its cruelty sets the tone for Macbeth's development into
the "butcher" he in part becomes. What we find in the
speech is a determination, a devotion so strong, not only
to one's word, but to one's desires no matter what they
are, as to deny the moral structure of the universe and to
formulate another universe of another kind. Here desire
and will are united into the heartless daring Lady Macbeth calls "valour" or "courage" or "manliness." Her next
speech, in which she dictates to him her plan for murder,
shows him how to put the "manly" image into action:

> When Duncan is asleep—
> Whereto the rather shall his day's hard journey
> Soundly invite him—his two chamberlains
> Will I with wine and wassail so convince
> That memory, the warder of the brain,
> Shall be a fume, and the receipt of reason

> A limbeck only. When in swinish sleep
> Their drenched natures lie as in a death,
> What cannot you and I perform upon
> Th' unguarded Duncan? what not put upon
> His spongy officers, who shall bear the guilt
> Of our great quell?   (I.vii.61-72)

Lady Macbeth's resoluteness, daring, and ingenuity act as a challenge to her husband, but—equally important for the present argument—he identifies all three traits as masculine attributes he is compelled to demonstrate himself, while failing to note that it is, after all, a woman who has spoken. In adopting her example, the perversion of her own female nature escapes his attention. Ironically he responds:

> Bring forth men-children only;
> For thy undaunted mettle should compose
> Nothing but males. Will it not be receiv'd
> When we have mark'd with blood those sleepy two
> Of his own chamber and us'd their very daggers,
> That they have done't?   (I.vii.72-77)

Macbeth takes her "undaunted mettle" for his own and adds his bit of reasoning to the argument for murder. The image she displays to him has become a kind of tool to obtain the crown, in a sense one of the murder weapons. It is with this manly image in mind that he screws "his courage to the sticking place" and makes his final decision. Therefore it is perhaps justifiable to suggest that Duncan's murder, though in one light simply a means to the crown, in another is subconsciously understood by Macbeth as the act which will prove him worthy of it. For the crown's worth, as far as Macbeth is concerned, consists mainly in its symbolical value to the wearer, that is, as a kind of indelible stamp of valor. It is the "ornament of life," but carries with it no obligations, makes no demands but one—to be worn. In a sense the crown may be said to "crown" the compelling image. Indeed, for Macbeth the crown is never anything more than an object of desire, either to get or retain. In the words of Wilson Knight, "Macbeth's crime . . . is almost an inverted, an introverted, lust or love; a self-desire, expressed by an action which aims at grasping glory forms to itself."[11] The crown is symbolically engulfed by the imaginary world Macbeth seeks to display in resolute and daring action. There it remains separated from the precincts of moral reality where its spiritual counterpart, Macbeth's jewel—his soul (or better yet, his conscience) still lives its tortured and isolated life.

According to this analysis then, the crown itself becomes synonymous with the act that achieves it. But the area of reality in which both crown and action exist in Macbeth's mind may be contrasted with that where Macbeth's sense of humanity exists. In this humane part of his mind, the prediction that Macbeth shall be king requires no immediate action whatsoever. In fact, he is the first to admit this:

> If chance will have me King, why, chance may
>   crown me
> Without my stir.   (I.iii.143-144)

The witches' prophecies, for whatever they are worth as actual prophecies, never suggest a means for obtaining the crown. The weird sisters do not even plant the seed of desire in Macbeth, but rather, their "All hail's," incantatory and enigmatic, act as an objectification of a desire already resident within Macbeth. Thus the guilty start at

11 Knight, *The Imperial Theme*, p. 132.

"things that do sound so fair" which Banquo remarks on the part of his companion.

But "manliness" demands action, direct, physical, and executed by the soldier-hero himself. Action means everything, verifies everything that Macbeth must have verified. And in order for the seal of "valour" to be set, the necessary action must not only be carried out by Macbeth, it must be fully acknowledged by him. Without acknowledgment of responsibility on Macbeth's part, the act would fail to prove him worthy of the crown. Thus at moments in the play we get the distinct impression that Macbeth instead of being subject to fate is in reality wrenching it into a pattern of his own determination, forcing it to obey *his* will.

This idea is first suggested immediately after Duncan names Malcolm Prince of Cumberland in Act I. Macbeth's reaction to the announcement is an acknowledgment of both the will to act and the responsibility for action:

> The Prince of Cumberland! That is a step
> On which I must fall down, or else o'erleap,
> For in my way it lies.   (I.iv.48-50)

But the lines following these are the more remarkable, for in a sense they point away from "willed" action as much as they point toward it. In them we obscurely see conscience battling with desire, and losing:

> Stars, hide your fires;
> Let not light see my black and deep desires;
> The eye wink at the hand; yet let that be
> Which the eye fears, when it is done, to see.
> (I.iv.50-53)

Here action is willed, the end suggested, the inner sensation of resolution sustained; but the culprit escapes into a blackness which hides both the reality of the deed and the doer from detection, even from Macbeth himself. The speech is a masterpiece of self-deception in which language and syntax themselves function as the mask which hides the killer from his conscience. The "black and deep desires" are acknowledged by Macbeth, but "the eye" and "the hand" seem detached from him, while the nameless deed itself "is done." It appears to do itself or is done by an act of prestidigitation. The magician's hand acts, but his eye winks. Only half the mind connecting the two is aware of the action. The other half in its blindness is aware of nothing, and thus is innocent. Who is to hold the right hand responsible for the deeds of the left? Macbeth's mind divides in this subtle attempt to put the deed outside the precincts of prohibitive conscience: to pass the guilt off to a part of himself he does not for the moment choose to recognize, and otherwise to see this part as a kind of magic outside himself—like the power of the witches, who accost him on the plain with "supernatural soliciting" which, according to Macbeth's interpretation, "cannot be ill, cannot be good," but simply "is," just as the deed "is done."

However, this interior pressure toward self-disguise and self-hypnotizing is not in reality so much amoral as it is a condition of willed amorality. The life of the soul is implied by Macbeth's necessity to stamp it out.[12] What

12 Stein ("Macbeth and Word-Magic," p. 278) suggests that Macbeth distorts his power over words when hypnotically incanting himself into killing Duncan or Banquo. However, as the play goes on, Macbeth "seems dimly aware of . . . the threat that the submerged alliance between his eloquence and his moral nature may regain its former ascendance." Consequently he seeks to smother language

we have in this speech is a mixture of the two ethics previously discussed, that informed by humanity and that of pure desire and resolute action. We are faced in language with a conflict of conscience and desire which the latter wins by managing to hide the physical reality of the deed from the potential doer, thus preventing the appropriate response of horror to it. The result is achieved through the establishment of a state of self-absorption that lays bare to *us* the nakedness of pure will while dissolving for Macbeth the concreteness of the act of murder and, in consequence, the concreteness of the potential murderer as well. Moreover, with the evaporation of these, personal responsibility vanishes too. We have no case against the killer because, so to speak, the *corpus delicti* is missing. Responsibility, thus, is willed— in every sense of the word—to the atmosphere.

This abstraction of soul and its consequent suppression of the pangs of conscience has its reverse counterpart during those moments when conscience asserts itself as a repellent objectification of Macbeth's guilty desire. Essentially we are still dealing with a conflict of conscience and desire, but in this case a shadow wells out of the hero's disturbed mind and locks him "rapt" in unspeakable "imaginings."[18]

---

and with it thought, to eliminate the "intellectual element involved in language" (p. 283) and with it right reason. Thoughtless action is to be the substitute, not to avoid conscience, but to avoid thinking itself for fear it will bring out his moral nature. Hence his effort to avoid words, to act on the moment. Bradley also sees this alignment between Macbeth's moral nature and the language he speaks. Muir (New Arden edition of *Macbeth*, pp. xxxiii-xxxiv) notes images reflecting the idea of disguise and self-disguise implicit in the drama. These images are "linked" with the themes of "equivocation, deceit and treachery."

[18] Brents Stirling (*Unity in Shakespearean Tragedy*. p. 139) traces

> . . . why do I yield to that suggestion
> Whose horrid image doth unfix my hair
> And make my seated heart knock at my ribs,
> Against the use of nature?   (I.iii.134-137)

The "horrid image" (in a sense "the future in the instant") seems to assault Macbeth as if it were not a
creature conjured up by his own mind, and his yielding
to this projection appears the result of a spontaneous
fascination, uncontrollable and overpowering. The "horrid image" in fact possesses him. But the context of the
image: "If good, why do I yield to that suggestion. . . ?"
clearly implies a recognition of evil, and in this instance
conscience momentarily triumphs and restores Macbeth's
moral balance. He recoils and invokes a fate that will
take care of everything.

> If chance will have me King, why, chance may
>   crown me
> Without my stir.   (I.iii.143-144)

But in the scene directly before the murder of Duncan
another frightful hallucination assails Macbeth; and in
this case (the more crucial one where immediate action
is concerned) desire wins its conflict with conscience. The
fused objectification of these, a bloody dagger, appears to
lead Macbeth on to the murder chamber: "Thou mar-
shall'st me the way that I was going." The knife is a
hypnotic metaphor, gathering to itself all Macbeth's
sensations until the "gouts of blood" on the "blade and

---

the "themes" of darkness, sleep, raptness, and contradiction in *Macbeth*. He finds the instances of "raptness" in the play vary from
"simple abstraction to near hypnosis." Note also Holloway's remarks
on the image of "the bloody man" which haunts Macbeth's imaginings in the form of "the horrid image" (pp. 58-59).

dudgeon" force him to reject the image as something too repellent to visualize. But the illusion has served its purpose. It has drawn him to the point of action while at the same time plunging him into his typical state of "raptness." As in the speech beginning "Stars hide your fires . . . ," where will was disguised as a kind of magical force outside Macbeth, it is now disguised as a "witchcraft" in the night which makes him *its* own. Although the hero never shifts responsibility for the deed onto Lady Macbeth's shoulders despite her role as "spur" to the sides of his intent, he allows the black night's mood of "bewitchment" to bear the burden of it:

> Now o'er the one half-world
> Nature seems dead, and wicked dreams abuse
> The curtain'd sleep. Witchcraft celebrates
> Pale Hecate's offerings, and wither'd Murder,
> Alarum'd by his sentinel, the wolf,
> Whose howl's his watch, thus with his stealthy pace,
> With Tarquin's ravishing [strides], towards his design
> Moves like a ghost.   (II.i.49-56)

And like a ghost moves Macbeth, petitioning the earth not to hear his footsteps. The incantatory language lifts him momentarily beyond will, so that he becomes a thing of the night, possessed by it, fulfilling its mood in the same way the "present horror" suits with the time. Momentarily he lives in his own mind as a pure object— ravishing Tarquin—the tool of fate.

Wilson Knight says of Macbeth: "He lacks spiritual courage to meet . . . the evil on its own spiritual terms, and hence projects his disordered soul into action and murders Duncan. Undue horror and fear of the deed drives him to it. . . ."[14] In a very real sense Knight is correct. Macbeth acts in order to free himself of the agonizing and guilt-ridden compulsion to act. He would have this blow be the be-all and the end-all here, not only out of fear of retribution, but to rescue himself from feeling the painful moral conflict he faces and the dreadful sense of paralysis his conscience imposes upon him. Simultaneously, however, his conscience demands pain as the price for action, as a kind of punishment before the crime which in some magical way can replace and prevent the punishment that might follow afterward. Yet it is this same suffering, self-directed, indeed self-imposed, that Macbeth perhaps feels can be eliminated by action—the murder itself.

Or to adopt a slightly different perspective, we might suggest that by means of the bloody dagger he stimulates sufficient horror to satisfy conscience, indeed more than enough, so that ultimately he can reject the vision as something too terrible to bear and still feel justified in the rejection:

> There's no such thing.
> It is the bloody business which informs
> Thus to mine eyes. (II.i.47-49)

But in this refusal to feel lies the freedom necessary to act. With conscience momentarily satisfied, the incantatory and hypnotic lines which follow drug it completely. Similarly, release from feeling is a release from the sense of moral responsibility that impelled the devious maneuvers of Macbeth's mind in the first place. Only the sudden realization that Duncan still lives awakens him

---

[14] Knight, *The Imperial Theme*, p. 128.

and converts the image we have of Macbeth as soul possessed to one of the active man responsible for his fate. His words recapture the tone of his wife's cruel logic:

> Whiles I threat, he lives:
> Words to the heat of deeds too cold breath gives.
>
> (II.i.60-61)

For an instant we are faced with two Macbeths, one controlled, the other controlling, each living a life of his own. They recombine, preserving their separate integrities, in a statement reminiscent of the "Stars, hide your fires" passage:

> I go, and it is done. . . .
>
> (II.i.62)

Then the problem of action stands out in a purity quite innocent of moral coloration for Macbeth. All he need do in order to live with himself is kill Duncan, for he has used the "dagger of the mind" to kill the soul. Desire has won the conflict. Macbeth is free to act.

After Duncan's murder the tone of *Macbeth* changes. There is a distinct hardening on the part of the hero chiefly attributable to the brutalization of Macbeth's soul caused by murder. But equally important is the suppression of prohibitive conscience which permitted the murder originally. In the succeeding portion of the play conscience ceases to function as an agent capable of preventing further crime; nor does it promote repentance.[15] Instead we begin with a repression of conscience which in fact necessitates further violence. Conscience lives a

---

[15] See Farnham, p. 108. See also Dolora G. Cunningham, "*Macbeth*: The Tragedy of the Hardened Heart," *SQ*, XIV (Winter 1963), 39-47.

ghostly life perverted to Macbeth's own uses: ". . . instead of acting directly in the form of remorse," it "comes to act through imaginary terrors, which in turn react on his conscience, as fire is made hotter by the current of air which itself generates."[16] The memory of Duncan's murder, those "terrible dreams" that shake the hero nightly, must be wiped out. Macbeth would be like the dead king, whom "nothing can touch . . . further." But in order to achieve this state he must either die himself or destroy anything that reminds him of Duncan or seems to threaten the static and unfeeling position he seeks to attain.

Furthermore the hero stands in a new relation to time after the king has been dispatched. This new relationship helps intensify the hardening of Macbeth's character. Before the murder Macbeth could look upon his past with satisfaction, while the future, with its promise of kingship, opened out desirably before him. The limitation imposed by the witches—the prediction that Banquo's issue will ultimately reign, no son of Macbeth succeeding—though impressive to Macbeth, had not yet become an obsession. Now, however, the new king has a new future as well as a new past, and both cannot be countenanced. The past, like a "new gorgon" turning Macbeth's heart to stone, is matched by an equally horrifying possibility in the time to come: the accession of Banquo's children.

[16] H. N. Hudson, *Shakespeare: His Life, Art and Characters* (New York, 1872), II, 334. Hudson also makes the interesting suggestion that Macbeth's terrible visions may indicate a repressed remorse, "conscience working in disguise," but that there is scarcely any manifestation of remorse *per se* barring the hero's momentary wish that he was sleeping as peacefully as Duncan (after the murder of the king).

Upon my head they plac'd a fruitless crown,
And put a barren sceptre in my gripe . . . .

(III.i.61-62)

Thus Macbeth has placed himself in a position where in order to preserve his inner peace and his throne, he must annihilate both the past and the future. He is in a very real way confined by the present moment. He has to prevent his mind from moving backward and time from moving forward; he must prevent the events of the past from determining the future. Working against the natural force of time in this way, he finds himself constrained within his own human limitations, and the hardening process he suffers is the result of his agonizing and futile attempt to push out the walls of time on either side, to make his present state engulf the past and the future, to establish himself as a kind of unreflecting and "memory-less" eternity.[17]

Because of these two factors, conscience and time, Macbeth is led once again to the frontiers of "manly" action as Lady Macbeth has defined it. Once Macbeth wears the crown, the fear of Banquo intensifies. Banquo becomes for Macbeth the frightening symbol of both the threat of the past (he may be suspicious of the circumstances surrounding Duncan's death) and the threat of the future. Action calls to the hero with a new insistence if he is to maintain his present state and throne.

[17] See Knight, *The Imperial Theme*, pp. 150-151 and John Lawlor, *The Tragic Sense in Shakespeare* (London, 1960), p. 123. William Blisset's excellent study, "The Secret'st Man of Blood. A Study of Dramatic Irony in *Macbeth*," *SQ*, X (Summer 1959), 397-408, contains a worthwhile treatment of time images in conjunction with blood images and their interlocking development in the play. See pp. 406-408.

To be thus is nothing,
But to be safely thus. . . .   (III.i.48-49)

In addition, Macbeth's desire for security is related to at least one other matter of significance besides the simple preservation of his throne. His "security" is also connected with the preservation of his sense of himself— of his "manhood." Banquo, says Macbeth, possesses (as Duncan did) "a royalty of nature" and "wisdom that doth guide his valour to act in safety." Those fears of Macbeth which stick deep in Banquo are conceived, then, in terms of "valor," and to a degree Macbeth sees himself in competition with his friend. The threat to the crown is thus established as a threat also to the hero's conception of himself as "valorous" and "dauntless." Macbeth, it would seem, like Marc Antony, must be the "foremost man."

My genius is rebuk'd, as, it is said,
Mark Antony's was by Caesar.

(III.i.56-57)

Thus the idea of safety is presented in two important ways: once in regard to Macbeth's security and once in connection with the quality of Banquo's wisdom and valor. The conflict between the two kinds of manliness is working here. Brute strength and daring confront once again physical power united with justice: "wisdom" and "a royalty of nature." But in this scene conscience does not attempt to arbitrate in a direct manner between the two as it did before the murder of Duncan. Instead conscience expresses itself merely in Macbeth's attempt to establish a rationale for his projected murder and an "alibi." This effort to prepare an "alibi" is perhaps the more characteristic where the habitual workings of the

hero's mind are concerned. Macbeth employs several murderers to kill Banquo, and in this way tries to dissociate
himself from the deed itself as much as he can, indeed
more than he was wont before the murder of Duncan.
Once more he attempts to will responsibility for the deed
to a force outside himself; yet this time he goes one step
further—he assigns the deed to his emissaries instead of
using his own hands, and subsequently makes them
rather than himself tools of the destroying night. It is a
case of murder twice removed:

> Come, seeling night,
> Scarf up the tender eye of pitiful day,
> And with thy bloody and invisible hand
> Cancel and tear to pieces that great bond
> Which keeps me pale! Light thickens, and the crow
> Makes wing to th' rooky wood;
> Good things of day begin to droop and drowse,
> Whiles night's black agents to their preys do rouse.
>
> (III.ii.46-53)

This attempt at dissociation is revealed in Macbeth's
almost immediate response to the appearance of Banquo's
ghost in the great banquet scene:

> Thou canst not say I did it; never shake
> Thy gory locks at me.   (III.iv.50-51)

Apparently Banquo cannot accuse Macbeth of murdering
him because Macbeth was not at the scene of the crime;
the king hires the murderers to kill Banquo, as Muir
says, "not for money, but out of hatred, so that they can
share some part of the guilt, so that he can cry 'thou canst
not say I did it,' "[18] and Macbeth's absence at the scene

[18] Muir, New Arden edition of *Macbeth*, p. lxviii. Also Bradley,
Shakespearean Tragedy, pp. 360-361.

of the murder in this light further substantiates his guiltlessness. Once again Macbeth has tried to hide from the world and himself behind an objective force with which he seemingly has no connection. He disguises himself, so to speak, as two murderers who kill Banquo for their own reasons and who at the same time are possessed of the "seeling night's" dire cruelty, of which they become the agents. Thus is conscience, already more suppressed than it was in the first two acts, satisfied—while in fact it is utilized to effect a more Machiavellian murder than that of Duncan. At the same time the manly image is more fulfilled according to Lady Macbeth's prescription. For now Macbeth is strong enough to make his decisions alone, and conscience has ceased to function in a prohibitive way:

> Be innocent of the knowledge, dearest chuck,
> Till thou applaud the deed.   (III.ii.45-46)

Macbeth, then, moves even closer toward enacting without moral reservation the ethic of pure desire. This second crime is easier for two reasons: first, conscience simply no longer has the positive force it had prior to Duncan's murder (although it has sufficient negative force); secondly, Macbeth's power as king allows him to enact the deed without involving himself physically. Yet, although he seems to himself "so much more the man" because he can plan the deed quickly, resolutely, and fairly efficiently without the help of his wife and without great inner turbulence, to us he seems so much less the man precisely because of his lack of physical involvement. He does not need to face the horror of spilling blood with his own hands.

Furthermore, if it is true that conscience in a preventative sense "gives up the ghost" at this point in the drama, it is equally true that conscience as an impulse toward repentance is undemonstrated when the murder has been "done." After the first crime Macbeth is still capable of saying:

> To know my deed, 'twere best not know myself.
> Wake Duncan with thy knocking! I would thou
>   couldst!   (II.ii.73-74)

But after the murder of Banquo he can think only of Fleance's escape:

> Then comes my fit again. I had else been perfect,
> Whole as marble, founded as the rock,
> As broad and general as the casing air;
> But now I am cabin'd, cribb'd, confin'd, bound in
> To saucy doubts and fears.   (III.iv.21-25)

The penitential function of conscience, in fact, is taken over symbolically by other characters in the play. The first of these is Lady Macbeth, who endures the burden of Macbeth's sense of guilt in addition to her own and who demonstrates the resulting punishment in the sleep-walking scene. Banquo, Macduff, and Malcolm serve in a related capacity. In their case conscience is translated into Nemesis, which is aligned with God, nature, and fate. What we see in these characters is the sacrificed "goodness" or "nobility" or "justice" of Macbeth objectified and set in natural motion against him. Thus if Macbeth at moments attempts to will his responsible conscience to a force outside him, the forces of good respond by actually taking on the function of conscience as the power of retribution. Just as Macbeth selects "black agents" to carry out his will and calls them fate's, fate selects its own agents, "white" ones, to carry out its justice.[19]

This view of Macbeth's predicament implies the significance of a scene undiscussed so far—the banquet scene in which Banquo's ghost appears. Here, for the first time conscience does not manifest itself merely as a horrid image in Macbeth's mind. Although the rest of the company, including Lady Macbeth, do not see the ghost, Macbeth does and so do we. Its objective presence is clearly indicated by Shakespeare's stage directions. This, of course, may be explained as simply an example of the theatrical conventions of the day, i.e. by employing an objective ghost Shakespeare was acquiescing to popular tastes which demanded supernatural sensationalism. Nevertheless, the effect of the ghost's objective reality upon the audience perhaps supersedes theatrical conventions and the fact that others at the banquet do not see it. For the truth is that we do not doubt its reality any more than we do that of Caesar's spirit, or any other spirit in Shakespeare for that matter. And what is important about this ghost is our ability for the first time to see by means of it the results of Macbeth's evil confronting him as a creature disjoined from himself. Indeed, when we recall it was Macbeth who so carefully attempted to dissociate himself from the act he perpetrated and its result, the appearance of the ghost in an objective form disjoined from him seems ironically appropriate.

Furthermore, the role of Banquo is so tightly related to the role of fate, and thus Nemesis, that his actual presence at the banquet (a presence the hero himself

---

[19] Ribner (*Patterns in Shakespearian Tragedy*, p. 155) says that "the audience comes to feel that Macbeth is destroyed by counter-forces which he himself . . . sets in motion."

invited) tends to objectify these forces in their full complexity—to cast an image of the future which recounts the past. This image points backward not only as far as Duncan's murder, but even beyond to the first meeting with the witches, where it was predicted that Banquo's sons would be kings. It points forward to the future, auguring not only Macbeth's destruction, but the fulfillment of the prediction.

Finally, the ghost appears to objectify Macbeth's current moral state. It reflects an image of Macbeth himself —of what he has become and will become.[20] To a degree it suggests that Macbeth's Nemesis, though it becomes a force outside him, actually derives from his own distorted soul. In the ghost's torn and bleeding shape we see the outcome of Macbeth's evil: the mutilated Banquo. But the ghost of the good Banquo can also be understood as a kind of analogy for Macbeth's mutilated soul, for that, too, once combined the virtues of valor and justice. In fact, through the ghost we can actually *see* Macbeth's end—*his* bloody and mutilated body, which is merely a reflection of his own inner state. It is his own "dire cruelty" that will destroy him: in the end he is his own Nemesis.

But both these conceptions of Nemesis, "subjective" and "objective" are connected with the "manly" image which has formed the basis of our discussion. To repeat, the results of Macbeth's bestiality are represented in the ghost of the "blood-bolter'd" dead man. We might say, then, that Macbeth's "manly image" casts for the moment the reflection of a beast:

[20] See Peter Dyson, "The Structural Function of the Banquet Scene in *Macbeth*," *SQ*, XIV (Autumn 1963), 375.

Hence, horrible shadow!
Unreal mock'ry hence!   (III.iv.106-107)

In these anguished words lies a recognition of self that
drains Macbeth's courage and leaves him trembling. For
the ghost's repellent form mocks not only the once-living
image of Banquo, but Macbeth's self-image as well. It
destroys Macbeth's "manhood" by instantaneously shat-
tering his self-conception, releasing the truth, and inadvertently suggesting his own end. Macbeth regains the
image and the self which accompanies it only after the
ghost makes its exit:

Why, so; being gone,
I am a man again. . . .   (III.iv.107-108)

In all of these ways does the actuality of Banquo's ghost
tend to illuminate and clarify the moral drama in which
Macbeth finds himself—to visualize the roles of conscience and Nemesis in relation to the hero's self-image.
But there is one more link to *Macbeth's* conception of
Nemesis and its part in the play. This concerns the
ultimately retributive roles of Macduff and Malcolm.
We recall how, horror-struck and trembling before the
apparition, Macbeth cries:

What man dare, I dare.
Approach thou like the rugged Russian bear,
The arm'd rhinoceros, or th' Hyrcan tiger;
Take any shape but that, and my firm nerves
Shall never tremble. Or be alive again,
And dare me to the desert with thy sword;
If trembling I inhabit then, protest me
The baby of a girl.   (III.iv.99-106)

The fact is that although it remains impossible for

Banquo to meet Macbeth in physical combat, Macduff can do so, and does, at the play's conclusion. It is Macduff who fights Macbeth sword against sword, not merely in fulfillment of the first apparition's warning of "Beware Macduff," but in answer to Macbeth's challenge to Banquo's ghost. And like Banquo, Macduff is invested with an aura of the supernatural, for he is the man unborn of woman Macbeth learns from the witches he must fear. Because of this Macduff also becomes a deputy of Nemesis, and he in turn is connected with Malcolm when he fights under the banner of Duncan's son, the true heir to the just king, the Prince of Cumberland, one of those innocent and brave children who ultimately lie beyond Macbeth's reach (like Fleance and Banquo's sons) and who form with Macduff, whose innocent children are murdered, suggestive links of a symbolic chain of Nemesis which ironically answers that especially cruel murder by binding the hero to his own death.[21] The Prince of Cumberland, a "step" the hero failed to "o'erleap," brings back to Scotland with him forces from the saintly English king, a sovereign in possession of "the healing benediction" and "a heavenly gift of prophecy"; a king whose "sundry blessings hang about his throne" and who, like the late Scottish king, is filled "full of grace."

Thus does Shakespeare establish the role of the outward universe while revealing its relationship to the

[21] Both Blisset (pp. 405-408) and Knight (*The Imperial Theme*, pp. 151-152) point out the connection between the time theme and the theme of sterility and future fruitfulness as they appear in *Macbeth*. Each suggests that the idea of the fruitfulness of the future is represented by the living children in the play, just as barrenness and sterility are represented by the murder of innocent children and mothers. These murders suggest a future unnaturally cut off.

inward world of the hero. We see Macbeth working in the universe and the universe working in Macbeth, their separate motions joined in the depth and darkness of his soul. The impulse toward evil throbs like the beat of a heart, sending out waves of action, each determining the next, which strike the shoals of heaven, then travel relentlessly backward to their source, inundating it, drowning it in the bitter waters of retribution.

So it is that with the death of Banquo and the subsequent appearance of his ghost, Macduff's function in the drama begins to assume new proportions. In Macbeth's mind, Macduff's failure to appear at the banquet suddenly connects itself with Banquo's unexpected and revealing (in every sense of the word) attendance. By not appearing at the banquet, Macduff becomes a "substitute" for Banquo. He acts as Macbeth had expected Banquo would. But with Macduff the failure to attend becomes ominous. Macbeth shores up his courage and focuses upon Macduff as a new object of "action"— a surrogate for Banquo. To such an extent has Macbeth bedeviled himself into suppression of memory and conscience that action, resolute and bloody, has become an automatic response to anyone or anything that even appears a threat. It is as if Banquo's ghostly and terrible appearance had revealed too much for Macbeth ever to look back without losing the sense of identity he must preserve in order to retain a crown which has never really been his. His language at this point figuratively bleeds in its harsh rededication to Lady Macbeth's ethic:

> For mine own good
> All causes shall give way. I am in blood
> Stepp'd in so far that, should I wade no more,

Returning were as tedious as go o'er.
Strange things I have in head, that will to hand,
Which must be acted ere they may be scann'd.

                                                    (III.iv.135-140)

In this passage Macbeth takes fate more fully into his own hands than he has before. Yet "equivocation" is still present. The last two lines indicate the typical relationship between the head, hand, and eye, the last, once again, refusing to "scan" the "horrid image" lest action be prevented. Between the head and the hand remains the willed blindness earlier associated with the imagery of the "bewitching" night.

Yet despite the force of Macbeth's rededication, he does not act. In the time elapsing before he attempts to realize his desires, Macduff makes his way to England and Malcolm. Action comes too late, and then in the most futile and unjustifiable form. The savage slaughter of Lady Macduff and her children completes the gesture that began with plotting Macduff's death. Moreover, with their murder, surely Macbeth's most cowardly and incriminating, action becomes more than a method of self-protection and a means of annihilating conscience; it becomes an end in itself. For what can Macbeth hope to accomplish in the realm of self-protection and preservation of the crown by such an act? Rather it is meant to punish Macduff for an offense not yet committed. As a practical measure, it is all but gratuitous. An effort of the will to rule the mind is realized through an attempt to control the objective world with action *per se*—any action, no matter how useless and brutal it may be in the face of reality:

> Time, thou anticipat'st my dread exploits:
> The flighty purpose never is o'ertook
> Unless the deed go with it. From this moment
> The very firstlings of my heart shall be
> The firstlings of my hand. And even now,
> To crown my thoughts with acts, be it thought and
>   done.   (IV.i.144-149)

In this speech the elements of time and action are perhaps at their most explicit. The "flighty purpose" must engage the future *before* fate can. If Macduff is a threat he must be summarily dealt with; but since he has managed to flee, Lady Macduff and her children will have to substitute for him. The last lines are a brilliant fusion of Macbeth's typical psychology as we have read it so far. "Thoughts" must be "crowned" with "acts"; "thinking" and "doing" must become the same "act." The murder of Lady Macduff fulfills the promise to do those things "which must be acted ere they may be scann'd." With it Macbeth becomes "valorous" with more ease than ever; and Lady Macduff and her children are murdered because Macduff is a threat; because Macbeth must do something to relieve his mental anguish. They are sacrificed in an irrational gesture against fate and the recalcitrance of time.

With this crime conscience is all but repressed completely. No "horrid image" raises its head. Macbeth's only acknowledgments of conscience are reflected in the haste imposed upon the decision and in his failure to commit the deed himself. Haste prevents the possibility of "wading back" in any sense, of permitting conscience to function properly. His delegating the deed to emissaries indicates at once the increasingly mechanical quality of his crimes and the impulse to hide behind his chosen agents. On the other hand, there is no protracted verbal effort to will responsibility for action to the atmosphere; nor does Macbeth make believe he is guiltless because he is not present at the scene of the crime. The customary state of "raptness" is missing, while the content of the speech in which Macbeth plots the destruction of Lady Macduff and her brood is somewhat reminiscent of the suggestive force of Lady Macbeth's portrait of exemplary valor: the idea of the slaughter of innocents is integral to both:

> The castle of Macduff I will surprise;
> Seize upon Fife; give to the edge o' th' sword
> His wife, his babes, and all unfortunate souls
> That trace him in his line.   (IV.i.150-153)

This murder, so shocking in its purposeless cruelty, is Shakespeare's most telling condemnation of Macbeth. For if the hero conforms more closely than ever to the standard of valor predicated by his wife, he deviates more completely than ever from the civilized standards of humanity and justice. Even Macbeth's conception of valor itself begins to show signs of wear that reveal uncompromisingly a shabbiness perhaps not as clearly revealed during the other murders. If this time fear has been utterly suppressed and action has become automatic, conversely physical participation is utterly missing and even were it present, it could scarcely, under the circumstances, mitigate our censure.

But the cumulative movement toward dire cruelty is also a movement away from rationality, with which conscience is connected. This idea of irrationality is further implied by Macbeth's reaction to those ambiguous and enigmatic apparitions invoked by the three witches in the scene prior to that of Lady Macduff's murder. It is this scene which provides the new pressure for the murder of Macduff, a pressure that leads to the death of his wife and children. But the scene also establishes the terms in which we are to read the last act. Macbeth refuses to acknowledge the confusing and contradictory nature of the apparitions' prophecies and chooses to see fate as propitious. He will take "a bond of fate" and "make assurance double sure" despite the fact that the first apparition's warning to "beware Macduff" and the vision of Banquo and his crowned sons, "stretch'd out to the crack o' doom" cancel out the advice of the other two apparitions. For the second and third have told him to "be bloody, bold, and resolute . . . for none of woman born/Shall harm Macbeth" and to "be lion-mettled, proud, and take no care . . . Macbeth shall never vanquish'd be until/Great Birnam wood to high Dunsinane hill/Shall come against him." As Arnold Stein suggests, these "verbal charms," the words of the witches and the apparitions which serve them, become Macbeth's single desperate reality. His "logic of action" is hinged to the witches' admonitions about Birnam wood and fearing no death by man born of woman.[22] Everything else becomes "walking shadows" and "sound and fury," agonizing, grotesque, meaningless. But Macbeth can repress all fear simply by recalling the apparitions' magic words. While the enemy approaches, he cries out to his attendants:

Bring me no more reports; let them fly all;
Till Birnam wood remove to Dunsinane

[22] Stein, "Macbeth and Word-Magic," p. 284.

I cannot taint with fear. What's the boy Malcolm?
Was he not born of woman?   (V.iii.1-4)

However, as the action proceeds, it becomes clear that
fate will not bear out Macbeth's allegiance to it. We have
seen Macduff and Malcolm readying themselves for an
invasion of the Scottish shores; now we see them on their
own soil. The death of Lady Macbeth symbolically re-
leases the burden of guilt she had borne for her husband and throws it back upon his shoulders. The cry of
her mourning women brings to him once again the
"taste of fears"; and almost immediately comes the next
blow: Birnam wood has "magically" begun to move toward Dunsinane, liberating even more powerfully a terror
whose ramifications project backward beyond the long
line of terrible deeds to that first "horrid image" which
assailed Macbeth's mind, and forward to the last one,
Macbeth's own head upon a pike.

The king's first reaction to the news concerning Birnam
wood is one of desperation, perhaps even panic:

Arm, arm, and out!
If this which he avouches does appear,
There is nor flying hence nor tarrying here.
(V.v.46-48)

But the gradual approach of the forces of Nemesis have
tied this "rebel against fate"[23] "to a stake." Baited like
a bear (image of the animal he has in part become), he
can do nothing but fight like an animal if he wishes
to keep the crown that has become his life; and if his
"acts" crown his life, as we have suggested, the crown
really *is* his life:

23 Dover Wilson's introduction to *Macbeth* (Cambridge, 1947),
p. lxv.

Ring the alarum-bell! Blow, wind! come, wrack!
At least we'll die with harness on our back.

(V.v. 51-52)

The call for the alarum-bell reminds us of the bell which
"invited" Macbeth to Duncan's murder, and we recognize
that slaughter has in a sense ultimately led to self-
slaughter. Now we are aware that the hero's only real
choice lies, after all, in the kind of death he selects; and
with this realization on our part, Macbeth's resolution,
although still bold, still bloody, takes on a new inflection.
It is difficult to prevent our admiration from going out
to him when we consider the odds he faces. It is almost
as if he were taking his punishment into his own hands
and refusing to relinquish his life to mysterious forces
outside himself. His last hope, the now more possible
impossibility that he might actually meet a man unborn
of woman (for Birnam wood has moved to Dunsinane),
seems almost a pitiable kind of dependency on supernatural support he himself can no longer trust. He begins "to doubt th' equivocation of the fiend/That lies
like the truth."

Nevertheless this dependency remains workable enough
for him to control fear automatically. He can still outface
the opposition and in doing so, dominate the scene.
Although our sympathies should lie unalloyed with
young Siward during Macbeth's fight with this soldier,
whose youth, tenderness, and valor align him solely with
the forces of good, we are instead overwhelmed by Macbeth's unrelenting belief in himself, his audacity even
to admit his own name:

Y.Siw. What is thy name?
Macb. Thou'lt be afraid to hear it.

Y.Siw. No; though thou call'st thyself a hotter name
   Than any is in hell.
Macb.   My name's Macbeth.
Y.Siw. The devil himself could not pronounce a title
   More hateful to mine ear.
Macb.   No, nor more fearful.
                           (V.vii.5-9)

Here, charged though the scene is with the suggestion
of the slaughter of innocents (for the fledgling soldier is
unequipped with anything but courage and a sword to
face the seasoned and dedicated warrior); though we
feel for young Siward and admire his valor, at the same
time we see him partly through Macbeth's eyes as an
interloper who would do better to confront adversaries
in his own class, who would be wiser to run at the sound
of the devil's name.

The scene, in fact, is an appropriate preliminary to the
meeting with Macduff, who comes to avenge his own
children and avenges young Siward as well by his conquest of the tyrant. But, for that matter, all the scenes
of the fifth act form appropriate preliminaries to Macbeth's meeting with Macduff. For despite the relentless-
ness of Macbeth's intonations in these scenes, the general
action sets him back to a point where conscience and
desire once again actively conflict. Indeed, looked at in
its entirety, the last Act can be understood as a kind of
pulsating release of conscience seen both in the subjective guise of fear and the objective guise of Nemesis.
In Act V Nemesis, via its representative characters, moves
in increasingly swift and powerful waves toward the
hero, always exciting the reaction of fear, which must
be quelled immediately in order for Macbeth to make
action take precedence. In Macbeth's speeches we sense

not only fearlessness, but the fearfulness that impels hardihood, the effort to make the manly image real. Thus at the point where Macbeth encounters Macduff, Nemesis, the object, and fear, the subject, coalesce, and Macbeth for the first time since Duncan's murder falls back into the morass of guilt:[24]

> *Macd.*   Turn, hell-hound, turn!
> *Macb.* Of all men else I have avoided thee.
> But get thee back: my soul is too much charg'd
> With blood of thine already.   (V.viii.3-6)

Macbeth draws back, confronted once again with a victim of his cruelty who is in a sense not only Macduff, but the ghost of Banquo, and the ghost of himself. The recognition that he is at last face to face with the man unborn of woman of whom he must beware "cows" Macbeth's "better part of man" as did Banquo's ghost, thus forcing him to relinquish the image of valor he has held before him like a shield. Macbeth's "valor," nurtured in part on the false sense of security the witches have given him, dissolves and Macbeth is denuded of his most valuable weapon, his conception of himself as a man whose courage and worthiness are the decree of fate:

> And be these juggling fiends no more believ'd
> That palter with us in a double sense,
> That keep the word of promise to our ear,
> And break it to our hope. I'll not fight with thee.
>   (V.viii.19-22)

But Macduff's jibe, "Then yield thee, coward," reverses the movement toward paralysis just as did Lady Macbeth's in Act I. Macduff's words inflame the portion of

[24] See Holloway, p. 69.

the hero's heart where the image of valor lies. The possibility of a penitent death, though open to Macbeth, is beyond his ken. Macbeth forgets that his soul is already too much charged with his adversary's blood and chooses the end fate has prepared. With his decision to fight Macduff, he embraces "action" more completely than ever before. For in the face of sure death, his determination to "lay on" rather than "kiss the ground before young Malcolm's feet/And . . . be baited by the rabble's curse" is an act of will that denies fear, the justice of Malcolm's cause, and mortality as well:

> Though Birnam wood be come to Dunsinane,
> And thou oppos'd, being of no woman born,
> Yet I will try the last. Before my body
> I throw my warlike shield. Lay on, Macduff,
> And damn'd be him that first cries, "Hold,
>   enough!"   (V.viii.30-34)

Still there is something awesome in the choice Macbeth makes. We know what the end will be, and we can see that in a way it is not another's death Macbeth wills, but his own. Untouched by remorse or repentance he becomes his own victim, his own damnation; Macduff is only the sword he uses. But we are prevented from accusing or condemning Macbeth for this ironic "suicide." Even as he takes resolute manliness for his shield this last time, he becomes his own source of punishment, so that after their long separation in his soul, valor and justice, as it were, unwittingly unite. The subject of the drama, Macbeth, and the object, Nemesis, become one. Through this paradoxical return to wholeness we find the hero to be what we have thought him all along—in some inexplicable way the source of his own fate.

For this reason we cannot accurately describe Macbeth's last valiant stand as an instance of "false courage."[25] It is far too complex for this sort of labeling. In fact, the quality of Macbeth's last stand all but defies human judgment. As suggested already, while action, immediate and automatic after Macduff's accusation of "coward," sacrifices conscience and repentance in the name of a distorted image, at the same time it automatically chooses the most just recompense for Macbeth's crimes. Macbeth, according to this view, delivers his own judgment upon himself. Of course, we can if we wish contrast his death with that of his namesake, the traitor Cawdor, who also "threw" away his life "as 'twere a careless trifle," but in a very different sense. We have been told by Malcolm in Act I that:

> . . . very frankly he confess'd his treasons,
> Implor'd . . . [Duncan's] pardon, and set forth
> A deep repentance. Nothing in his life
> Became him like the leaving it.   (I.iv.5-8)

Clearly the second Cawdor's death is in studied opposition to this one. Repentance is lacking, so is remorse. But justice is not. Somehow the will of fate has become

25 Lily B. Campbell (*Shakespeare's Tragic Heroes* [Cambridge, 1930], pp. 236-237) finds that in the last stages, Macbeth, who has "supp'd full with horrors" moves toward despair, "which is the final stage of fear and which manifests itself as fury. . . ." For Miss Campbell, Macbeth in this final scene fights only with the courage of an animal, "not with the fortitude of a man controlling passion by reason." Virgil K. Whitaker (*Shakespeare's Use of Learning*, p. 297) agrees with Miss Campbell and expresses his ideas in much the same terms. Nevertheless, although this interpretation may be doctrinally accurate, it seems hard to accuse Macbeth of being merely an animal here. Animals do not make speeches with the tone and sense of control in a desperate situation that Macbeth's "before my body/I throw my warlike shield . . ." illustrates. Certainly this has a heroic ring, despite everything that has gone before it.

Macbeth's will, and what is godly in his death impinges upon the relentless world he has himself chosen. Though stripped of the "supernatural" bolstering the witches had given him, in the last analysis he faces, alone and with dignity, the dreadful end his own acts have determined. And oddly enough, the manly image now holds true: it seems a heroic one.

The "usurper's cursed head" severed from his body like the "merciless Macdonwald's" at the beginning of the play, may well become a metaphor accurately representing Macbeth's self-contained universe of will and desire, an appropriate reflector, bestial and bloody, of the distorted image itself. But it does not explain everything. It fails to tell us why the image of valor seems not false but true in this last moment upon the banks and shoals of time. What we can say in Macbeth's defense is this: that in the end what is heroic about him is his refusal to put himself at the mercy of others outside himself, to passively will away his death to agents of any mysterious force as he had self-deceptively attempted to will away the lives of others. Having chosen himself as his own god and killed without mercy, he ironically becomes subject to the rigor of his own judgment, or perhaps misjudgment, and at the same time, his own blind justice. We may well conclude that it takes a king to kill a king. Time and fate, despite Macbeth's struggle to willfully annihilate them, have closed in. He accepts their edict even in defying it, and without blaming them or hiding behind them as hitherto he has. He takes them, as has been his custom, into his own hands. But like the noble Macbeth who fought and slew the "merciless Macdonwald" in Act I, he once again openly risks everything. The manly image indeed becomes his end.

III

OTHELLO AND *CORIOLANUS* :

THE IMAGE OF THE WARRIOR

From one perspective the title characters of *Othello* and *Coriolanus* form a distinct contrast. Where Othello seems warm and generous in his dealings with men at large, Coriolanus is cold and unyielding; where Othello shows emotional richness, Coriolanus reveals emotional poverty. Othello is the man whose open nature comes to exclude his wife at Iago's promptings. Coriolanus is the man whose closed nature can be opened only by his mother's promptings, and then too late.

Yet despite such differences, these characters reveal certain interesting similarities. In each play Shakespeare takes a soldier hero and places him in a situation with which his military training cannot cope. Othello is confronted with the complexities of love; Coriolanus is faced with the temporarily "peaceful" state of Rome. Action in these plays centers, therefore, to some extent upon the unfamiliarity of the situations themselves, and there is an invisible dividing line between the traits of the characters and the kind of action the new situations require. Secondly, Othello and Coriolanus are above all soldiers, men of action; the esteem in which they are held by Venice's signory and Rome's senate respectively gives them some warrant to believe in their own power and their own righteousness of conduct. They have "done the state some service," and each is highly aware of the state's obligation to him. Their belief in themselves and their success on the battlefield may be construed, consequently, as factors in the kinds of intellectual and emotional blindness they come to demonstrate. How Othello finally chooses to act upon the supposed infidelity of his wife, how Coriolanus chooses to act upon the problem of the consulship, become in each case a measure of their failure, not simply as soldiers, but as men.

Othello and Coriolanus can best be contrasted to such highly reflective types as Brutus or Hamlet. Although Brutus and Hamlet also meet with strikingly unfamiliar situations, action is possible for them only after a period of introspective thinking. The student Hamlet must avenge his father and assume the obligation of curing a sick state; the philosopher Brutus believes he must assassinate Caesar and is forced to assume the political and military responsibilities which follow the murder. However, for these two, violent action is not a way of life but a moment of strained and tormented self-realization; it is the breaking of a habit, a forced march in the face of destiny. For Othello and Coriolanus, action, warlike action, is the habit which fails to acknowledge other potential modes of being, and which therefore becomes a killing habit.

The approval Venice and Rome give to the active military roles of Othello and Coriolanus is perhaps a factor in their singular lack of introspection. It is as if their recognized distinction as soldiers and their necessity to the state have dislocated their self-criticizing faculties. This is less true of Othello than it is of Coriolanus, who is incapable of seeing himself as anything but a soldier, that is, in his public role. But Othello also manifests the dislocation, as witnessed by his references to his military accomplishments. Yet if Othello and Coriolanus are admired, if they admire themselves for their military abilities, this admiration comes at the expense of certain important internal powers. Their public selves are very much isolated from their personal ones. Of all Shakespeare's heroes, excluding perhaps Timon, they are the men who remain most permanently unaware of their own natures. The violent and destructive feelings of which they prove capable are hidden by the accepted military forms and tactics they use in defense of their respective countries. War is their fulfillment, not merely an occupation. This is not to say Shakespeare is criticizing soldiers *per se,* but rather the kind of mind which cannot penetrate the secret of its violence because it has gone rigid with self-approbation.[1]

Therefore, if Iago in his brilliantly corrupt manner can say of himself, "I am not what I am," Othello and Coriolanus, though in part suffering from the same kind of dissociation, cannot make such a statement because they are incapable of the realization. To Othello, all men, including himself, "are what they seem to be"; this logic, ironically, actually holds true for Othello's condemnation of Desdemona. The "evidence" Iago gives against Desdemona makes her *seem* a whore—in consequence Othello must *be* a cuckold and Desdemona must die. By the same token, if the plebs in *Coriolanus* seem as a class to be "dissentious rogues," they must therefore be devoid of any human qualities and can be abused as worthless "scabs." Finally, if one seems to be a hero, if all one's community agrees one is a hero, the awareness of this title can give him "positional assurance," to

[1] See Robert B. Heilman, *Magic in the Web* (Lexington, Ky., 1956), p. 185.

quote Robert Heilman.[2] By the term Heilman means a feeling of moral righteousness, of unassailability which allows a man to believe his conduct is automatically beyond reprobation. The soldier hero, in short, selects as his total reality the reality his title gives him. He visualizes himself in a word, but fails to recognize the word does not cover all of him as a human being. Thus can he believe that "direct," "forthright," and "righteous" action—the action of the soldier's manual and military tribunals, or of punitive assaults against one's country, is appropriate to situations which actually demand reserve and sensitivity.

In *Othello* Shakespeare places the soldier hero in a close human entanglement, the kind of human entanglement for which his background and sense of himself have in no way prepared him.[3] The action is internal: it is increasingly detached from the military problem of defending Cyprus and more and more focused upon the inner domain of the bedchamber and the heart. As Bradley puts it: "His deed and his death have not that influence on the interests of a nation or an empire which serves to idealise, and to remove from our own sphere, the stories of Hamlet and Macbeth, of Coriolanus and Antony."[4] Othello's jealousy of Desdemona achieves precisely what he said his bringing her to Cyprus would not achieve. He does "scant" the state's "serious and great business . . ./When she is with" him, but only because, strangely enough, he

[2] *Ibid.*, p. 142. Heilman describes "positional assurance" as "a sense of status, of propriety of attitude."

[3] Supporting arguments are given by J. Dover Wilson and Alice Walker, eds., *Othello* (Cambridge, 1957), p. xxxix and F. R. Leavis, "Diabolic Intellect and the Noble Hero: A Note on Othello," *Scrutiny*, VI (December 1937), 283.

[4] A. C. Bradley, *Shakespearean Tragedy*, p. 148.

puts her away from him. The results, however, insofar as the state is concerned, are minimal. The setting, despite the early threat of the Cyprus wars, is a "peaceful" one, and when war really breaks out, it breaks out full-blown and bloody on the domestic front.

In *Coriolanus* dramatic action is almost wholly external: there is little "love interest" of any kind in this play. The entire working out of Caius Marcius' tragedy is presented as part of the panorama of state. Coriolanus' expulsion from Rome, though significant in a number of ways, may and should be apprehended first on the political level. For it is only by relating the political factionalism of the plebs and the patricians to the personal factionalism of Coriolanus (if it can be said that one man makes a party) that a unified understanding of the play can be attained, that we can comprehend how fully *Coriolanus* is a tragedy of state. Hence disunity in the peaceful Othello household is complemented by disunity in the state of Rome. Both *Othello* and *Coriolanus* are tragedies of domestic war, and although war in the bedchamber is not the same as war in the streets, the two kinds of conflict are morally related. *Othello* and *Coriolanus* are counterparts because in each case the truest enemy ultimately resides within the "peaceful" state, while in the beginning the greatest threat seems to be a force outside it: for Venice, the Turk; for Rome, Antium. But *Othello* involutes the theme one step further. Iago is the villain in the state of Venice; but Othello is his marriage state's own worst enemy. By the end of the play he sees himself as such, and in his last speech he converts himself into the kind of outward enemy he is capable of handling. An identification is made, not only with

Venice's traditional enemy, the Turk, but with that "Spartan dog," Iago; yet it is Othello who dies:

> And say besides, that in Aleppo once,
> Where a malignant and a turban'd Turk
> Beat a Venetian and traduc'd the state,
> I took by th' throat the circumcised dog,
> And smote him—thus.   [stabs himself.]
> (V.ii.352-356)

In Kenneth Burke's words, "the villain and hero here are but essentially inseparable parts of the one fascination."[5] On the island of Cyprus Iago is the outer force of evil; but the villain within Othello is that portion of himself which clasps the evil in a corrupt and deadly embrace.

Likewise, just as Othello in welcoming Iago to his bosom becomes the great enemy of his own domestic bliss, in *Coriolanus* it is Caius Marcius himself, the great defender of Rome, who ultimately becomes that state's chief threat. However, in his self-righteousness Coriolanus never sees himself as a traitor to Rome, while Othello comes, at least in part, to recognize his guilt and wrong-headedness. Coriolanus instead of recognizing his own treachery, sees Rome and only Rome, as the vicious party. The case is a simple one for him: it is he who is defending himself from his city's treacherous "ingratitude," and his defense is to march against not only the plebs who have exiled him, but the patricians who have loved him.

[5] Kenneth Burke, "*Othello*: An Essay to Illustrate a Method," *HR*, IV (Summer 1951), 166. John Holloway (*The Story of the Night*, p. 56) also notes the identification made between Othello and that "circumcised dog"—the "turban'd Turk." See also Derek A. Traversi, *An Approach to Shakespeare*, 2nd edition (New York, 1956, Copyright: Sands & Company, Ltd.), pp. 128-129.

ief, *Othello* and *Coriolanus* share a common moral
tive despite the different materials they deal with.
... *ello* the limitations of the soldier hero are explored
on the personal level, and tension is engendered by means
of the very closeness of the characters and the intimacy
of the language and imagery they use. *Coriolanus*, on the
contrary, circumvents the personal to a large extent and
treats its hero's limitations almost solely in social and
military terms. Tension is created by means of the distance between the various elements of the state and by
the use of a language often as harsh as it is durable. In
Othello the hero's personal self is exposed. In *Coriolanus*,
because the hero all but has no personal self, since it has
been lost in its military and aristocratic functions, that
self either must be inferred or cannot be found at all.
And this, perhaps, is the major distinction between the
two characters: Othello, for all his self-deception, still has
something of a personal self to expose, while what is exposed in *Coriolanus* is the terrifying emptiness of the
central character.

If the element scrutinized most deliberately in *Othello*
is the central character's inner life, that element is mani-
fested dramatically, of course, in his relationship with
Desdemona and Iago. Before the signory in Act I Othello
demonstrates his typical public character. His conduct,
restrained and self-possessed in the face of Brabantio's
accusations, is both accepted and admired by the senators, and in Othello can be discerned the grandeur and
nobility which must have attracted Desdemona. Yet his
conduct throughout the rest of the play—his acquiescence
to Iago, his trust in him (particularly in view of what the
audience knows of Iago's villainy) and his thematic relationship to the gulled Roderigo suggest about him the

quality of foolishness Emilia points out in the last act. It is a quality he himself acknowledges after having heard the true story of his wife's "infidelity." "O fool! fool! fool!" he cries as his previous blindness becomes increasingly apparent to him.

The "flaw" within Othello that allows for his gulling, according to Heilman, is a kind of internal insecurity whose roots cannot be categorically identified.[6] This "insecurity" exists, nevertheless, clearly enough for those, like Iago, who can see below the surface of things and who know the difference between seeming and being. Ironically, it exists as clearly as the blackness of the Moor's face and is printed as indelibly upon his soul as his color is printed upon his flesh. Yet to say so is not to identify Othello's problem as a racial one in the contem-

[6] Heilman, p. 139. Heilman argues that ". . . Othello's scope is lost sight of if we can understand him only by racial psychology. . . . Othello's Moorishness, if it is anything more than a neutral heritage from Cinthio, is less a psychological or moral factor than a symbol of characteristic human problems currently denoted by such overly familiar terms as 'insecurity' and 'rejection.' Moorishness, in this sense, is one of the ills the flesh is heir to." Two views which do notice the Moor's blackness as a racial issue, and a social issue as well, are Laurence Lerner's "The Machiavel and the Moor," *EIC*, IX (October 1959), 339-360 and Allan D. Bloom's "Cosmopolitan Man and the Political Community: An Interpretation of *Othello*," *APSR*, LIV (March 1960), 130-157. Lerner feels that the "conventional" Venetian view of Othello as a black man and an outsider is justified in the end. Othello proves himself the black savage he was thought to be (pp. 358-359). Eldred D. Jones in "The Machiavel and the Moor," *EIC*, X (April 1960), 234-238, answers Lerner's article. Bloom's piece depicts Othello as a "cosmopolitan man" attempting to break through societal boundaries. For a good answer to Bloom see Sigurd Burckhardt, "English Bards and *APSR* Reviewers," *APSR*, LIV (March 1960), 158-166. For Bloom's response to Burckhardt and the give and take which follow, see the same volume of *APSR*: Bloom, "Political Philosophy and Poetry," pp. 457-464; Burckhardt, "On Reading Ordinary Prose," pp. 465-470; and Bloom's final statement, "A Restatement," pp. 471-473.

porary sense, or necessarily as a racial problem at all. Rather, the Moor's blackness might be more fully explained as representative of some latent evil which is part of the human soul, and which can come to dominate the whole man when stimulated effectively.[7] In Act III, when Othello momentarily looks inside to find the cause of Desdemona's supposed disaffection, he offers the following possibilities:

> Haply, for I am black
> And have not those soft parts of conversation
> That chamberers have, or for I am declin'd
> Into the vale of years. . . .   (III.iii.263-266)

But he rejects these suggestions immediately with the remark "yet that's not much," and it becomes difficult to say whether he is merely repressing a sense of inadequacy he cannot bear, or whether he actually feels and means precisely what he says. Traversi states that Othello is subject to a sense of "mortifying social inferiority"[8] with which he cannot cope, and such an interpretation is plausible, provided we do not lay too much stress on the word "mortifying" (for Shakespeare treats the matter most delicately, if he is really treating it at all), and provided we do not reduce the play to a symposium on race relations or a sociological treatise on Old Venice.[9] In

[7] Heilman, p. 139.

[8] Traversi, *An Approach to Shakespeare*, p. 142.

[9] Wilson and Walker, eds., *Othello*, p. x. Wilson feels that "The marriage between an African with a 'sooty bosom' and an Italian girl with 'whiter skin than snow' sets the racial problem in its extremest form, and most of Act I is given to bringing this out." On p. xii Wilson says I.iii.397-400 sums up "the relations between African and European for the past three and a half centuries." Arthur Sewell (*Character and Society in Shakespeare*, pp. 91-97) does not give a "sociological" interpretation of the play, but he does see the society of Venice as playing a significant part in the drama, primarily

order to prevent ourselves from doing so, we might turn to Kenneth Burke, who by means of adept phraseology manages to combine in his explanation of Othello's blackness both the "sociological" and the "universal" points of view: "So, in contrast with the notion of the story of a black (low-born) man cohabiting with (identified with) the high-born Desdemona, we should say rather that the role of Othello as 'Moor' draws for its effects upon the sense of the black man in every lover."[10] "Effects" here is the focal word, for it allows Shakespeare to gain from his audience (Elizabethan, modern, indeed any Western audience) certain emotional responses to the Moor's blackness, while in no way attempting to define Shakespeare's racial prejudices. It allows, moreover, the more universal perspective mentioned earlier. The black man in every lover may be interpreted as the complex figure of Iago, the white man whose soul is black, the principle of evil which appeals to and can be accepted by even an admirable man, a man like Othello himself.[11] However, although the evil is elicited from Othello, although Othello's jealousy can be designated "secondary" rather than "primary," as Heilman would have it, it must be agreed that Heilman is also correct in suggesting that this in no way contradicts the idea that evil is there to be elicited and that, in consequence, Othello remains at least partially responsible for his actions.[12] The suggestion that Othello

---

as a kind of "director" of Othello's and Iago's values. See also Wyndham Lewis' description of Iago as the "villain Everyman" in *The Lion and the Fox* (New York, n.d.), pp. 188-189.

[10] Burke, "*Othello*: An Essay to Illustrate a Method," p. 182.

[11] See Leavis, p. 264.

[12] Heilman (pp. 38-39) says "secondary jealousy" is "induced, not spontaneous, and it takes root and gains strength not because of an addition to sexual suspiciousness but because of other charac-

truly comes to *believe* in Desdemona's infidelity, whether
"tricked" into this belief by Iago or not, does not entirely
mitigate his guilt. In fact, it is difficult to say exactly how
justifiable his conduct would appear had his wife actually
been unfaithful. Undoubtedly there would be a tendency
to sympathize with him more in these circumstances; murder to our eyes, nevertheless, scarcely seems the answer to
the problem of adultery even when taking the Elizabethan
conception of masculine honor into consideration. The
impulse to kill as a means of release from his difficulty
comes as a spontaneous reaction on the part of Othello.
Moreover, it is the kind of solution to which, it can be
assumed, constant experience in war has accustomed him
—a traditional method of punishing "traitors." The very
real humiliation he feels in regard to Desdemona's betrayal must necessarily make his response that much more
automatic and violent.

Othello's failure to treat Desdemona more humanely
can be in part explained as the result of the limited sort
of training he has had and the limited sort of experience
to which he has been accustomed.[13] "On trial" before the

---

teristics." It has to do with the "inner trouble" which "makes him
prone to acquiesce in the invention of a great imaginary evil for
himself. . . . 'Primary jealousy' is not induced, but spontaneous;
it is not occasional but chronic; it is not the product of exceptional
circumstances acting upon the character, but the character's essential mode of responding to circumstances. It is the basic determinant
of moral direction. It has been called . . . envy." Clearly, it is Iago
who fits this latter description. Lily B. Campbell (*Shakespeare's
Tragic Heroes*, p. 153) notes much the same element in Iago.

[13] Heilman, p. 187. Bradley, of course, noted the "strange life of
war and adventure" which Othello "has lived from childhood"
(*Shakespearean Tragedy*, p. 153); however, Bradley understands this
life, not as a limitation, but as something which makes Othello
"by far the most romantic figure among Shakespeare's heroes."

signory, Othello begins the defense for his surreptitious marriage in the following way:

> Rude am I in my speech,
> And little bless'd with the soft phrase of peace;
> For since these arms of mine had seven years' pith
> Till now, some nine moons wasted, they have us'd
> Their dearest action in the tented field,
> And little of this great world can I speak
> More than pertains to feats of broils and battle,
> And therefore little shall I grace my cause
> In speaking for myself.   (I.iii.81-89)

Othello's words suggest that the ways of love have been as foreign to him as those of the drawing room, and his statement can be accepted as a recognition of this limitation and thus as an expression of self-effacement. Clearly this seems to be the manner in which Othello expects his words to be taken. Conversely, this kind of admission (and Othello makes several of them) can also be looked upon as an attempt to point up his superiority in the realm of military life, and in doing so, to suggest circumspectly the "obvious" and "primary" importance of this realm and his success in it, thus excusing himself from any failure in other areas of experience. To be brief, such statements can be viewed as a defense of the self which seems to apologize for personal weakness while actually congratulating the self upon its strength. Also, whatever Othello says, he surely does "grace" his cause in speaking for himself. It is the very rhetoric he uses in describing his courtship of Desdemona that wins the duke to his side. As the duke puts it, "I think this tale would win my daughter too." Yet the speech describing the courtship bears a certain similarity to Othello's "apology." The choice of such words as "dearest action in the tented field" and "feats of broils and battle" is significant because it is the same kind of language the Moor uses when explaining how he won Desdemona:

> Wherein I spoke of most disastrous chances,
> Of moving accidents by flood and field,
> Of hair-breadth scapes i' th' imminent deadly breach,
> Of being taken by the insolent foe
> And sold to slavery, of my redemption thence
> And portance in my travel's history;
> Wherein of antres vast and deserts idle,
> Rough quarries, rocks, [and] hills whose heads touch heaven,
> It was my hint to speak. . . .   (I.iii.134-142)

This speech, we assume, reflects the tone Othello used with Desdemona herself, and clearly its terms are calculated to reveal the Moor in his own best light. There would seem nothing untoward about this, considering how Brabantio requested Othello in the first place to tell the story of his life. On the other hand, Othello apparently felt no disinclination to hold forth, to create a heroic picture of himself for his young, lovely, and attentive listener. Curiously, she seems to have functioned more as an audience for him than as a recipient of his devout praises. It is this element of self-dramatization which Traversi regards as "a contribution to the rhetorical fiction whose justification is the main purpose of his life,"[14] the fiction being that he is something more than an ordinary mortal. Brabantio absurdly accuses Othello of having used sorcery to entrance his daughter; Othello responds that his "story" was the only witchcraft he used.

---

[14] Traversi, *Approach to Shakespeare*, pp. 133-134.

Nevertheless, it may be felt that Shakespeare is in some measure indicating the efficacy of rhetoric in its own right to create a potent image capable of moving the heart, an image which somehow is not quite wholly accurate in regard to the individual it purports to represent. For is this not very like, though not identical to, Iago's method in the temptation scene? He changes Desdemona's image, but even more daringly for the broader gap between the image and the reality. Yet, to complicate matters even further, is it not also true that the rhetoric with which Othello inadvertently disguises part of the truth, the part earlier described as his own self-doubt, at the same time measures the impulse toward dignity and grandeur felt so strongly in the Moor?

Another example of Othello's attempts at self-effacement which may reveal as much pride as modesty occurs a few lines later. The duke has just announced the imminent invasion of Cyprus by the Turks and has informed Othello his services as general are required. Othello replies:

> The tyrant custom, most grave senators,
> Hath made the flinty and steel couch of war
> My thrice-driven bed of down. I do agnize
> A natural and prompt alacrity
> I find in hardness, and do undertake
> These present wars against the Ottomites.
>
> (I.iii.230-235)

Certain words in this speech like "tyrant custom" and "agnize" give warrant for an interpretation that sees Othello acknowledging a doubtful trait in himself. The question is, how honest is this acknowledgment? We might feel it is somewhat odd, considering Othello's newly married state, that he accepts his orders not as a man who wishes to do his duty in spite of his personal feelings, but rather as one who admits these orders are most attractive to him, perhaps even more attractive than the new wife standing at his side. Of course, it can be explained that he hopes to take Desdemona with him to Cyprus; yet why the aura of self-consciousness surrounding the speech? Why the vague tone of apology when in truth he lives for the "pride, pomp, and circumstance of glorious war"? Does the statement, in short, become self-laudatory in the end, another pointer toward those "disastrous chances" and "moving accidents of flood and field" which give Othello the distinction of heroic accomplishment, the sense of which is latent in the language he uses: the "flinty and steel couch of war" and the attraction toward "hardness"?

If such is the case, the real personal limitations a life of "hardness" breeds are in fact unexplored verbally by Othello at any point in the play, although the play itself surely reveals these limitations. The metaphor of war's hard but beloved bed exposes Othello's true feeling for his occupation and for himself, while at the same time predicting through its confusion of the battlefield and the marriage bed what is actually to become the play's climactic action, the slaying of Desdemona in a real marriage bed. It is, then, at the expense of love that war is idealized,[15] and what Othello fails to recognize is that a life of "hardness"—an outer life of heroic accomplishment, can make men hard, that is, unfeeling and insensitive to the subtleties of personal experience, even as it can make them heroic on the battle line.[16]

[15] See G. R. Elliot, *Flaming Minister* (Durham, N.C., 1953), p. xxxi.
[16] Heilman, p. 14.

Thus it appears that the stance Othello habitually takes is a romantically heroic one, whatever the man himself may be. The showmanship of his rhetoric diverts attention from the internal failings he demonstrates in the portion of the play yet to come,[17] failings he himself identifies in the first act without really being aware of their meaning. In his language can be seen the latent insecurity, self-protectiveness, and lack of self-possession instrumental in causing the tragedy.[18]

[17] *Ibid.*, p. 140 and p. 166. See Heilman on "showmanship" in reference to Othello's last speech. See also Traversi, *Approach to Shakespeare*, p. 128. The question occurs as to whether the "rhetoric" in Othello's speeches is to be attributed to him, or whether it is simply a necessary element in the writing of poetic drama. S. L. Bethell ("Shakespeare's Imagery: The Diabolic Images in *Othello*," *SS*, V [1952], 64) notes that where tragic heroes like Othello are concerned, "The poetry is not an outcome of their characters but their characters are created by poetry." Bethell's point is well-taken; yet in drama, once a character speaks, he becomes not only responsible for what he says but how he says it. The kind of language a character uses inescapably impresses an audience; they identify him, his consistency, and inconsistency not only by means of his actions but also by the way he speaks. Surely the poetry in poetic drama is a convention; nevertheless, if characters are to have an integrity of their own, an integrity which can be evaluated and judged, we must be able to take their words seriously as *their* words; and these words must reflect their characters. This is especially true for the central figures in a play.

[18] E. E. Stoll argues that Othello is "lacking in a predisposition, a psychology." See *Shakespeare and Other Masters* (Cambridge, Mass., 1940), p. 190. His suggestion, however, that Othello "is led to hearken to Iago, not with a psychological justification, but by means of time honored convention" in fact begs the question. For the point is, of course, that Othello has no *real* justification at all, no rationally concrete motivation of the kind Stoll demands. Rather he acts, as many of us do in critical situations, out of emotional "motivations." As William O. Raymond says, although theatrical exigencies play a part in the "incompleteness" of motivation, if such "motivation" were basically faulty or incomplete, the quality of the play would certainly suffer ("Motivation and Character Portrayal in *Othello*," *UTQ*, XVII [October 1947], 95). For a further view of Stoll's concept of psychology, see *Art and Artifice in Shakespeare*

Othello's self-glamorizing remains a consistent trait until the very end. The speech describing how he won Desdemona, his speech of farewell to military life, and even his terminal speech are all cases in point. If each is resonant with sound and full of color, these very qualities "color" the truth: they deflect our scrutiny from Othello's limitations by pointing up the one role in which the Moor has always been a success. These speeches captivate with a kind of theatricality, a flair for the grand manner which manages to engage the imagination, but at the expense of part of the human truth.[19] In the end, Othello's public life as a soldier—his "battles, sieges, fortunes"—his having done the state some service—is used by him to extenuate the story of jealousy he would have Lodovico relate, apparently, without reservation. Othello's sense of

---

(New York, 1933), p. 53 and "*Othello*: An Historical and Comparative Study," *The University of Minnesota Studies in Language and Literature*, No. 2 (March 1915), 1-70. Leo Kirschbaum (*Character and Characterization in Shakespeare* [Detroit, 1962]) argues against the position which fails to find some element in Othello's nature at least partially responsible for the tragedy. Kirschbaum makes the astute observation that although everyone finds Iago "honest," only Othello is capable of believing that Desdemona could be promiscuous. Kirschbaum notices three times in the play when it is suggested to characters, namely Cassio, Emilia, and Roderigo, that Desdemona is unchaste. In each case, however, the characterization is rejected. Only Othello comes to believe in the characterization. Kirschbaum implies that the three rejections are purposeful contrasts to Othello's acceptance of the idea of an unchaste Desdemona and that this acceptance indicates a flaw in Othello (pp. 148-150). Kirschbaum also notices a contrast between Cassio's ability to acknowledge his guilt for drunkenness at II.iii.268ff. and Othello's incomplete acknowledgment of his guilt in his last speech (pp. 147-148).

[19] Leavis (pp. 266-267) suggests that Othello takes the noble warrior in himself to be "the whole of reality." Marvin Rosenberg argues against the entire Leavis-Traversi-Heilman interpretation in his discussion of the "modern Moor" in *The Masks of Othello* (Berkeley and Los Angeles, 1961), pp. 185-205.

his own "foolishness" is converted into a rhetorical triumph which reveals the hero's instinctive drive toward dignity and order while also indicating his persistent impulse toward ennobling self-disguise. It becomes, in fact, impossible to separate these two impelling forces:

> Then must you speak
> Of one that lov'd not wisely but too well;
> Of one not easily jealous, but, being wrought,
> Perplex'd in the extreme; of one whose hand,
> Like the base [Indian], threw a pearl away
> Richer than all his tribe; of one whose subdu'd eyes
> Albeit unused to the melting mood,
> Drops tears as fast as the Arabian trees
> Their medicinal gum. Set you down this;
> And say besides, that in Aleppo once,
> Where a malignant and a turban'd Turk
> Beat a Venetian and traduc'd the state,
> I took by th' throat the circumcised dog,
> And smote him—thus.   [stabs himself.]
>   (V.ii.343-356)

In Leavis' words, the final portion of this speech is a "superb *coup de théâtre*" for Othello as well as Shakespeare. "That he should die acting his ideal part is all in the part." Still, although we may agree with Leavis that Othello's last magnificent attempt at self-demonstration feels right because Othello the actor and Othello the man of action symbolically blend and affirm his heroic reality; although we may admit that "Othello dies belonging to the world of action in which his true part lay,"[20] we

[20] Leavis, p. 276. Conversely, Traversi (*Approach to Shakespeare*, p. 148) writes that in the end the last speech can be interpreted as "the dupe's attempt at self-justification in an irrelevant pose"

must also agree with Heilman that somehow Othello's self-recognition is not quite complete. The blindness instrumental in Desdemona's death is perceived by him as helplessness in the face of destiny:

> But, O vain boast!
> Who can control his fate?
> (V.ii.264-265)

This sense of helplessness is transformed into a kind of excuse when he speaks of himself as "one not easily jealous, but, being wrought,/Perplex'd in the extreme."[21]

Thus the speech preceding Othello's death reveals his limitations even as it frees his last noble act. It is by converting the personal tragedy of Desdemona's murder into a public one that he finds a sufficiently familiar identity amid the welter of unfamiliar private emotions to carry out his justice. The Venetian and the turban'd Turk who "do battle" in Othello's last lines are public forms of a self which still cannot apprehend personal realities in their own right. They are the hero and villain of the private drama in which Othello has, so to speak, taken both parts; but these parts are reconceived by means of their public names. Desdemona is lost to these last lines; nevertheless they raise the Moor toward the level of dignity he demonstrated in Act I. They act as a "cue" for Othello, releasing the great soldier he is. Once again, as in the case of Brutus, the point of death is the point

---

in addition to being "a piece of splendid self-centered poetry. . . ." T. S. Eliot, of course, said that Othello was merely "cheering himself up" in his last speech (*Selected Essays* [New York, 1932], p. 111). Dover Wilson, however, gives a good argument against the Eliot-Traversi interpretation (*Othello*, p. liii). Wilson says that it would be difficult for the actor to "act *the acting* of a regained nobility, satanic or otherwise."

21 Heilman, p. 163.

of "freedom." The will Othello lamentably ceded to Iago is now once again his own.

Othello's great limitation, then, like that of Brutus or Macbeth, is a habit of mind he comes to adopt. His fault lies in his way of "seeing" things, and as Heilman says, this manner of perception is associated with Iago's way of "seeing" things. According to this interpretation, Iago manages to impose upon Othello a point of view which accepts "facts" as "proof" of Desdemona's infidelity, but in a situation demanding not proofs but the delicacy of the instincts.[22] Iago's mind, mechanistic and legalistic in its limitations, succeeds in transferring these limitations to Othello's mind. In Heilman's words, "When Othello decides to follow Iago and be 'wise' and 'cunning,' he adopts . . . a new code; he will 'see' the facts, get the 'evidence,' 'prove' his case, and execute 'justice.' "[23]

This "new" code, however, proves to be related to Iago's style of speaking. Iago's "facts" and "proofs" in the crucial temptation scene are actually rhetorical devices by means of which Iago encourages Othello to create a damaging conception of himself. Actually the "facts" and "proofs" of Desdemona's infidelity cannot exist because Desdemona has not been unfaithful. Therefore the chief tool in the temptation scene is language, or the rhetorical use of language: it is by means of words alone that Iago convinces Othello of Desdemona's infidelity. These words become the "facts" and "proofs" in the case.

Iago's rhetoric, potent with an imagery of sensuality, animality, and disgust, is diametrically opposed to Othel-

[22] See Winifred M. T. Nowottny, "Justice and Love in *Othello*," *UTQ*, XXI (July 1952), 330-344; Moody Prior, "Character in Relation to Action in *Othello*," *MP*, XLIV (February 1947), 233; and Traversi, *Approach to Shakespeare*, p. 140.
[23] Heilman, p. 226.

lo's rhetoric of dignified self-glorification. Yet the rhetorical impulse is displayed by each. Iago is constantly making speeches to Roderigo, and though they are in "prose," they are as much speeches as those Othello makes in "blank verse." Just as Othello uses language to reflect the image of himself he wishes to see, likewise, Iago, when speaking to Othello, uses language in much the same way; but his language reflects Othello's fears and insecurities; it establishes an image Othello would rather hide and not see. The key to Othello's conduct lies in his response to the spoken imagistic word, because for him it is not merely a word, but reality. And in a sense this is equally true for Iago. Iago's idea that all women are faithless and all men, barring himself, are fools is based not on facts, but on a stereotyped conception of reality which is mirrored in the very language he uses. He envisions people as "types" and acts on his assumptions in order to individualize himself, to bolster his own ego and justify his misdeeds.[24] It might even be said that Iago's "realism" is actually an inflation or exaggeration of the world's corruption. His realism is as "romantic" as Othello's idealization of Iago (for does not Othello believe men what they seem to be?). In this light Iago appears to be as much a believer in his own images as is Othello, and what Othello adopts from Iago seems, after all, not simply a "legalistic" or "mechanistic" viewpoint, but a set of images which make concrete and demonstrable feelings and attitudes already latent in him. Othello is literal-minded only to the extent that he accepts the lying images Iago gives him literally. His mind, like Iago's, is in reality stridently "metaphorical." His reaction to symbolic metaphors is symptomatic

[24] *Ibid.*, pp. 39-41. See the discussion of Coleridge's term "motiveless malignity."

of imaginative powers beyond the ordinary. The legalistic attitude adopted is merely an intellectual guise for attitudes essentially emotional in nature, just as Iago's intellectual cleverness disguises a perversion rooted somehow in his own hard-bitten sensuality.

It is, then, by means of "symbolic words" that Othello's "doubts" are stimulated and made "proofs"; moreover, we might suggest that such words could very well stimulate doubts in anyone. Hence, a central problem in *Othello* concerns the way the mind functions on the "metaphorical" or "symbolic" level.[25] How can a reality be created where supporting facts do *not* objectively exist, and what can such a false reality lead to? These questions, which might be approached through psychology alone, can be equally well approached by referring to the use of language in *Othello*, precisely because Shakespeare makes words the central issue in the temptation scene—the words that lead Othello to his ultimate self-destruction.[26]

[25] Susanne K. Langer, *Philosophy in a New Key* (Cambridge, Mass., 1960), pp. 40-52. Mrs. Langer's philosophical and aesthetic position is pertinent to the use of language as I have been describing it in *Othello*, and indeed, the rest of the tragedies. Her description of the human mind as first and foremost a symbol maker, a description that implies the essence of language is "poetic" rather than "discursive," and that discursive language is actually a development out of the symbolistic function of the human mind, seems especially applicable to *Othello*. See especially the first five chapters of *Philosophy in a New Key*. Another philosophical view of language which seems useful here is Croce's. Croce says: "Logical thought is not language, but it never exists without language, and it uses the language which poetry has created; by means of concepts (here Croce uses the word to mean thinking on an abstract plane), it discerns and dominates the representations of poetry, and it could not dominate them unless they, its future subjects, had first an existence of their own" (Benedetto Croce, "Aesthetics," *Encyclopaedia Britannica*, 14th edition, I, 265).

[26] Irving Ribner analyzes the temptation scene from his own perspective in *Patterns in Shakespearian Tragedy*, pp. 105-108.

In the temptation scene, Iago plays upon Othello quite literally "by ear." He does not plan the temptation in great detail; but he does pour the poison of his language into Othello's ears. The allusion to *Hamlet* is significant. Although Claudius murders the old king by pouring poison into his ear, the story of the terrible deed is the poison the ghost of the king pours into Prince Hamlet's ears. In *Hamlet*, the poison is the truth; in *Othello*, the poison is the series of "dangerous conceits" Iago refers to at line 326 of the temptation scene: "Dangerous conceits are, in their natures poisons. . . ." These "conceits" are the instruments which help Othello make a "lie" of his wife's life and his own. This "lie," nevertheless, proves to be an underlying truth about his own nature.

Iago's use of language implies the submerged principle upon which Othello's transformation is based. It might be said that Iago prompts the Moor to redefine his conception of himself. Plainly, the new conception must be one which will do the Moor great harm. But as a prelude to Othello's redefinition, Othello's conception of Desdemona must first be redefined; for Desdemona is the most substantial element of Othello's total life context barring his military occupation. If Iago can make Othello reconceive his wife's relationship to Cassio and himself, he can, in forcing Othello's vision back upon his own black face, make him reconceive his own identity, redefine his "name" and choose a "role" which seems suitable to the new "situational drama" in which he finds himself.[27]

27 See Anselm L. Strauss, *Mirrors and Masks* (Glencoe, Ill., 1959), pp. 47-48. Strauss shows how the process of self-definition is related to the roles one assumes and the roles "assigned" to others in the various situations the individual encounters. Where the issues of "roles" and "status" are concerned, Strauss discusses the process of "coaching," that is, the situation in which an individual attempts to teach someone else how to "act out" or "become" a new

Othello's attachment to Desdemona in the light of her loyalty is the context Othello brings to the temptation scene. The transformation of this context begins with an ambiguous repetition of certain key words. Through the process of repetition these words shake loose their usual meanings and establish a new suggestiveness informed by Iago's "doubts" and his feigned reluctance to come to the point. Repetition of these key words in the context of doubt is Iago's method of dislocating his general's sense of reality. Moreover, it is not enough that Iago alone repeat these words if they are to help establish a new context for Othello. Iago must provoke Othello into repeating them too. Othello must engage actively in this context-building if the "situation" is to seem real, if it is truly to command his way of "seeing" things.

Thus the first hundred and fifty lines or so of the temptation scene reveal the constant reiteration of various abstract words such as "thought" and its variations "think" and "thinking"; "words" and its variations "say" and "name"; the important word "honest" and its variation "honesty"; the words "seem" and "know"; and the word "conceit." It is interesting to notice that many of these examples suggest manners of perception which become confused as Othello passes from his "old self" to his "new." Also they may be construed thematically as markers pointing out one central issue around which *Othello* revolves: the perception of truth and its relation to subjective and objective reality. However, the point at present is this: the process of reconceiving Desdemona in or-

---

identity. This, of course, is something like the predicament Othello is in with Iago. Language plays its part in both situations. The coach, malevolent or benevolent, uses language to seduce or induce —the words he uses reflect and color the image to be attained.

der to redefine Othello is initiated by Iago's conferring a threatening ambiguity upon these and other ordinarily "clear" words. The process can be traced more concretely by observing an illustrative exchange between Iago and Othello:

Iago. My noble lord,—

Oth.   What dost thou *say*, Iago?

Iago. Did Michael Cassio, when [you] woo'd my lady,
  Know of your love?

Oth. He did, from first to last. Why dost thou ask?

Iago. But for a satisfaction of my *thought*;
  No further *harm*.

Oth. Why of thy *thought*, Iago?

Iago. I did not *think* he had been acquainted with her.

Oth. O, yes; and went between us very oft.

Iago. Indeed!

Oth. *Indeed*, ay, *indeed*. Discern'st thou aught in that?
  Is he not *honest*?

Iago.   *Honest*, my lord?

Oth.   *Honest*! Ay, *honest*.

Iago. My lord, for *aught* I *know*.

Oth. What dost thou *think*?

Iago.   *Think*, my lord?

Oth.   *Think*, my lord!
  [By heaven, he *echoes*] me,
  As if there were some *monster* in [his] *thought*
  Too hideous to be shown.—Thou dost *mean some-*
  thing.   (III.iii.93-108)

Here italicized are several words which through the process of "echoing" become ambiguous and then ultimately take on more specific meanings. And it is to be noted that although Othello accuses Iago of "echoing"

him, he "echoes" Iago even as he makes the accusation.
Italicized also are a few words of thematic significance.
The central word seems to be "thought," which by the
end of the passage comes to "mean something" monstrous.[28] At first "thought" implies little more than an
undefined and perhaps doubtful idea ("But for a satisfaction of my thought"). "Think," however (as in "I did
not think he had been acquainted with her"), because the
word "acquainted" has a secondary sexual meaning, becomes suggestive in an ambiguous way.[29] Moreover, it implies this "acquaintance" has been purposefully hidden
from the rest of the world and that there is some secret
involved in it. Conversely, it also implies, illogical though
the implication may seem, that Iago is somehow aware of
the secret. Iago's "Indeed!" accentuates the context of
doubt and its repetition stresses that context so that
"honest" begins to take on the meaning of "dishonest"
while the sexual implications become clear in the repetitions that "echo" the word. By means of the sexual re-
verberations the "thought" Iago "thinks" becomes less

[28] Paul A. Jorgensen, in " 'Perplex'd in the Extreme': the Role
of Thought in *Othello*," *SQ*, XV (Spring 1964), 272, points out that
the words "think" or "thought" appear eighty-four times in *Othello*
and that "think" is used thirty-one times in the temptation scene.
Jorgensen adds that the control of thought by Iago accounts for a
great deal of the "psychology of the temptation scene" (p. 267).
Note Jorgensen's parallel analysis of the temptation scene (pp.
273-274) and John Lawlor's suggestion that in this scene Iago attempts to emphasize "thought" over "knowledge" (*The Tragic
Sense in Shakespeare*, pp. 93-94).

[29] There is no listing for "acquainted" in this sexual sense in
the *OED*, but under the listing for "To Know" there is the sub-
heading "To have carnal acquaintance or sexual intercourse with."
Illustrations are given from *Measure for Measure* (V.i.203) and
All's Well (V.iii.288). I believe it possible, considering this potential meaning for "know," that "acquainted" might have had a
similar connotation in the right contexts, or that Shakespeare
was capable of implying such a connotation.

ambiguous than it had been; indeed, by the end of this exchange "think" is actually suggestive of the verb "know." The acts of "thinking" and "knowing" are slowly identified, and Iago's earlier "for aught I know" takes on the meaning "I know something, perhaps everything." Iago "means" something, and Othello sums up this meaning in a word that symbolically "names" the "thing"; there is some "monster" in Iago's "thought," a "horrible conceit" worth Othello's knowing. The final "meaning" in this passage, it should be noted, is established and held by a symbolical word, a kind of name whose suggestive force has been defined by a "translation" of the meanings of the various words which have led up to it. In a sense, Othello passes from one world to another, his vehicle being language itself. But the self he brings has not yet been transformed coherently. The transformation is merely implied thus far, ironically, by the very word he uses to characterize Iago's "thought"—that is, the word "monster."

The subsequent repetitions of "thought" and "honest" plus those of other significant words reenforce the definitions worked out in the illustration cited above. It is a tribute to Iago's cleverness and a recognition of the "danger" in language to note that Iago seldom states his "thoughts" directly, but allows his words to speak for themselves—to deliver their special meanings as if they were symbols or metaphors rather than words used in an ordinary discursive conversation meant to give information to the receiver (which is, of course, Iago's feigned purpose). In short, it is the silences, the hesitations, the questioning attitude surrounding Iago's words, in addition to the words themselves, which are eloquent in their reverberative meanings. They are the membrane, if such a term may be used, between Othello's conscious and unconscious minds, which catches, vibrates, and helps define language into meaning.

Thus Desdemona's guilt shapes itself largely through language used metaphorically—symbolically. These abstract words come to be her infidelity, although Iago never literally says she has been unfaithful. In fact, even the crucial description of Cassio's dream later in the scene is really a kind of metaphor, too—an image in action constructed of words which "stands for" and becomes the act of infidelity. The strawberry handkerchief in its turn becomes a symbol of that act.

The intensity of Othello's reaction to Iago's words lies, therefore, not simply in what he sees in any tangible way (the handkerchief, for instance, or the interview between Iago and Cassio or Cassio and Bianca). The intensity derives from what he is capable of conceiving, of envisioning. And what he is capable of conceiving is founded, on the one hand, upon certain preconceptions he has in regard to himself, plus others he learns from Iago in regard to "Venetian wives," and on the other upon the "poetic" sensibility Bradley has pointed out as one of Othello's virtues:[30] that is, a strong receptiveness to emotionally loaded language which accompanies his marked inclination toward the creation of it. This imaginative sensibility is clearly a factor in Othello's downfall, just as Iago's imaginative use of language is the instrument of that downfall. Dover Wilson states it this way: "When moved, indeed, there is in his mind no frontier between reality and imagination."[31] In fulfilling his capacity as a

[30] Bradley (*Shakespearean Tragedy*, p. 154) is, to be strictly accurate, speaking of Othello's imaginative receptivity to experience. The term "Venetian wife" is Leavis'. See p. 129 of my text.

[31] *Othello*, p. xiv.

human being for "conceptual" thinking ("conceptual" here meaning simply the mind's ability to conceive images) and in fulfilling this capacity on the highest plane —the imaginative—Othello ironically becomes to all intents and purposes crueler than any beast. Furthermore, he becomes bestial in his conduct precisely because he delivers himself into an imagined state of affairs without giving sufficient attention to the kinds of "evidence" Iago proposes. His attitude is not truly "legalistic" at all, although he thinks it is. For these reasons, it can be said that language itself is in a very special way the web of Othello's destiny; that what he finally comes to conceive of himself through language actually becomes his end. "Monstrousness," not through his cuckolding, but through his reduction into a barbarous killer, is the fate which awaits him.

The kind of words by which Othello grasps his fate changes during the course of the temptation scene, although Iago does persist in using "abstract" language throughout. Iago's new device makes itself apparent after, more or less, the first one hundred and fifty lines. The new stage is signalled by increasing concretization of terms and by the use of categorizing titles or "names." In fact, Iago's famous speech on the value of a "good name," whatever his use of it may be, helps substantially to explain the semantical-psychological predicament the new stage elicits:

Good name in man and woman, dear my lord,
Is the immediate jewel of their souls.
Who steals my purse steals trash; 'tis something, nothing;
'Twas mine, 'tis his, and has been slave to thousands;
But he that filches from me my good name

Robs me of that which not enriches him,
And makes me poor indeed. (III.iii.155-161)

"To name," sociologist Anselm Strauss writes, ". . . is not only to indicate; it is to identify an object as some kind of object. An act of identification requires that the thing referred to be placed within a category."[32] In a broad sense the "good name" to which Iago refers supplements the actual name of the character involved and gives it a specific character, i.e. "the divine Desdemona" or "Desdemona the fair warrior." Rhetorically speaking, Desdemona's "good name" is an epithet which places her in the category of divine or "soldierly" things, as the case may be. Semantically speaking, the filching of Desdemona's good name means the substitution of a new epithet for the old, that is, the positing of a new category: "Desdemona the lewd minx" or "Desdemona the fair devil" or "Desdemona the whore of Venice." However, these new

[32] Strauss, p. 24, quoting Kenneth Burke, *A Grammar of Motives* (New York, 1945), continues, " 'To tell what a thing is, you place it in terms of something else. This idea of locating, or placing, is implicit in our very word for definition itself: to define, or determine a thing, is to mark its boundaries.' " The boundaries are marked, of course, either by a noun or adjective which indicates a recognized or recognizable category. The significance of "names" in conjunction with the ideas of identification and self-identification is illustrated, according to Strauss, by the change of names people go through upon important occasions like marriage or conversion: that is a change not merely of social status, but of "identity" as well. Of names as symbols, Mrs. Langer says, "A word fixes something in experience, and makes it the nucleus of memory, an available conception. Other impressions group themselves round the denoted thing and are associatively recalled when it is named . . . a mnemonic word establishes a *context* in which it occurs to us; and in a state of innocence we use it in the expectation that it will be understood with its context" (p. 136). Thus the name of a thing or an abstract quality evokes associations whether the original experience with the thing was direct or indirect. Othello's experience with Desdemona as a "whore" fits the latter case.

titles are not applied by Iago; rather what he says of Desdemona's conduct toward her father, of the singularity of
her marriage, of the supposed infidelity of all wives in
Venice, and finally of "Cassio's dream" implies them,
and Othello does the rest:

> Damn her, lewd minx! O, damn her! damn her!
> Come, go with me apart; I will withdraw
> To furnish me with some swift means of death
> For the fair devil.   (III.iii.475-478)

The categorical titles derived from Iago's implications
support the new context Iago has established for Othello.
They create for the name "Desdemona" a new image, and
since this image is in the mind of the beholder, not in the
reality of Desdemona; since, in brief, the filching is a
purely subjective matter which, unlike pickpocketing,
can be executed without the victim's being present, Desdemona is left totally defenseless. Nothing can make "Desdemona" mean all the virtues her name formerly con-
noted other than a change of perception (indeed of "conception") on the part of Othello. In this way has Othello
not only failed to enrich himself, but has symbolically
robbed his wife of all her virtue.

Furthermore, if the filching of Desdemona's good name
makes her poor, it robs Othello as well. For the act of
vandalism places Othello in a new context. "Desdemona"
now means the "whore of Venice"; therefore "Othello"
must mean "cuckold." The stealing of Desdemona's name
steals Othello's too. To his own eyes, Othello the great
soldier and fond lover progressively disappears until in
the great "farewell" speech the old identity is given up
completely: "Othello's occupation's gone."

However, Iago uses another potent group of categorizing titles along with those implied ones referring to Desdemona. These refer to Othello himself and they are stated aloud. Kenneth Burke explains Iago's technique in the following way: "Iago proves himself a master of the 'say the word' device whereby the important thing is to see that the summarizing word, the drastically relevant motivating title is spoken."[33] The speaking of these titles further undermines Othello's rapidly diminishing self-respect by fleshing out the implications Iago has already made by means of a more abstract kind of language. Their very utterance gives reality to horrors which, were they to remain submerged (because unspoken) might yet be laid to rest; for the speaking of a suspicion somehow does make it more real, as if language itself could somehow render tangible the objects of amorphous fears and doubts. Thus Iago implies that Othello will become a "green ey'd monster" if he partakes of the green-eyed monstrousness of "jealousy" (III.iii.165-166). Moreover, he notes how "that cuckold lives in bliss/Who certain of his fate, loves not his wronger" (III.iii.167-168), and with this statement Iago for the first time directly associates Othello with the image of the cuckold. Othello then makes his contribution: he would be exchanged for a "goat" if he believed Iago's imputations (III.iii.180); but some lines later he finds he would rather be a "toad" than allow any part of the thing he loves "for others' uses" (III.iii.270-273). And strangely, for Othello even the mere statement of such words in any context, in-

---

[33] Burke, "*Othello*: An Essay to Illustrate a Method," p. 193. Stoll, as usual, is extremely astute in picking out the significant details in a scene. He explains the scene much as Burke does, focusing on important words Iago repeats, but only to show how *unlikely* the whole thing is. See "*Othello*: An Historical and Comparative Study," p. 24.

cluding the context of denial, establishes an area contagious with animality and monstrousness, the images of
which infect his mental vision. Moreover, Othello infects
himself with the disease increasingly as his inner tranquility deteriorates.

The new self-image forged by means of this combination of animal titles and monstrous innuendoes is that of
the cuckold, the beast with horns. Yet up to this moment
the image of Othello's ignominy has not been formulated
solidly enough for Othello to act. It is the great farewell
speech which reveals to Iago the Moor's readiness for a
more decisive onslaught. For the farewell speech, as implied earlier, gives up the old identity of the great warrior and the devoted lover and leaves Othello open to new
attacks. With his "occupation" gone, Othello is primed
to receive a new job of work. His demand to "see" so he
may "prove" is a demand for a new positive identity; but
in order to conceive this identity he must first have the
"ocular proof" of his disgrace. If Othello can actually
have the verification of his own eyes that Desdemona is
the "Venetian wife" whose "country disposition" he is
familiar with through hearsay, if her name can be *seen*
to mean "whore" and his "cuckold," his name can come
to mean "a great one bent on revenge" and he will be able
to act accordingly.

The "ocular proof," however, is not merely the strawberry handkerchief, which serves as a "tangible" sign of
Desdemona's infidelity; it is this sign in combination with
the "sight" of the guilty sex act itself—that is, the defining conceptual image toward which the entire revelation
of the temptation scene has been building, the image in
action which *shows* Othello he is a cuckold and Desdemona a whore as if it were an event itself. This image in

action is "Cassio's dream." So it is that when Othello cries, "[Her] name, that was as fresh/As Dian's visage, is now begrim'd and black/As mine own face," and calls for satisfaction, shrewd Iago responds immediately, "How satisfied, my lord?/Would you, [the supervisor], grossly gape on—/Behold her topp'd?" But without additional hesitation he begins to make the impossible and the morally repulsive take place. He initiates his visualization of the scene of lust by means of images reminiscent of the animal titles mentioned previously:

> It is impossible you should see this,
> Were they as prime as goats, as hot as monkeys,
> As salt as wolves in pride, and fools as gross
> As ignorance made drunk.   (III.iii.402-405)

The context of denial in which these images appear merely heightens the semantic points made thus far. For even in light of the "impossibility" Iago refers to, clearly the force of his words impresses Othello. The extremity of the language, the conceptual resonance of the images in combination with Othello's fears and desires make for reality. Nevertheless, Othello, still seeking irrefutable proofs, demands "a living reason she's disloyal." Iago's response, his "reason," completes with increased specificity the process begun with the images. Moreover, it is important to notice that Iago's "reason" (a word morally significant in its own right) is not one in the conventional sense at all. It is, instead, as we have already suggested, a kind of symbolic or metaphorical representation of the sex act which makes Othello "understand" by viewing the scene as if he were really present at it, indeed, almost as if he were a participant in it. Cassio's dream is this "living reason"—a reality Othello accepts not by virtue of discursive logic, but by virtue of the conceptualizing power of language, a power which can make words look like real things to those who are inclined already, through insecurity or self-doubt, to see them that way. To repeat, Iago's description of Cassio's dream is *the* defining image or complex of images explored, as it were, in action, toward which all the innuendoes, abstract words, and categorizing titles have been pointing all along. The description explodes forth in a shocking manner because its content is a highly developed and vivid conceptual revelation of Othello's new "truth," and because this new truth indelibly identifies Othello with his new "name":

> *Iago.* In sleep I heard him say, "Sweet Desdemona,
> Let us be wary, let us hide our loves;"
> And then, sir, would he gripe and wring my hand,
> Cry, "O sweet creature!" then kiss me hard,
> As if he pluck'd up kisses by the roots
> That grew upon my lips; then lay his leg
> Over my thigh, and sigh, and kiss; and then
> Cry "cursed fate that gave thee to the Moor!"
> *Oth.* O monstrous! monstrous!
> *Iago.* Nay, this was but his dream.
> (III.iii.419-427)

The effect of the speech lies in the "concreteness" of its sensual imagery, the imagery itself being seen, as it were, "through a keyhole." These elements account for the extraordinary sense of participation evoked by Iago's dialog. In reality, the scene of the sex act involving Desdemona and Cassio is perceived through the little drama of Iago and Cassio in bed. It is like a play within a play. The homosexual undertones heighten the repulsiveness of the "dream" itself as they draw Othello, now in the position of a "voyeur," *into* the double image of corruption. Othello's "O monstrous! monstrous!" identifies at long last Iago's hidden "thought" and himself at the same moment. The appalling act makes him the monster he thought he was—a horned beast. Ironically, however, although incorrect about the state of "monstrousness" he is in, Othello, because of his reaction to Cassio's dream, does in truth become another kind of monster: the green-eyed variety he swore he would not become: the kind that watches, and seeks, and sees what is not, in reality, present.

Iago's reply to Othello's anguished ejaculation further intensifies the effects of his account. "Nay, this was but his dream," Iago says. On its simplest level the statement appears to be a mollifying one. Iago implies that, since what he has described was only a dream, it should not be taken seriously. Conversely, the remark also suggests that if the dream is horrible, the reality must be that much worse. The focus here is on the distance between the dream and the reality. What strikes the audience, though, is another discrepancy; for the audience is aware that there is *no* reality behind the dream. With Iago's statement Shakespeare seems to point out the tremendous capacity the dream has for manufacturing a reality out of nothing tangible at all. It is as if Cassio's dream were a nightmare Othello had experienced in his own bed, so that the dream attains reality for him in the way all dreams are real to men while they are having them: it has the validity of experience itself. Yet this dream, in fact, represents a reality thrice removed from the truth: it is a dream within a dream within a dream. Iago recounts the circumstances in which Cassio supposedly had the dream, and Iago's description has a nightmarish quality.

But the scene with Cassio and Iago in bed probably never took place; through Iago's description of it, however, the vision of Cassio's dream is exposed—the dream of Cassio in bed with Desdemona. But this dream represents, supposedly, a real event; yet it is clear that such an event never occurred at all. The foundation event itself is a dream—a "dreamt-up" event without any objective existence whatsoever. Nevertheless, this wisp of nothing, this "conceit" without the slightest concrete foundation in the character of Desdemona as it has actually been experienced by Othello (Desdemona who because of her love has given up her father) acts as "proof," temporarily relieving Othello's mind of doubt and projecting him into a fantasy of Iago's and his own making. In Iago's words, Cassio's dream helps "to thicken other proofs/That do demonstrate thinly." Othello's reaction, "I'll tear her all to pieces," marks the extent to which he has accepted the dream as proof, the extent to which the word "dream" has come to mean "proof" to Othello, though the dream has consisted of nothing but words. And the profound illogicality and illegality of the whole sequence is only accentuated by our realization that even had the dream been true in any sense, it could be legitimately used to prove nothing. Othello's "I'll tear her all to pieces" demonstrates the dream's success in achieving a conceptual reality, and it points up as well the monstrous release of a ferocity bestial in nature—as if the labels Iago had forced his general to apply had indeed been appropriate. In his response to the dream, Othello becomes the goat, toad, monkey, wolf, and fool evoked by the motivating titles he has been associated with. He becomes a cuckold by virtue of his *own* awakened passion and the true adulterer of his own marriage.

Therefore, although Leavis is correct in saying that "Othello acquiesces in considering Desdemona a type—a type outside his experience—the Venetian wife,"[34] we can also say that Iago nevertheless makes that experience take place. The contradiction resolves itself when we recall that "types" and "dreams" are both kinds of symbolic reality. The self Othello creates is based upon a symbol supported by a symbol. In short, the real "proof" resides inside the man. Objective reality, what Othello concretely knows from personal experience outside the dream world, simply will not bear out the conclusion to which he arrives. He does precisely what Iago suggested he could not do: he "grossly gapes" upon a "scene" of lust to make his "proof," but the real grossness lies within himself. His prurience is a shadow of Iago's lust, but it is a shadow which has been present all along, cast in his own complexion.

Iago's crucial account of Cassio's dream is followed by the description of Cassio wiping his beard with Desdemona's handkerchief (in reality another "dreamt-up" event). For the time being, this second demonstration of Desdemona's guilt clinches the case. "Now," says Othello, "do I see 'tis true," and having confirmed his monstrous identity, action becomes imperative. But action is only possible through a recasting of the monstrous and paralyzing cuckold's image into a more positive mold. The name "cuckold" must now be reinterpreted into a role which can justify and impel action at the same time. To continue to love Desdemona helplessly in the face of his ignominy would bind Othello

---

[34] Leavis, pp. 268-269. Holloway (p. 159) attempts to repudiate Leavis' remark by suggesting that Leavis is working from pure inference. I would agree with Leavis, however, that it is Othello who is working from inference.

to the inactive, humiliated creature, he has, ironically, chosen as himself. But the rejection of love can release the hatred capable of achieving Othello's end: action, immediate and definitive—in order to set his mind at rest and recapture his lost identity, in which action itself has played such an important part:

> Look here, Iago;
> All my fond love thus do I blow to heaven.
> 'Tis gone.
> Arise, black vengeance, from the hollow hell!
> Yield up, O love, thy crown and hearted throne
> To tyrannous hate! Swell, bosom, with thy fraught,
> For 'tis of aspic's tongues!   (III.iii.444-450)

Upon this hatred Othello builds a new role, the active and far more acceptable one of the just avenger. It is a role which also has the virtue of familiarity, reminiscent as it is of his lost "occupation"—that of the good soldier fighting for a just cause. But in back of this image remains the acceptance of Desdemona's guilt and Othello's necessity to believe himself just and great. The image itself gives impetus to action by encompassing the psychological pressures and directing them toward the wonted end:

> Like to the Pontic Sea,
> Whose icy current and compulsive course
> Ne'er [feels] retiring ebb, but keeps due on
> To the Propontic and Hellespont,
> Even so my bloody thoughts with violent pace,
> Shall ne'er look back, ne'er ebb to humble love,
> Till that a capable and wide revenge
> Swallow them up.   (III.iii.453-460)

By identifying himself with the relentless course of the Pontic Sea, Othello confers nature's sanction upon the new self of the just avenger. By implication patience and "humble love" are rejected as "unnatural," and vengeance is exalted in their stead. But the "nature" Othello adopts here is not the orthodox one Christian humanism posited, the one we have come to identify with Shakespeare. Othello's "nature" is anything but benign, orderly and creative. It is more like Edmund's "nature," something to be made use of by the human reason and will, which is in a sense exactly what Othello does, rather than something which informs human reason and will, dictating to them ethical modes and procedures.[35] But unlike Edmund, a highly self-conscious and intelligent creature, Othello appears less aware of the "nature" he makes his goddess. And unlike Edmund, too, Othello is for the moment through with any attempts to make passion look reasonable. He becomes, like the icy and compulsive Pontic Sea, a law unto himself, and disorder is the order of the day.

Yet having drawn upon "nature's" authority to endorse his revenge, it is but one more step for Othello to call what is "natural" just, to invoke heaven's name itself in his cause:

> Now, by yond marble heaven,
> In the due reverence of a sacred vow
> I here engage my words.   [kneels.]
>   (III.iii.460-462)

---

[35] See John F. Danby's discussion of the "two Natures" in *Shakespeare's Doctrine of Nature: A Study of King Lear* (London, 1949), pp. 15-53 and Paul N. Siegel, *Shakespearean Tragedy and the Elizabethan Compromise* (New York, 1957), pp. 3-78.

In his own eyes, Othello becomes a soldier of justice.[36] The interior process of self-justification allows Othello to reestablish temporarily his old, dependable rhetorical self—and the public role which for him makes action possible.

The Moor's vow to heaven consummates his divorce from Desdemona; and the identity of his new life's companion is revealed when Iago kneels to take his part in what appears a mock marriage ceremony:[37]

> Do not rise yet.
> Witness, you ever-burning lights above,
> You elements that clip us round about, [kneels.]
> Witness that here Iago doth give up
> The execution of his wit, hands, heart,
> To wrong'd Othello's service!   (III.iii.462-467)

Iago's imitation of Othello's rhetorical style locks the two characters in a linguistic embrace that suggests the present affinity of their souls. Yet the audience knows that Iago is using Othello's "style" against him, just as by inciting Othello to use *his* style earlier, Iago managed to achieve a refashioning of the Moor's identity. However, the relationship of Othello's "rhetorical style" to Iago's "plain speaking" is implicit in the way the characters exchange dialects. The metaphorical and conceptual devices which characterize both men's language are in a very real way the links between Othello and Iago. These devices reveal that Othello is not merely the slave of a passion—jealousy—but, like Cassius and Brutus, a slave

---

[36] Ribner (*Patterns in Shakespearian Tragedy*, p. 95) and Kirschbaum (*Character and Characterization*, p. 154) make similar statements.

[37] Ribner (*Patterns in Shakespearian Tragedy*, p. 108) notes the "union" of Othello and Iago at III.iii.462-467.

of the very idiom he speaks and its reverse counterpart, the idiom Iago speaks. Furthermore, the extent to which the normal conceptualizing function of language has been distorted is illustrated at the beginning of Act IV, when Othello's language itself disintegrates into the confused babbling of the delirious:[38]

> Lie with her! Lie on her! We say lie on her when they belie her. Lie with her! ['Zounds,] that's fulsome!—Handkerchief—confessions—handkerchief—To confess, and be hang'd for his labour;—first to be hang'd, and then to confess.—I tremble at it. Nature would not invest herself in such a shadowing passion without some instruction. It is not words that shakes me thus. Pish! Noses, ears, and lips.—Is't possible?—Confess—handkerchief!—O devil! [Falls in a trance.]
>
> (IV.i.35-43)

The trance into which Othello falls, melodramatic though it is, emphasizes the state of moral isolation the hero has unhappily achieved. It is a state bordering upon madness. The words themselves, in their disconnection and incoherence, become symbols for this moral degeneration. Othello's statement that "Nature would not invest herself in such a shadowing passion without some instruction. It is not words that shakes me thus" drives, ironically, straight to the heart of the matter. For it is precisely words that *have* shaken him throughout the temptation scene and continue to shake him now with all their symbolical import. In having shaken loose their old meanings, words blur his intellectual and moral

---

[38] R. M. Rossetti, in "A Crux and No Crux," *SQ*, XIII (Summer 1962), 301, suggests that Othello is trying to handle the situation here through "the conceptual power of words."

vision, and he finds himself locked in the purely subjective context of a private nightmare.

To summarize, Othello's recognition of his role as "monster" (for to Othello "a horned man's a monster and a beast") causes the necessary demoralization for the more active role of "soldier of justice" to be formulated. This second role relieves his anxiety not only in that it provides a means of "justifiable" action, but also in that it is the means by which he can reassume an identity similar to his old familiar one. His vision of himself as "a great man" substantiates the older image and compensates for the feeling of distress caused by the cuckold image. Similarly, the physical "wiping out" of Desdemona can be looked upon as the destruction of the supposedly corrupt force besmirching his "good name."[39] By destroying her, he can, as it were, "uncuckold" himself—rid himself and the world of the influence undermining his identity. Yet it is through the assumption of this last and most self-deceptive role that Othello commits his monstrous deed. The scene of Desdemona's death, for all its highly ritualized beauty and for all Othello's later protestations that he "lov'd not wisely but too well" is at its heart a scene of the utmost cruelty.[40] Othello cannot

---

[39] Stirling (*Unity in Shakespearean Tragedy*, p. 129) says that the "inner fountain" Othello speaks of in the "brothel scene," that place where Othello must "live or bear no life" (IV.ii.57-62) is the self. His good name is, of course, a symbolic reflector of the self. It could be said, then, that the necessity for Desdemona's death springs not from the violation of his love alone, but from the undermining of his ego. "The consecration, the ritual, becomes an enshrinement of self," according to Stirling.

[40] *Ibid.*, pp. 111-138. Stirling notes the development of ritual and anti-ritual in the play, especially in the brothel scene and the scene of Desdemona's murder. About the murder scene Stirling says, "Othello's ritual . . . is an elaborate one. In addition to casting himself as lightbearer and minister of Justice, he suggests the role

even find time to allow his wife the "one prayer" he offered her at the scene's commencement. The sacrifice remains murder despite the rhetorical and ritualistic trappings with which Othello invests the deed.

The movement of *Othello*, finally, is one through a forest of words—of titles, images, metaphors, and dreams, —and there can be little question that these words are part of the psychological impetus for the hero's deeds. Shakespeare was clearly concerned with language's potential for creating a kind of reality in its own right. As a poet and dramatist he must have been. Moreover, he saw how this potential was related to theater and how theater was related to action: how the theater of the mind and the role chosen by the "actor" (in this case Othello) can impel action, can make the image in the brain a reality tangible enough to kill. And in imaging forth that killing, in action, he knew how to move an audience.

The temptation scene in *Othello* allows the audience a clear and terrifying view of its hero's internal life, but there are few, if any, scenes in *Coriolanus* which offer such point-blank apprehension of inner realities. Unlike Othello, Coriolanus is seen always in his public role. His concerns are always public concerns: battles, the assumption of the consulship, the betrayal of his country; even his death at the hands of Volscian conspirators in a public square may be contrasted with Othello's suicide in the bedchamber of the murdered

---

of priest. . . ." (p. 133). Stirling earlier said: ". . . the dramatist's point of view is ironical: he does not, of course, imply the ritual is evil in itself, but he bases . . . his tragedy upon subjective delusion fortified by objective ceremony. Personalized violence seeks to become impersonal action" (p. 126).

Desdemona. Yet the two men have more than their occupations in common. They are each capable of using their public roles for quite private purposes. Othello transforms the problem of Desdemona's supposed adultery into a public problem. As God's justicer he kills his wife in order to save mankind from the corruption of her nature; yet at the heart of this "sacrifice" is his own private revenge. In *Coriolanus* the hero seeks honor, not out of a sense of public responsibility, but to "ennoble" himself. As William Rosen puts it, "Through Marcius' speech and through the comments of others, Shakespeare emphasizes the fact that personal rather than public considerations motivate his great services to Rome."[41]

Coriolanus' Rome is a very different place from the sea-encircled Island of Cyprus. The road from Rome to Corioli, as we shall see, is not a long one, and those who frequent it do so as soldiers, statesmen, or traitors, not as vengeful lovers. Nevertheless, the imagery in Iago's language, which becomes Othello's imagery, too, is not entirely absent from the later play. In Coriolanus' scurrility, always forcefully directed against the plebs, the beast raises once again its head:

> What would you have, you curs,
> That like nor peace nor war? The one affrights you,
> The other makes you proud. He that trusts to you,
> Where he should find you lions, finds you hares;
> Where foxes, geese. (I.i.172-176)

Plainly Coriolanus' intonations are not Iago's, nor is Coriolanus a "villain," though Farnham is correct in identifying him as one of Shakespeare's "deeply flawed"

[41] William Rosen, *Shakespeare and the Craft of Tragedy* (Cambridge, Mass., 1960), p. 182.

heroes.[42] More significant for our purpose is the idea that this scurrility is used in a political battle, not a private scheme. In *Coriolanus* it might be said that the inner idiom characteristic of *Othello* is translated into an idiom first and foremost political in suggestiveness. In Coriolanus' speech above, the lion and the fox, Machiavelli's symbolic animals, make a telling appearance. However, this "translation" does not occur at the expense of a major insight into personal reality. Rather, the personal world of Coriolanus, or the lack of it, must be inferred from seeing him in political and social action and to some extent from an examination of the imagery he uses. Rosen is correct in pointing to the "outer" perspective Shakespeare establishes in regard to his hero. The many remarks evaluating Coriolanus and the various assessments which characters give of him, force the audience, perhaps more than in any other Shakespearean tragedy, to judge the hero objectively.[43] It is this exterior perspective that gives the play its peculiar sense of distance; moreover this perspective accounts to some degree for the definite lack of involvement between the audience and the major character.

At the same time, "distance" helps the audience focus its attention upon the broad public concerns of the state, the political panorama. A whole view of *Coriolanus* cannot relinquish judgment of *all* the participating factions in the state and their joint responsibility for the ensuing tragedy. Rossiter is partially correct when he suggests that with *Coriolanus* ". . . you are past the great tragic phase

---

[42] Willard Farnham, *Shakespeare's Tragic Frontier*, pp. 253-254.

[43] Rosen, p. 190. Rosen adds that this "objective framing" places the audience in the position of judge.

and back in history again."[44] This is not to say that
Coriolanus is more a history play than a tragedy or that
Shakespeare has given up his interest in tragic character;
it is only to suggest that the concern with conducting the
state in *Coriolanus* is reminiscent of basic interests in
the histories and to some extent in *Julius Caesar*. Still,
it is important to remember that for Shakespeare, as for
any writer of tragedy, political problems are in fact
directly related to the inner moral dilemmas of individuals, of Man himself. In this light, Othello's failure
to recognize Desdemona in her human reality is a philosophical question different only in degree, not in kind,
from Coriolanus' failure to recognize the human reality
of the plebs. In *Coriolanus* the scope of the human problem is deliberately magnified beyond the personal, and
the participation of the community in the tragedy is more
than implied. Caius Marcius' immense military heroism
and immense limitations as an individual are literally a
problem of Rome. But Rome has other problems too:
the division of the plebs and the patricians over the distribution of corn precedes the difficulties Coriolanus
offers. Yet the two problems become inextricably related.
The senate's refusal to feed the populace is congruent
with and complicated by Coriolanus' refusal to "feed"
the plebs any form of political, indeed, human recognition.[45] Thus does *Coriolanus* offer a distinct correspond-
ence between the warped relations in the body politic
and the distortions in the anatomy of its main character's soul. The story of Caius Marcius is a tragedy of

44 A. P. Rossiter, *Angel With Horns and Other Shakespeare Lectures* (London, 1961), p. 22.

45 G. Wilson Knight, *The Imperial Theme*, pp. 176-178. See also
Charney's remarks on food imagery, *Shakespeare's Roman Plays*,
pp. 143-145.

state more fully developed in its public concerns than any of the plays discussed so far; paradoxically, it is the severe inner limitations of its major character that make it such.

Coriolanus' primary difficulty as a human being is his inability to see the ambiguity either in the situations he encounters or in himself. The supremacy of his military prowess and his knowledge of what it can accomplish wall him in from the rest of mankind; his aristocratic background divides him from the "common man." "Honor" and "aristocracy" are the backbone of his existence; "And I am constant" is his most characteristic remark. This "constancy," in which he believes so devoutly, takes a number of forms. First of all, he is always "his own man," or at least he attempts to be, whether on the battlefield or in the public forum. For Caius Marcius, personal valor on the field of battle is the meaningful center of life; but if he fights well, he fights well alone, and this is never more clearly demonstrated than during the assault on Corioli's gates. The great soldier charges into the town, allows himself to be cut off from his own troops, and takes on the town's defenders by himself. Admittedly his act is audacious and heroic; nevertheless it is also foolhardy and irresponsible, a means first of all for accruing honor to his own name. Rome surely benefits from his action, but the benefit comes as a dividend, not as the principal aim.[46]

Similarly, though Coriolanus is a member of the patrician class, his dedication is not chiefly to the ruling group in Rome, but to himself, to his own sense of dignity

---

[46] Rosen, pp. 191-192. Rosen further notes that "Plutarch's Coriolanus . . . enters Corioli with very few men to help him; he is not completely isolated and alone."

and honor. He can speak effectively about the anarchy which results ". . . when two authorities are up,/Neither supreme. . . ," but his refusal to buy the plebs' mercy with "one fair word" derives not from any pristine loyalty to the patrician cause (which might be better served with temperance, if not temporizing), but from his absolute loyalty to himself. After castigating the plebs for annulling his election as consul, he says to his mother:

> Why did you wish me milder? Would you have me
> False to my nature? Rather say I play
> The man I am.   (III.ii.14-16)

Coriolanus' "constancy," his reluctance to temporize, to play the man he is not, though from one point of view a trait which might well be admired, from another is suggestive of the persistently negative quality of his personality, a quality reinforced by his scurrility. Barring the speeches later in the play when he acquiesces to his mother's plea to spare Rome, scurrility remains his most characteristic idiom. Like his sword, it acts as a weapon both offensive and defensive in nature. It "cuts up" the plebs, but its use, passionate and vindictive, prevents constructive thinking on his part and defends him from the necessity of investigating his own moral stance. Here is Coriolanus addressing his "enemy," the people:

>   Who deserves greatness
> Deserves your hate; and your affections are
> A sick man's appetite, who desires most that
> Which would increase his evil. He that depends
> Upon your favours swims with fins of lead
> And hews down oaks with rushes. Hang ye! Trust ye?
> With every minute you do change a mind,

And call him noble that was now your hate,
Him vile that was your garland.   (I.i.180-188)

Coriolanus, admittedly, has his point where the inconstant nature of the plebs is concerned. But as Second Officer says before the consular election:

> . . . he [Coriolanus] seeks their hate with greater devotion than they can render it him, and leaves nothing undone that may fully discover him their opposite. Now, to seem to affect the malice and displeasure of the people is as bad as that which he dislikes, to flatter them for their love.   (II.ii.20-25)

The intense loathing Coriolanus expresses for the plebs appears, among other things, a method of self-definition, a way of "proving" his heroic superiority over the "reechy" people. This method of self-definition, one by which he seeks to undermine the plebs in order to glorify himself, is carried over to his relationship with the senators. Here too the primarily negative quality of his character is constantly reiterated as he points out in one situation after another what he will not do, what he cannot seem, what he is not. More honorable in his own eyes than any man, Coriolanus, nevertheless, seldom tells us what he *is* (his "modesty" precludes this); honor itself is negatively defined.[47] After Corioli he cannot bring

[47] Derek A. Traversi, "Coriolanus," *Scrutiny*, VI (June 1937), 45. Clearly Coriolanus' language is that of the man playing God, as the tribunes later point out. Traversi finds in certain speeches "a perversion of the traditional speech of war-like heroes" which is a "masterpiece of irony." Another point connected with the language of the play in general is this: one must not impute to Shakespeare the difficulties Coriolanus has with language. In creating the kind of hero Coriolanus is, Shakespeare has made him speak at all times appropriately. It is true that *Coriolanus'* language lacks the oral magnificence of *Macbeth* or *Hamlet*. G. Wilson Knight finds it "ice-

himself to accept acknowledgment for his heroism publicly. To Cominius he says:

> I thank you, General;
> But cannot make my heart consent to take
> A bribe to pay my sword. I do refuse it,
> And stand upon my common part with those
> That have beheld the doing.   (I.ix.36-40)

When it comes to donning the ceremonial robe of humility as part of the consular election, he immediately refuses:

> I do beseech you,
> Let me o'erleap that custom; for I cannot
> Put on the gown, stand naked and entreat them
> For my wounds' sake to give their sufferage.
> (II.ii.139-142)

Nor can he repent for his surly language during the election:

> For them! [the plebs] I cannot do it to the gods;
> Must I then do 't to them?   (III.ii.38-39)

And when it comes to smoothing over the situation after he has completely disaffected the plebs, this too is impossible for Coriolanus:

---

cold, intellectual, cold as a mountain torrent and holding something of its iron taste" (*The Imperial Theme*, p. 155). But to speak of the *character* Coriolanus, this is just as it should be, although I am not sure his language is always "intellectual." Traversi ("Coriolanus," p. 43) describes the play's verse as one of "consistency and artistic success." L. C. Knights (*Some Shakespearean Themes* [London, 1959], p. 150) says, "the verse, close packed and flexible, has that power of compressed definition that we associate with the plays of Shakespeare's maturity, so that the immediate action is felt as the focus of a vision of life that is searching and profound."

I'll know no further.
Let them pronounce the steep Tarpeian death,
Vagabond exile, flaying, pent to linger
But with a grain a day, I would not buy
Their mercy at the price of one fair word;
Nor check my courage for what they can give,
To have 't with saying "Good morrow."

(III.iii.87-93)

It can be seen, therefore, that even the "fair words"
Coriolanus gives himself are generally not stated directly,
but must be inferred from his negative delivery of them.
By such statements he implies his honor is great, but he
will not say as much in so many words. His "modesty" is
a case in point. Coriolanus will not boast, but his refusal
to do so impresses us less as true modesty than as an
attempt to hide his enormous estimation of himself. His
incredible speeches to Cominius after the heroic conduct
within Corioli's gates are self-conscious enough to make
us feel he is posing. Surely modesty could not be responsible for such a barrage of language:

May these same instruments, which you profane,
Never sound more! When drums and trumpets shall
I' th' field prove flatterers, let courts and cities be
Made all of false-face'd soothing!
When steel grows soft as the parasite's silk,
Let him be made [a coverture] for th' wars!
No more, I say. For that I have not wash'd
My nose that bled, or foil'd some debile wretch,—
Which, without note, here's many else have done,—
You [shout] me forth
In acclamations hyperbolical,
As if I lov'd my little should be dieted
In praises sauc'd with lies. (I.ix.41-53)

As Cominius says, "Too modest are you;/More cruel to your own good report than grateful/To us that give you truly."

But Coriolanus can see no ambiguity in himself or in his language. At those points in the play during which he is willing to make a positive identification of himself, such as at the play's conclusion when he calls himself an "eagle," or earlier, upon his departure from Rome into exile, when he calls himself a "lonely dragon," there is no recognition that eagles and dragons (like lions or, for that matter, foxes) are predatory creatures which kill their prey, not for the sake of honor, but because it is in their nature to kill.[48] Eagles and dragons remain for him the symbols, simple and unambiguous, of a noble ideal and of the embodiment of that ideal in himself. Similarly, invective is for him a simple reflection of the purity of his nature and his motives (while for the audience it becomes an index of his willfulness, his passion, his spitefulness, his interior defilement, and his blindness to his own human nature). Nor is there for Coriolanus any possibility of self-recognition. For the truth of the matter remains that Coriolanus *is* constant, and the image he casts is unified. Unlike Othello, he has only one occupation—that of war. Othello, for all his faults, can love, and because he can, in the end he is capable of seeing at least part of the truth. Othello can momentarily envision the ambiguity in the role he has chosen and see the "other side of the picture." The just avenger, he finds, can be a fool: "O, blood, blood, blood!" he cries, dedicating himself to the life of violence. But

48 Charney, in *Shakespeare's Roman Plays*, on the other hand, believes the animals "represent traditional primacies" and that, generally, noble animals go with the patricians, ignoble with the plebs (pp. 166-169).

recognition comes with the direct parallel, "O fool, fool, fool!" However, as Rosen states, ". . . there is no . . . journey toward painful discovery in *Coriolanus*. The Coriolanus of the first scene is the same Coriolanus at the end of the play. His opinions and attitude undergo no change."[49] To Coriolanus, the "picture" can have only one interpretation. It is up to the audience to infer the other side.

The single image the audience receives of Coriolanus contains in fact three parts, but these parts are inseparable and cast the same shadow. There is his relationship to war, his relationship to the community, and his relationship to his mother, the quality of the first two deriving from the strength of the last. There can be no question of Volumnia's importance in Shakespeare's story of Caius Marcius. Plutarch recognizes her, but Shakespeare makes the relationship of mother and son the core of the play.[50] In more than one respect, out of it everything develops:

> *Vol.* Thy valiantness was mine, thou suck'st it from me,
> But owe thy pride thyself.   (III.ii.129-130)

This judgment of Coriolanus by his mother is interesting not only because it suggests something about the intensity of their relationship, but also because it is not wholly accurate. Coriolanus' pride may not derive completely from his mother, but she is certainly involved in it. By having encouraged him to be the surpassing warrior she desires, she has helped to create the breach between

---

[49] Rosen, p. 187. See also A. C. Bradley, *Coriolanus*. British Academy: Second Annual Shakespeare Lecture (London, 1912), pp. 9-12.

[50] On this point, see Harley Granville-Barker, *Prefaces to Shakespeare* (Princeton, N.J., 1947), II, 164.

him and the community which characterizes her. Coriolanus, when expressing his inability to flatter the plebs, can say, "Let them hang!" But Volumnia, despite her criticism of her son, can respond with equal vehemence, "Ay, and burn too!" Clearly, Volumnia's aristocratic separation from the Roman populace is magnified in Coriolanus. Furthermore, her ambitions for him play a significant part in his life. It is Coriolanus who stands for consul; but it is Volumnia who desires the honor for him more than he desires it for himself:

> *Vol.*   I have liv'd
>> To see inherited my very wishes
>> And the buildings of my fancy; only
>> There's one thing wanting, which I doubt not but
>> Our Rome will cast upon thee.
>
> *Cor.*   Know, good mother,
>> I had rather be their servant in my way
>> Than sway with them in theirs.   (II.i.214-220)

To be brief, Volumnia's aristocratic and masculine spirit informs Coriolanus' character, and the extent of her influence can be seen even in the kind of education she chose for her son. Like Othello's, but far more severely, that education limits Coriolanus' emotional possibilities, positing, as it does, physical valor as the prime value of life. In the "hardness" which results are implicit both the heroism Coriolanus attains and his moral separation from the rest of the community. Volumnia describes the education she envisioned for Caius Marcius in the following way:

>   . . . When
> yet he was but tender-bodied and the only son of my
> womb, when youth with comeliness pluck'd all gaze

his way, when for a day of kings' entreaties a mother
should not sell him an hour from her beholding, I,
considering how honour would become such a person, that it was no better than picture-like to hang
by th' wall, if renown made it not stir, was pleas'd
to let him seek danger where he was like to find
fame. To a cruel war I sent him; from whence he
return'd, his brows bound with oak. I tell thee,
daughter, I sprang not more in joy at first hearing
he was a man-child than now in first seeing he had
proved himself a man.   (I.iii.5-19)

The intensity of Volumnia's language surely witnesses
her attachment to her son. However, perhaps it is fair to
say that what appears from one point of view a positive
human bond, from another assumes a negative quality. In
sending her son out to fight at a time ". . . when for a day
of kings' entreaties a mother should not sell him an hour
from her beholding," she impairs permanently his ability
to relate to the rest of mankind. Involved in soldiering,
in fighting, in killing from his youth, Coriolanus persistently associates "honor" with the amount of havoc he
can cause among the ranks of his "enemies." The nobility
of Volumnia's sacrifice is undermined by the "hardness"
in it, a "hardness" mirrored in Coriolanus' typical solution for the problems he comes to face: destruction, be it
verbal or real, for his adversaries.

Honor for Coriolanus, then, lies not so much in defending his country, but in the simple fact of being a warrior.
In him the military occupation of the aristocrat is discon-
nected from its value as a service and is made valuable in
its own right—somewhat in the same manner this disconnection is made in *Macbeth*. And in battle Coriolanus is

a veritable holocaust, a power all but immortal in its capacity to destroy. But if there is something "immortal" in his military prowess, by definition there is something inhuman as well, and this "inhuman" feature also develops out of the great soldier's relationship with his mother. Their bond, which should be the basis of human understanding and sympathy, is charged by Volumnia with a "divinity" in the epic sense. "Juno-like" Volumnia produces a "Mars-like" Caius Marcius, and their bond instead of representing the kind of human interconnection applicable finally to mankind at large, restricts the two in a tight relationship that will acknowledge no connection with the common herd. The mother invests herself with more than human powers of maternal sacrifice (quite blind to the possibilities this sacrifice might lead to), and the son attempts to enact the "divine" manliness the mother delivers to him as the utmost value in life.

Nevertheless, ironically, Coriolanus' sense of honor is even more restrictive than that of his mother. The end of Coriolanus' education was to Volumnia's way of thinking not simply a question of honor, but one of fame as well. For Volumnia honor is useless unless "renown" stirs it, and it seems fair to assume that honor stirs renown as well. Thus honor and fame are interlinked, and Volumnia's ideal portrait of her son incorporates the idea of "reputation." This emphasis on renown is symptomatic of her pride, to be sure; on the other hand, to a degree it humanizes her. For Volumnia, the honor of the consulship and the fame it will bring are worth a soft word or two to the plebs:

> *Vol.*   You are too absolute;
> Though therein you can never be too noble,

> But when extremities speak. I have heard you say
> Honour and policy, like unsever'd friends,
> I' th' war do grow together. Grant that, and tell me
> In peace what each of them by th' other lose
> That they combine not there.
>
> *Cor.*   Tush, tush!
>
> (III.ii.39-45)

But if Volumnia can admit "fame" into the complex of her values, Caius Marcius cannot; or at least he will not acknowledge such an admission. As we noticed earlier, he is incapable of accepting the praises of Cominius even when according to his own standards he deserves them; he even receives the laudatory title "Coriolanus" with the greatest reluctance. To Coriolanus, acknowledgment of a desire for fame would be in one sense the acknowledgment of a human weakness; in another it would be an admission of dependence on the rest of the world. These are both admissions Coriolanus simply cannot make.

To the degree, then, that Coriolanus claims for himself an integrity which cannot be touched by popular acclaim, he, as Volumnia says, makes his pride his own. Conversely, to the degree that Coriolanus' sense of honor is bound up with Volumnia's attempt to make her son the living image of honor, she remains the hereditary source of this pride. It is ironically appropriate, therefore, that she should be present during each of the critical moments of the play's action: when Coriolanus rebels against donning the robe of humility, when he refuses to speak the plebs fair in order to retain the consulship, and when he is about to march against Rome with the Volscian army.[51]

Considering the importance of Volumnia's influence

[51] See Ribner's remarks on Volumnia, *Patterns in Shakespearian Tragedy*, p. 200.

upon her son, it is also appropriate that she should deliver to the audience in language the commanding image
of Coriolanus, the one, unstated by him, that directs his
actions. She does so with the vigor and intensity we have
grown to expect of her:

> Death, that dark spirit, in 's nervy arm doth lie,
> Which, being advanc'd, declines, and then men die.
>
> (II.i.177-178)

It is a powerful image, deeply admired by Volumnia, but
for the audience it is not entirely ingratiating. Nevertheless, one thing is clear—no matter how the image is interpreted, Coriolanus always fulfills it. Even when he is, in
O. J. Campbell's word, "satirized,"[52] he maintains the
image Volumnia has shaped for him. And in this image is
reflected the perversion of relationship between mother
and son which carries over to the hero's relationship with
the populace. As Traversi puts it, for Coriolanus war is
a "splendid and living ecstasy,"[53] and it might be added
that equally for him, peace is destruction. Cominius also
sets forth the image, but like Volumnia, without any
awareness of its negative implications. He is speaking

[52] O. J. Campbell, *Shakespeare's Satire* (London, 1943), pp. 198-
217. According to Campbell, in *Coriolanus* Shakespeare was not constructing a conventional tragedy. The hero does not evoke our
sympathy, he alienates it. Shakespeare's method is not to ennoble
Coriolanus but to mock him, and the play is filled with derision.
He calls the play, like *Timon*, a tragical satire and aligns it with
Jonson's tragedies in the same vein. Other critics whose points of
view are related to Campbell's are Norman A. Brittin, "Coriolanus,
Alceste, and Dramatic Genres," *PMLA*, LXXI (September 1956),
799-807; Edwin Honig, "Sejanus and Coriolanus: A Study in Aliena-
tion," *MLQ*, XII (December 1951), 407-421; and John W. Draper,
"Shakespeare's *Coriolanus*: A study in Renaissance Psychology,"
WVUB, III (September 1939), 22-36.

[53] Traversi, "Coriolanus," p. 53.

of Coriolanus' military heroism at the recent battle for
Corioli:

> His sword, death's stamp,
> Where it did mark, it took; from face to foot
> He was a thing of blood, whose every motion
> Was tim'd with dying cries. Alone he ent'red
> The mortal gate of th' city, which he painted
> With shunless destiny; aidless came off,
> And with a sudden reinforcement struck
> Corioli like a planet; now all his.
>
> .   .   .   .
>
> And to the battle came he, where he did
> Run reeking o'er the lives of men, as if
> 'Twere a perpetual spoil; and till we call'd
> Both field and city ours, he never stood
> To ease his breast with panting.
>
> (II.ii.111-126)

This is the image of Coriolanus most admired by plebs
and patricians alike, and since in Coriolanus' case action
speaks louder than words, it might be said that it is the
image most admired by Coriolanus himself; for it is precisely this image he enacts during the carefully developed
battle scenes. It is, furthermore, the picture he would
present once again in living action at the climax of the
play to the city he has spent his blood defending. Beneath
the commendatory purposes of the speech, however, Cominius' purposes, lies a vision of destructiveness accentuated by the language Shakespeare puts into Cominius'
mouth. This vision of destructiveness appears in such ex-
pressions as "death's stamp," "he was a thing of blood,"
"every motion was tim'd with dying cries," "struck Corioli
like a planet," and "he did run reeking o'er the lives of

men." We have here the image of the lion truly running rampant, though Cominius might be inclined to create of it a heraldic device. The horror of the scene is reminiscent of the first description received of Macbeth, that from the bleeding captain:

> For brave Macbeth—well he deserves that name—
> Disdaining Fortune, with his brandish'd steel,
> Which smok'd with bloody execution,
> Like Valour's minion carv'd out his passage
> Till he fac'd the slave;
> Which ne'er shook hands, nor bade farewell to him,
> Till he unseam'd him from the nave to th' chaps,
> And fix'd his head upon our battlements.
>
> (I.ii.16-23)

But the description of Coriolanus is, at least for sheer quantity of destruction, even more impressive than that of Macbeth. Moreover, the destructive element in Coriolanus is unqualified by Duncan's gracious presence, a presence which leads the audience to believe the political and moral state of affairs at the beginning of *Macbeth* is unreservedly good and worth practically every conceivable form of defense. Considering the niggardliness of the patricians where the distribution of corn is concerned and the vacillating conduct of the plebs, it is hard to make the same statement about Coriolanus' Rome. The great soldier's impulse to destruction should be read, therefore, as a reflection of the discord in the state rather than as symbolic of the power of goodness. Indeed, Coriolanus in his very heroism seems to represent sheer power itself —an amoral force; and as things turn out he is willing to consider the use of that power not only against his enemies, but against his friends as well.

Finally, the issue of Coriolanus' "constancy" forces us to return to his language momentarily. Even the scurrility he directs against the populace is derived from his center of destruction. This scurrility does not reverse the image of the destroyer; it supports it. Aggressive, passionate and repellent, his words are meant to "annihilate" the people:

> All the contagion of the south light on you,
> You shames of Rome! you herd of—Boils and plagues
> Plaster you o'er, that you may be abhorr'd
> Further than seen, and one infect another
> Against the wind a mile! You souls of geese,
> That bear the shapes of men, how have you run
> From slaves that apes would beat! Pluto and hell!
> All hurt behind! Backs red, and faces pale
> With flight and agued fear! Mend and charge home,
> Or, by the fires of heaven, I'll leave the foe
> And make my wars on you.   (I.iv.30-40)

Although this speech should be examined in its proper context (the plebs, cowed by the Volscian forces, have begun to retreat), and admittedly Coriolanus has some justification for his disgust and rage, the extremity of his language casts some doubts on his qualifications as a military leader and reveals how far his hatred for the plebs goes. It is not every general who threatens to "leave the foe" and make war on his own men. Furthermore, the statement acts as a prediction here, for by the end of the play, he decides to make war on all of Rome for the sake of the plebs.

Coriolanus, therefore, in spite of his ultimate betrayals, remains "constant" to the very end. But our interpretation of this constancy is somewhat different from his own.

To our eyes his constancy lies in this: he is always the potential killer whether defending his country or planning to destroy it. Nor does he ever probe the ambiguity in his impressive self-conception. This lack of recognition holds true in spite of his acquiescence to Volumnia's pleas for Rome at the climax of the play. If there he makes any discovery of his essential humanity, that discovery is never consciously projected outward toward the rest of mankind. Unlike the situation in *King Lear*, the hero makes no connection between the diseased and scabrous state of the world and the condition of his own soul.

But this question of recognition is important in reference to the entire state of Rome as well. What both Coriolanus and the community as a whole fail to see is that the dynamic image delineated in statements such as those by Volumnia and Cominius contains a threat to themselves as well as to their enemies. Neither the patricians nor the plebs understand how the cultivation of pure physical might, even in an outwardly acceptable military guise, in a sense prepares the soul for any violence. They do not comprehend that the strong man whose strength is his only asset lives through violence purely, though that violence be restricted to the formal patterns of war. Finally, they seem unaware that at its heart such violence is irrational and may turn, even in its being cultivated for the defense of a country, against those who enshrine it in any form.

The only qualification of the frightening image the audience receives of Coriolanus occurs in the figure of Virgilia. Only she seems to feel in Coriolanus something other than the hero or the god. What Virgilia understands about her husband that no one else grasps or cares to grasp, including himself, is that he is not a kind of divinity, but a human being. To Volumnia's epical portrait of her son at war, "His bloody brow/With his mail'd hand wiping," Virgilia can only reply, "His bloody brow! O Jupiter, no blood!" or "Heaven bless my lord from fell Aufidius!" She would not be satisfied with a "good report" for a husband, were Coriolanus to die, as Volumnia would be satisfied with that report for a son. In short, by recognizing that Coriolanus can die and that his death would be an irremediable loss to her, Virgilia affirms his connection to humanity and that human tenderness he has almost buried from sight. And it is significant to note that Coriolanus consistently treats his wife with gentleness. Equally significant, this affirmation suggests that across the gulf which might appear to separate two such different people as Coriolanus and Virgilia, there is a bridge, and that this bridge also connects Coriolanus with the plebs whether he chooses to see it or not. Hence, Virgilia, like Cordelia in *King Lear* or Desdemona in *Othello* (who forgives Othello's anger because "we must think men are not gods") represents a reality which ultimately "transcends the political and personal,"[54] and at the same time becomes a point of reference from which we can judge the action of the play. The tears Virgilia constantly sheds are analogous to Cordelia's divine tears. In her silence (characterized as "gracious" by Coriolanus himself) and in the limited number of appearances she makes on stage, Virgilia becomes the small, almost negligible human heart of Coriolanus.[55] Her demeanor and

[54] John F. Danby (*Poets on Fortune's Hill* [London, 1952], p. 149) mentions Cordelia as such a reality. For a more detailed study of Cordelia as framed by the traditional Christian humanist view of nature, see Danby's *Shakespeare and the Doctrine of Nature, passim* and pp. 114-140 especially.

[55] Bradley (*Coriolanus*, p. 19) notes ". . . that kind of muteness in which Virgilia resembles Cordelia, and which is made to suggest a world of feeling in reserve."

her typical language form a clear contrast to Volumnia's attitude toward her son. Volumnia can say:

> The breasts of Hecuba,
> When she did suckle Hector, look'd not lovelier
> Than Hector's forehead when it spit forth blood
> At Grecian sword. . . .   (I.iii.43-46)

Shakespeare has taken deliberate care through the exaggerated quality of Volumnia's language to show what violence looks like and to reveal the excesses in her standards. If Virgilia can be accused of sentimentalizing her repulsion for violence, surely Volumnia can be accused of sentimentalizing war. Indeed, Virgilia's "squeamishness" is more than simply comic and more than naive. At the bottom, it is an instinctive awareness that pain hurts, weapons kill, and men can die.

The violation of the human body Virgilia sees in the potential wounds of her husband suggests, of course, a parallel in the violated body of the disrupted Roman state; and surely the action of the play concerns the body politic of Rome. As practically every critic points out, Menenius' speech on the "stomach and the members" is central to any interpretation of *Coriolanus*.[56] This is not to say that Menenius is entirely justified in using the metaphor to defend the position of the patricians. Rosen tells us that ". . . Menenius and Coriolanus are alike in their lack of sympathy and understanding for the citizens' troubles. Menenius, like Coriolanus, feels no responsibility for the existing conditions: 'For the dearth,' Menenius rationalizes, shifting responsibility, 'the gods, not the patricians, make it.' "[57] Rosen's point is well taken.

---

[56] Charney (*Shakespeare's Roman Plays*, p. 146), for instance, calls the fable "a point of reference for all the disorder and distemper in the state."

[57] Rosen, p. 180.

If the political function of the patricians is like the distributive function of the good stomach in the metaphor, they are no more fulfilling their obligations to Rome than the plebs are. Unlike the good stomach, the patricians fail to send the "general food," the corn, through the "rivers" of the plebs' "blood." Similarly, the patricians fail to give the plebs political nourishment by refusing to acknowledge the justice of the plebs' request.

However, if Menenius misapplies the metaphor, the metaphor itself remains an apt description of what the condition in the state of Rome *should* be. Yet to say as much is not necessarily to agree with O. J. Campbell that the play is merely an Elizabethan political exemplum,[58] unless, of course, the definition of "political" can be made to suggest more than it conventionally does. Fortunately, we have L. C. Knights to do this for us. Knights understands Shakespeare's "politics" as not limited to an investigation of the political scene or even those elements of conducting the state which were the traditional concerns of politics in the Renaissance. Above all, Shakespeare is not concerned with politics in the sense contemporary Americans are. Knights' idea is that Shakespeare works through the great Renaissance political metaphor to what lies behind the ostensibly "political" situation; that is, he exposes the social, moral, religious, and most of all, the human and personal relationships in the community that actually inform "politics." And behind all this, F. N. Lees might add, is a conception of man and society which sees their adjustment as rooted in nature itself.[59] Knights

<hr/>

58 O. J. Campbell, pp. 203-204.

59 L. C. Knights, *Shakespeare's Politics: With some Reflections on the Nature of Tradition.* Annual Shakespeare Lecture of the British Academy (London, 1957), pp. 115-132. Knights finds a similar conception to Shakespeare's, and the one from which the poet most

says, "Behind hierarchy and authority, behind formal justice and public order, is a community of persons bound by
'holy cords . . . which are too intrinse t' unloose.' The
basic political facts . . . are that men can feel for each
other, and that this directness of relationship—expressing
itself in the humblest of ways as well as in the most exalted forms of loyalty and sacrifice—is the only alternative to a predatory power seeking whose necessary end is
anarchy."[60] Thus the traditional image of the perfect
state Menenius delineates is singularly appropriate because it reflects the processes of "feeding" and "eating"
fundamental not only to man's political nature, but to
nature itself. Political recognition and the responsibilities which go with it are a "natural competency." But the
metaphor itself is an ideal, not a reality, and both parties
violate the ideal by exercising their power in the un-
thinking manner they do.

Knights' view of Shakespearean "politics" is also espe-

---

probably derives, in the medieval political ideas in Dante's *De
Monarchia*, St. Thomas Aquinas, John of Salisbury (*Policraticus*),
and in the contemporary views of Hooker. (Danby, in *Shakespeare's
Doctrine of Nature*, also discusses the views of Hooker in relation
to Shakespeare.) All these thinkers show the "tendency to transform
the political world into the social, and the social into the religious" (p. 127). F. N. Lees ("Coriolanus, Aristotle, and Bacon,"
RES, New Series, I [April 1950], 114-125) presents a view similar to
Knights' and reveals the part "nature" plays in the body politic
metaphor. Lees suggests that Shakespeare's political ideas on the city
and the state may come from "I.D.'s" translation into English of
Aristotle's *Politics* in 1598. He finds significant parallels between
the belly fable and Aristotle's conception that it is "natural" for man
to be social and take a positive part in the life of the city. The key
remark in Aristotle is: "He that is incapable of living in a society is
a god or a beast." Lees finds this a "fitting brief commentary on
the play" (p. 117).

60 Knights, *Shakespeare's Politics*, p. 120. Knights refers here to
King Lear in particular, but it would seem his statement could be
applied to Shakespeare's political vision in general and certainly to
Coriolanus.

cially pertinent in light of Coriolanus' feeling for the plebs. More than anything his hatred is a breach of the human connection which sustains the state. His military image, so to speak, invades Rome's domestic privacy, and his unwillingness to compromise, to surrender anything to his foe, the plebs, serves only to exacerbate a situation that has deteriorated far enough. This refusal to acknowledge the plebs both as a political element and as human beings is most plainly defined in Coriolanus' recalcitrance where donning the robe of humility is involved. Clearly he feels such a demonstration would undermine his dignity as an aristocrat and a soldier. Yet it might be submitted that Coriolanus' reluctance to take part in the ceremony has aspects deeper than those usually offered by the critics: the aspects of "honor" and "modesty." The refusal to put on the gown is finally more than a question of Coriolanus' carrying out an old custom that will "belie his feelings"; nor is the fact that he will not stoop to flattery or that he reveals "bull-headed integrity"[61] the whole of the truth, although these interpretations surely represent part of the truth. For, as a matter of fact, Coriolanus *does* put on the gown—and with only one intention in mind: to gain the people's voices no matter what his feelings. In other words, when he puts on the traditional gown, he does so, not in order to confirm his relationship with the people, to show that he recognizes them as a functioning portion of the community with its own claims, but rather as a political maneuver (which admittedly goes against his grain) that would tend, were he successful, only to place him further out of the people's reach than he is already. To be sure, Coriolanus is finally

---

[61] MacCallum, *Shakespeare's Roman Plays*, p. 579; Farnham, p. 250; and Honig, p. 421 respectively.

incapable of sustaining the maneuver. He insults the plebs, and their somewhat tardy realization that they have been insulted allows the tribunes to put up the cry for banishment which expels Caius Marcius from Rome. Nevertheless, both the use to which Coriolanus puts the gown and his inability to wear it with dignity and restraint are symptoms of the same difficulty. Given that the wearing of the gown and its concomitant exposing of wounds received for Rome have a certain sensational quality; given that they are, as Rosen says, a "vulgar and humiliating display"[62]—the custom still has a purpose and Coriolanus succeeds in violating it. The gown and the display of wounds "beg voices" in the name of a common bond—the state and humanity. The prospective consul must literally show evidence that he has cared for the people, that he is one with the community, and that he has been willing to sacrifice his blood for them. The wounds, in short, have a double meaning. If they are a mark of the bearer's heroism, they are also a mark of his humanity, of his citizenship, of his common bond. From this perspective, the refusal to expose wounds becomes a rejection of that common bond (and here the word "common" means both "ordinary" and "held in common"); but the word "common" can have no such meanings to Coriolanus. To him the word means "base" and that is all. To go one step further, the refusal to expose wounds may also be interpreted as a refusal to reveal the human self which received them, just as the refusal to accept praise, in its curious excessiveness, may be interpreted as a measure intended to hide the damning truth that Coriolanus is, after all, not simply the image of honor, but a man.

[62] Rosen, p. 170.

The result of Coriolanus' behavior during the affair of the robe is, of course, chaos—but not only because he fails at flattery or because in his "naked honesty" he will not conform to the customs of Rome.[63] For, as we have seen, the custom of donning the robe is not to be taken as a mere matter of form. Beneath this "vulgar display," a display which demonstrates the plebs' limitations, is something which demonstrates Coriolanus' limitations as well. Although the plebs may exhibit their "vulgar wisdoms" in demanding the ceremony without one jot abated, Coriolanus once again reveals his incapacity for accepting another class of human beings on their own terms in order to knit the state into the unity of diverse human beings it actually is. The concession to be made may be one of policy, and in his reluctance to employ policy Coriolanus may be admirable; but it is important to remember that Coriolanus' attitude toward the plebs makes the great metaphor of the body politic unworkable. There can be no true state with a man like Coriolanus at the head of government. Hence Coriolanus' behavior results in anarchy because he is incapable of recognizing that the plebs, though they may at times act like beasts, are human beings; because he is incapable of recognizing that he, though a great warrior, is a human being; and because he is incapable of recognizing that the plebs as well as the patricians are part of the state. Coriolanus' limitation turns out to be not simply a native integrity which prevents him from acting the hypocrite. It is a tremendously deep distortion of nature which can be detected in his position regarding his mother, the plebs, the state, and the world at large.[64]

[63] Brittin, p. 805.
[64] See L. C. Knights, *Some Shakespearean Themes*, p. 154 and Ribner, *Patterns in Shakespearian Tragedy*, p. 187.

As to the plebs—they are, to be sure, not without blame. They are vacillating and hydra-headed; they do allow themselves to be used by the tribunes. On the other hand, they are intrinsically generous and give Coriolanus every chance to prove himself interested in the state and their welfare. The price for the consulship is but "to ask it kindly" and when Caius Marcius does not ask it kindly, they confer the title upon him anyway. During the scene in which Coriolanus begs their voices, they reveal a nature simple and ingratiating; however this nature is their downfall. The entire election becomes confused with the issue of "gratitude" and their mistake turns out to be the same the patricians make. During the election both parties fail to remember that Coriolanus' true function in the state is that of warrior and that his greatest potentialities do not lie in the realms of peace. Because of the plebs' generosity, and because, as Third Citizen puts it, "ingratitude is monstrous," the people choose to forget that Coriolanus hates them. Yet were the plebs thinking coherently, they would perhaps see that "gratitude" for deeds done in the quest of honor alone (whatever the benefits to the state) may not be the best credentials for public office, especially from a man clearly hostile to them.

Ironically, it is the proud and self-seeking tribunes who remind the plebs of Coriolanus' hostility. The tribunes are rabble-rousers, real "Machiavellian" foxes, and more than satisfied to see Coriolanus demonstrate his ill-will toward the plebs during the ceremonial begging for voices. His conduct provides them with a new pretext for self-aggrandizement, and they waste no time in stirring up the plebs to repudiate the election. After Sicinius and Brutus have shown the populace how Coriolanus has used them, Sicinius says to his cohort:

> To th' Capitol, come.
> We will be there before the stream o' th' people;
> And this shall seem, as partly 'tis, their own,
> Which we have goaded onward. (II.iii.268-271)

They are even willing to take upon their own shoulders the blame for the plebs' rejection of Coriolanus, or so they tell the people; but this willingness is no reflection of a true sense of responsibility on their part. They are looking for power any way they can get it. If there is a breach between the patricians and the people, they can use Coriolanus as a wedge to broaden the gap and slip themselves into power.

Nevertheless, the tribunes, whose motives remain anything but pure, are right, righter than anyone else, in their estimation of the danger in Coriolanus. Brutus says to the plebs:

> Did you perceive
> He did solicit you in free contempt
> When he did need your loves, and do you think
> That his contempt shall not be bruising to you
> When he hath power to crush? (II.iii.207-211)

This Brutus, a very different sort of republican than his namesake in *Julius Caesar*, has enough basis in Coriolanus' past conduct to substantiate his judgment. Perhaps it is because the tribunes are so involved in their own self-interest that they are capable of seeing through Coriolanus. For it is they who say directly to him:

> You speak o' th' people
> As if you were a god to punish, not
> A man of their infirmity. (III.i.80-82)

However, their perspicacity does not excuse their own

dissentiousness. In their hunger for power they prove to be as much a threat to the state as the man they seek to have thrown from the Tarpeian Rock.

To be brief, all parties are responsible for the disunity in the city of Rome, but Coriolanus remains that disunity's commanding symbol (this, perversely enough, *because* of his "constancy"). At the same time, it is he who reveals, in an off-hand way, a recognition of his true function in the state. We have dealt with this quotation before, but for a different purpose. Coriolanus has just returned to Rome in triumph from the war with Corioli and is on his way to the capitol. His mother says:

> I have liv'd
> To see inherited my very wishes
> And the buildings of my fancy; only
> There's one thing wanting, which I doubt not but
> Our Rome will cast upon thee. [the consulship.]

To which Coriolanus replies:

> Know good mother,
> I had rather be their servant in my way
> Than sway with them in theirs.   (II.i.214-220)

But this momentary recognition, if indeed it can be called such, is scarcely assimilated by Volumnia and not really understood by Coriolanus. Like the patricians themselves, he forgets that his value as a servant rests in his military prowess. When the patricians try to convince him to speak the crowd fair and prevent his being attached as a "traitorous innovator," they disregard the fact that Coriolanus is first and foremost a man of war whose calling is not political to begin with. Indeed, this truth is not recognized by the patricians from the outset of the play. They become as much confused by the issue of "gratitude" as do the plebs. Thus, if in electing Coriolanus consul the people fail to remember that his potentialities lie in war and that in alienating him those potentialities might well be turned against them, the senators make the same mistake. The issue of Coriolanus' repudiation, like the altercation over the gown of humility, becomes confused with "flattery" and "gratitude," and the patricians, blinded by Coriolanus' heroic image, without understanding the full significance of that image, continue to support Coriolanus in the face of popular disapproval. It is not, unfortunately, until the belated moment of Coriolanus' banishment that the senators acquiesce, the result of which is Coriolanus' total disaffection from the state. As to Coriolanus himself—in spite of his statement that he "had rather be their servant" as a soldier than as consul, his treatment by the plebs reduces all to a question of "honor" for him. He sees his wounds bleeding for Rome (although he was unwilling to reveal those wounds to the Romans), and the plebs' banishment of him, plus the patricians' acquiescence to the plebs, impel his decision to avenge himself on the city as a whole.

The question of "honor" nevertheless remains a central paradox in the play. For in one sense Coriolanus *is* correct when he states he cannot flatter the people, that by doing this he would not be true to himself. He would lose his integrity first of all because he hates the common people, and second because he would be violating his true function in the community—the destroyer of Rome's enemies (this, given that perversely enough the people and even the patricians become Rome's enemies in their dissentiousness over the corn issue and over the public role Coriolanus is to play in the country). It is this very truth to himself that gives Coriolanus his heroic status. Like the case of Brutus in *Julius Caesar*, who is an honorable man, the honor Coriolanus seeks dishonors him. That for which under other circumstances the audience might admire him, causes the audience to condemn him. His honor so separates him from the ideal of the peaceful city that there is literally no place for him in it.

Conversely, if Coriolanus proves true to himself, it can be seen that, unlike the case of Brutus, there is never any moral conflict in him at all. He may rebel at using policy to attain his ends, but he never feels he should not hate the common people, nor does he feel that the limitation revealed by the one kind of service he can perform—that of killing—reflects a lack in himself. Thus if Coriolanus is true to his image, he is never true to what lies below that image—his own human nature. Feeling is perverted at such a deep level that all the judgments he makes against the populace, even those which are valid, turn against him and expose him as traitor to the people, traitor to Rome, traitor to Corioli, traitor to himself, and traitor to the human cause.

But he is true to his mother:

> O mother, mother!
> What have you done? Behold, the heavens do ope,
> The gods look down, and this unnatural scene
> They laugh at. O my mother, mother! O!
> You have won a happy victory to Rome;
> But, for your son,—believe it, O believe it—,
> Most dangerously you have with him prevail'd,
> If not most mortal to him.   (V.iii.182-189)

This, excluding the invective he uses at other points in the play, is some of Coriolanus' most passionate language.

With it he determines to leave Rome unharmed and chooses the death Aufidius makes for him. The statement, however, opens out beyond the immediate situation. For Volumnia has most dangerously prevailed with her son throughout his life; his values, his conception of himself, so much derived from her, have led to his predicament. Coriolanus, who would not give the plebs their grain and "politically" (in both senses of the word) feed the state, has had his human nature all but digested by Volumnia. Whatever love he most fully acknowledges is directed toward her, so that his human qualities have become isolated in her from the rest of the community. In a way they have been sacrificed for the aura of "divinity" which surrounds and unites the two. Only she, not even his wife, can make him merciful. In the close interdependency of Coriolanus and his mother are seen a kind of political and spiritual incest that reveals a distortion even in the one crucial relationship Coriolanus can demonstrably "feel" with great depth.[65] Here Coriolanus' hidden and isolated humanity acts the part of Nemesis and mortally betrays him to the enemies he has chosen for friends—Aufidius and his army.[66] The triplex image of Coriolanus which represents his relationship to the community, his relationship to war, and his relationship to his mother can be seen at this point, the point at which he is *most* human, to be one image, powerful and annihilating, the source of his own destruction.

But if this image, swordlike, points inward toward what is left of the feeling center of the hero's perverted humanity, it points outward too, through Rome, to Corioli. In this enemy city waits, so to speak, the same pas-

---

[65] G. Wilson Knight, *The Imperial Theme*, pp. 176-178.

[66] See Farnham, pp. 250-251 for a related, but slightly different interpretation.

sionate mob which set Coriolanus up as consul, only to
banish him. When he arrives it will welcome him with
the acclaim customary for heroes and gods. But just as
the tribunes had little difficulty convincing the Roman
populace of Coriolanus' enmity, Aufidius, as power-seek-
ing and envious as the tribunes, will have even less difficulty provoking the Volscian mob. Indeed, just as Coriolanus helped the tribunes in their cause, he will help
Aufidius in his. The Volscian general's public accusations
of "traitor" and "boy of tears" (which contain, it will be
admitted, more than a suspicion of validity) impel Caius
Marcius to expose himself as he has never exposed himself before. Surely now he is "most dangerously" less
than modest:

> "Boy!" False hound!
> If you have writ your annals true, 'tis there
> That, like an eagle in a dove-cote, I
> [Flutter'd] your Volscians in Corioli:
> Alone I did it. "Boy!"   (V.vi.113-117)

The climactic indiscretion of his words defines him clearly to the Volscian crowd as their great enemy; for they,
like the Roman plebs, had apparently forgotten how Coriolanus once fought against them, although in their case
the fight was military and not political. Their response
is tragically appropriate in view of their memories of
slaughter and carnage:

> *All the people.* Tear him to pieces! Do it presently!—
> He kill'd my son!—my daughter:—He kill'd my
> cousin Marcus!—He kill'd my father!
>
> (V.vi.121-123)

Aside from their capacity to create a sense of horror,

these lines function in another important way. By focusing our attention upon the slaughtered members of the various Volscian families, they emphasize the major thematic issue in the play. For "families" and the distorted relationships in them have been implicit thematically throughout—from the perverted relationship of Coriolanus and his mother to the political hostilities in the state of Rome to the betrayal by Coriolanus of his own land. The personal sense of pain and anger now felt by the Volscian populace paradoxically stretches this thematic issue one step further to the universal perversion in the universal human bond: the destruction of Man by Man. And at this point we recognize that the scene as a whole has suitably drawn all participants into the primary image of destruction which characterizes the play. Both Corioli and Coriolanus are responsible for this scene of death. And behind them stand all the Romans who have made their contribution. Unlike the situation in *Antony and Cleopatra*, where the conflict is between Rome and Egypt, in *Coriolanus* the two symbolic states are twins, and the enemy resides in each of them. Thus in *Coriolanus*, perhaps even more fully than in *Othello*, where the states of Venice and Cyprus are the "outer" and "inner" forms of the same state, it can be seen that the enemy, the potential killer, is Man; and nobody, not the plebs, nor the patricians, nor the tribunes, nor the Volscian crowd, nor individuals like Aufidius or Volumnia or Menenius, is to escape blame for the Volscian conspirators' blood-curdling cry as they overwhelm Coriolanus in what appears an epitome of the entire play's action:

> Kill, kill, kill, kill, kill him!
> (V.vi.132)

Only one character may perhaps be justifiably excluded from this scene of savage death and the condemnation that goes with it. The words on the body politic might be taken from Menenius' loquacious mouth and placed in that of Caius Marcius' "gracious silence"—Virgilia, the one truly "private" character in the play, and the only character who, paradoxically, fulfills a public role in a really meaningful way. Not only is it she who can still recognize the last impulse of humanity, faint though it may be, in her husband; but it is also she who most clearly represents in her tears and silence (which are her language) the natural, quiet, inborn humanity that transcends personality—of which she appropriately has so little—and is the essential root which grows through family, through class, into the flowering state.

IV

ANTONY AND CLEOPATRA:

THE HEROIC IMAGE

Of *Antony and Cleopatra* Sigurd Burckhardt remarks, "The sense of triumph which the play engenders springs from its immense daring, which, if it were not ultimately made good, would be mere defiance."[1] The statement is a useful gauge for the change in critical perspective which has developed since Dr. Johnson found the play ununified and structurally inept.[2] However, critics have always been struck by the extraordinary majesty of the play's language. Indeed, traditionally this language has been one of the primary instruments of apology for *Antony and Cleopatra* (until today, when critics find little necessity to apologize for it at all). Charles Bathurst's opinion is characteristic of the older point of view: "*Antony and Cleopatra* is carelessly written, with no attempt at dignity, considering what great personages are introduced; but with a great deal of nature, spirit, knowledge of character, in very many parts, and with several most beautiful passages of poetry and imagination: as for instance the dream of Cleopatra."[3]

More recently we have the work of Harley Granville-Barker and Una Ellis-Fermor to help explain *Antony and*

[1] Sigurd Burckhardt, "The King's Language: Shakespeare's Drama as Social Discovery," *AR*, XXI (Fall 1961), 385.

[2] Samuel Johnson, quoted in "Antony and Cleopatra," *A New Variorum Shakespeare*, ed. H. H. Furness (Philadelphia, 1907), XV, 477.

[3] Charles Bathurst, quoted in *New Variorum*, XV, 479. Samuel Taylor Coleridge (*Lectures and Notes on Shakespeare* [London, 1897], p. 315) gave the famous motto "Feliciter Audax" to the play's style and coined the phrase "happy valiancy of style" in honor of it.

Cleopatra's puzzling construction; and the result is a confirmation of Burckhardt's remark, although he is referring more to the part language plays in the drama than to structure. Granville-Barker showed us how the play is made up of a series of contrasting scenes, alternately representative of the attitudes and goals of Rome and Egypt, and how from this sequence of fluctuating points of view the principal theme of the play evolves—a conflict of those values characteristic of each state.[4] The late Miss Ellis-Fermor contributed the idea that the Elizabethan drama, rather than having characters in a "close-locked group" and a construction which attempts to bring out a definite theme (à la Ibsen), instead attempts to use ". . . characters widely differing as individuals or as groups, and so placed that our imaginations are induced to supply, it may be at unawares, intermediate and background figures or moods that complete a harmony of wide range and complexity, suggesting to our minds not a clear-cut image or a dominant theme, but the breadth of life and humanity."[5] Although Miss Ellis-Fermor's statement is a generalization perhaps less applicable to a play like

[4] Harley Granville-Barker, *Prefaces to Shakespeare*, I, 371. Hazlitt first suggested this idea when he pointed out a struggle between "Roman pride and Eastern magnificence" with the world suspended between the two. William Hazlitt, *Characters of Shakespeare's Plays* (London, 1817), p. 95. John Holloway (*The Story of the Night*, p. 107), finds the "oscillation" in the play due to the movement back and forth between lust and love.

[5] Una Ellis-Fermor, "The Nature of Plot in Drama," English Association *Essays and Studies*, XIII (1960), 67. Portions of this piece appear in an earlier form in *Shakespeare the Dramatist*: Annual Shakespeare Lecture of the British Academy (London, 1948). T. B. Stroup, in "The Structure of *Antony and Cleopatra*," *SQ*, XV (Spring 1964), describes the play's structure as derived from the morality play of the "world theater kind." The world was looked upon as a stage, and in relationship to its forebears, Stroup suggests, one can see in *Antony and Cleopatra* "a kind of unity within its 'Gothic' diversity. . ." (p. 291).

Othello than to *Antony*, it is derived from a careful study of Elizabethan dramatic techniques, and certainly it can be said that her idea is an astute one. She traces the spatial relations in the play with a wonderful acumen. It is true that for the sake of her argument she must put the action into a kind of static repose, but her analysis divines *Antony's* breadth superbly. When she says it embraces "the whole known world" through her technique of pictorially describing the play's structure, we can see precisely how much her view of things corroborates Granville-Barker's and clarifies the intrinsic amplitude of the major characters as well: "In the greatest plays, moreover, distance itself gives prominence to the chief characters; the attention of the subordinate agents is focused upon them. A whole universe, it seems, is intent upon the action of those foreground figures [*sic*] and their power, in turn, reaches to the uttermost bounds of the world, to figures upon the very border of invisibility."

These figures on the border of invisibility are no supernatural creatures, but merely the least significant of the play's characters, those at the end of a "continuous regression in the spatial grouping of minor figures."[6] Miss Ellis-Fermor traces the regression back from the hero and heroine, who stand in the foreground, through Caesar, Pompey, and Lepidus; through Enobarbus, Maecenas, Agrippa, and Alexas; through Scarus, Dolabella, Menecrates, Mardian, and Canidius; through Ventidius, Thyreus, the clown, the soothsayer, Dercetas, and Diomed; and furthermore through figures who become increasingly less distinct than those already mentioned, but most of whom retain some little individual distinguishing inflection of their own: servants, guards, messengers, soldiers,

6 Ellis-Fermor, "The Nature of Plot," pp. 71-73.

until we reach the "virtually invisible Taurus" with his one line, "My Lord?"[7] Finally, Miss Ellis-Fermor's suggestion that this particular structural technique gives us the sensation that all eyes are directed toward the focal characters seems to bear out Danby's observations concerning the great amount of commentary by subordinate characters upon the protagonists, a device we noted also in *Coriolanus*.[8]

However, if structural difficulties in *Antony and Cleopatra* have been explored and to some extent resolved, contemporary interpretations of the major characters themselves remain at odds. The principal difficulty here relates to what might be called a conflict between the major characters and their language, the foremost area of investigation for the critics being the last acts of the play. In Rosen's words "The exciting drama inherent in the poetry . . . competes with the more mundane drama of the play's action."[9] Burckhardt would surely agree; indeed, he finds that the "poetry" in the play achieves a kind of victory and fulfills its claims, although it does not "overcome" Caesar's more prosaic political empire. "For it is the peculiarity of this play that it dismisses us into the world of prose and Caesar not with the sense that too great a price has been paid to restore an order in which mediocre men can live, but with a certain composure, because no more is rendered unto Caesar than is his."[10] To interpret the play's competing elements in this style is not to underestimate those assessments of the principal conflict (by now traditional) which see the antagonism between Rome and Egypt (or policy and love,

[7] *Ibid.*, p. 73.
[8] John F. Danby, *Poets on Fortune's Hill*, p. 131.
[9] William Rosen, *Shakespeare and The Craft of Tragedy*, p. 146.
[10] Burckhardt, "The King's language," p. 386.

or military life and the flesh) as the play's coherent center of interest. Caesar's imperial milieu of calculating shrewdness is prosaic enough. For all his apparent high-mindedness where Antony's conduct is concerned, Caesar can break his pact with Pompey and rid himself of Lepidus with no moral reservations whatsoever. As Danby suggests, if one of the perspectives in the play is that of "insensate love," the other is that of "cynical Rome."[11] Similarly, the "poetry" latent in Cleopatra's sensual and heart-consuming Egypt is apparent enough not to warrant more than an allusion to Enobarbus' description of the queen on her barge: "O'er-picturing that Venus where we see/The fancy outwork Nature."

Yet even within Cleopatra herself and Antony himself, the poetic and prosaic elements compete. Both characters, each of whom can achieve enrapturing rhetorical flights, are capable of betrayal, falsehood, and policy. Antony can wed Octavia and plan immediately to return to Cleopatra, and well before Caesar breaks the pact with Pompey and speaks "scantly" of Antony. As for the queen, her career in the play is a progress of betrayals and apparent policies, from the two disastrous sea-battles to her patting palms with Caesar's messenger Thyreus. Yet in *Antony and Cleopatra*, as Maurice Charney concludes, where language is at issue (and thus the characters who speak it), Shakespeare appears to be deliberately extending his "imaginative resources" as far as he can. Charney contrasts the "style" of this play with that of *Julius Caesar*, where the author seems to be purposely limiting these resources. Charney describes the style of *Antony and Cleopatra* as "hyperbolical"—a "reaching out of the

[11] Danby, *Poets on Fortune's Hill*, p. 151.

imagination for superlatives."[12] In his own terms, he comes to a conclusion not entirely different from Burckhardt's. If Burckhardt feels that Caesar triumphs in his realm and Cleopatra triumphs in hers, Charney, concentrating on his own interests, maintains that *Antony and Cleopatra*'s style is "elliptical and complex, with an ability to suspend many ideas without seeking to resolve them into one."[13]

Thus the special "daring" of the play proceeds along a number of lines, including its structure, to the demands put upon poetry, on language at its most highly "conceptual." The triumph in *Antony and Cleopatra* lies not in its forcing us to dismiss the claims of a Caesar, or even those of Cleopatra, strumpet; it lies in the establishment of a realm of its own, the realm, for lack of another word, of the imagination—a force which, in spite of its apparent dissociation from literal reality, from the prosaic, nevertheless can manage to live with the prosaic and remain a fertilizing catalyst in the spirit of man.

Therefore if we cannot go quite as far as Stoll when he says that the love of Antony and Cleopatra "is greater than their natures,"[14] we might agree that their conception of their love indeed surmounts the limitations their natures impose upon it—that is, at least, during those portions of the play where Antony is not rejecting Cleopatra or Cleopatra belittling Antony. For, surely, observing the two in action often makes us doubt the complete worthiness of each as a love object in the

[12] Maurice Charney, "Shakespeare's Style in *Julius Caesar* and *Antony and Cleopatra*," *ELH*, XXVI (September 1959), 355-356. Charney presents his ideas on the "Roman" style of *Julius Caesar* and the "Egyptian" (hyperbolical) style of *Antony and Cleopatra* in a revamped form in *Shakespeare's Roman Plays*, pp. 11-29.

[13] *Ibid.*, p. 367.

[14] E. E. Stoll, *Art and Artifice in Shakespeare*, p. 146.

other's eyes. In the last analysis, if we are to accept Antony and Cleopatra on the terms they stipulate for themselves when they are about to die, "poetry" is going to have to do double duty. If we are to believe that Antony is "A Roman by a Roman/Valiantly vanquish'd" and that Cleopatra is "fire and air," her "other elements" given "to baser life," poetry will have to be something beyond a mere reflection of character: it will have to establish a realm of its own at some time for the lovers to live in forever, and we will have to accept that realm. In the words of Robert Speaight, the play is affirmative ". . . as only a supreme masterpiece can be, and we must see in what its affirmations consist. They do not consist in the unsaying of all that the more sombre plays had told us about human nature."[15] However, even as we take the failings of our major characters into consideration, we ought to recognize that the first postulate of these lovers' love *is* its eternity; and if the establishment of that eternity means a poetic magnification of the lovers themselves on some plane—even if that plane exists in their own imaginations—it is language that will have to make that magnification:

> *Ant.* Let Rome in Tiber melt, and the wide arch
> Of the rang'd empire fall! Here is my space.
> Kingdoms are clay; our dungy earth alike
> Feeds beast as man; the nobleness of life
> Is to do thus, when such a mutual pair
> [embracing.]
> And such a twain can do 't, in which I bind,
> On pain of punishment, the world to weet
> We stand up peerless. (I.i.33-40)

[15] Robert Speaight, *Nature in Shakespearean Tragedy* (London, 1955), p. 125.

The success of such language depends to some degree upon its power to disarm us. It is like a looking glass that creates and maintains its image despite the stones which may be cast at it. Such stones are flung not only by Philo, Enobarbus, Caesar, and Pompey; they are seized and cast, oddly enough, by Cleopatra herself, although, of course, not with the same disinterest. Indeed, Cleopatra is perhaps the most effective of Antony's satirists.[16] Thus, in response to Antony's immense inflation of himself, Cleopatra, and their love, the queen is capable of saying:

> Excellent falsehood!
> Why did he marry Fulvia, and not love her?
> (I.i.40-41)

We might, indeed, be prone to take Cleopatra at her word, did we not learn she is as capable of restoring illusions about Antony as she is of destroying them; and this is especially true at the end of the play. Antony and his image become her empire, and if her basic impulse is to control, subject, and confine Antony in "her strong toil of grace," it is also to become the interpretress of the image he leaves behind him. From this standpoint, it can be seen that Antony's more rhetorical speeches, whatever their afflatus, survive, as it were, in Cleopatra's hands, ultimately not merely in spite of her, but because of her:

> *Cleo.* His legs bestrid the ocean; his rear'd arm
> Crested the world; his voice was propertied
> As all the tuned spheres, and that to friends;
> But when he meant to quail and shake the orb,

16 Brents Stirling, *Unity in Shakespearean Tragedy*, p. 160.

He was as rattling thunder. For his bounty,
There was no winter in 't; [an autumn 'twas]
That grew the more by reaping. His delights
Were dolphin-like; they show'd his back above
The element they liv'd in. In his livery
Walk'd crowns and crownets; realms and islands
    were
As plates dropp'd from his pocket.   (V.ii.82-92)

If we feel that Cleopatra speaks of "her" Antony with
the same lack of self-awareness Othello demonstrates
when speaking of himself, this speech might truly re-
sound with hollowness, despite its poetic splendors. And
if it does not, perhaps it is because the queen remains
sublimely conscious of her exaggeration. She soars sky-
ward, defying her knowledge both of Antony and herself,
and her awareness somehow gives ballast to what otherwise might be pure rhetoric and nothing more. Her
question to Dolabella at the end of her speech, "Think
you there was or might be such a man/As this I dream'd
of?" indicates this awareness by setting up the response
she of course receives; but that response, "Gentle madam,
no," only provides a catapult for six more lines of extraordinary poetry. By allowing room for Dolabella's
gentle mockery in her question, she rids us of our smile
before we can deride her. The comic perspective is also
provided for by the intentness with which Cleopatra
builds up her description of Antony in the lines preceding the grand encomium itself. Dolabella's interruptions,
Cleopatra's refusal to acquiesce, to relinquish the world
she is creating before she has finished creating it, ring
with humor; but it is a humor that protects her language even as it reveals a Cleopatra who is enacting the

role of *grande dame* for her own benefit as well as Antony's, for Dolabella's as well as her own:[17]

> *Cleo.* I dream'd there was an Emperor Antony.
>   O, such another sleep, that I might see
>   But such another man?
> *Dol.*   If it might please ye,—
> *Cleo.* His face was as the heavens; and therein stuck
>   A sun and moon, which kept their course and
>   lighted
>   The little O, the earth.
> *Dol.*   Most sovereign creature,—
> *Cleo.* His legs bestrid the ocean .... (V.ii.76-82ff.)

Here once again, as in Antony's speech in Act I, we are contained by the spaciousness of the universe, but now that universe is Antony himself. The "little O, the earth" sings its own paradox—it is nothing, it is everything—it is as broad as Cleopatra's mind can make it, and narrow as the letter itself; but our feet are on that earth even as we hear her words. As her poetry battles with Dolabella's quietly realistic interruptions (a technique used in other scenes as well), we are struck dumb by our own amusement, stretched out on the oddly delightful rack of her rhetoric, pulled together again accordion-like as we slide down from Cleopatra's perspective to Dolabella's, and drawn out as we slip upward from Dolabella's to an even higher level of Cleopatra's. The result is a chastening of our resistance and a new willingness to accept the limitations of Dolabella's point of view even while recognizing that he is right in his realistic way. The same holds true in regard to Cleo-

[17] In L. J. Mills, "Cleopatra's Tragedy," *SQ*, XI (Spring, 1960), 156, footnote 20, see references to G. S. Griffiths and A. H. Tolman.

patra: we accept her Antony even while realizing he simply did not measure up in action to the dream she projects of him. Yet her final statement in answer to Dolabella's quiet refusal to indulge her fantasy winds sinuously about the entire question and by sheer force of will squeezes actuality out of what in fact has been only a "dream":

> *Cleo.* You lie, up to the hearing of the gods!
> But, if there be [or] ever were one such,
> It's past the size of dreaming. Nature wants stuff
> To vie strange forms with fancy; yet, t' imagine
> An Antony were nature's piece 'gainst fancy,
> Condemning shadows quite.   (V.ii.95-100)

Here Cleopatra charges that the imagination would defeat itself in attempting to create an Antony; it could not reach his noble proportions. In ordinary cases it is nature which loses in the competition with fancy, where the making of "strange forms" is at issue. But since only nature itself could produce an Antony, sublime artist that she is, fancy cannot hope to reproduce his monumental features. Yet in these lines Cleopatra claims a greater reality for her dream of Antony than Dolabella's limited perspective can offer.[18] If, she seems to say to Dolabella, reality is the point of contention, the inability of the imagination, Dolabella's or anyone else's, to imagine an Antony is due to some fault in the imagination, not to some fault in Antony. In short her language dislodges Antony from the world of mundane forms and raises him to "Platonic" proportions: "Platonic" in the

18 See *Antony and Cleopatra,* New Arden edition, ed. M. R. Ridley (Cambridge, Mass., 1954), p. 216 and Charney, "Shakespeare's Style," p. 363 for related interpretations of this speech.

sense of the *Symposium*, where art brings to birth new forms which mirror and immortalize the artist-lover and the beloved.[19] (And what else is Cleopatra but an artist in language in these speeches?) Moreover, Cleopatra implies that an imagination with sufficient capacity could engage this reality, an imagination at least something like her own:

> . . . yet, t' imagine
> An Antony were nature's piece 'gainst fancy,
> Condemning shadows quite.

Here the heightened human imagination fulfills nature's art, is Nature's art, because it is one of nature's most sophisticated tools: the natural impulse which recreates and perfects the creations of nature itself. And since, according to Cleopatra, the subject, Antony, is already perfect, the recreation of him will be sublime. Thus by using Dolabella's refusal to acknowledge the Antony of her dreams for her own advantage, Cleopatra launches a new world as wide as possibility, as broad as the mind, as infinitely expandable as her own imagination can make it—and leaves Dolabella below impressed at her devotion.

Yet this vision of Cleopatra's "man of men" is not presented until after Antony's death. Earlier Cleopatra spends a sufficient amount of time deflating Antony's self-image, not only by means of action, but by words as well. Her skill is not without significance, for Antony's whole effort throughout the play is directed toward reestablishing a past conception of himself which not only he, but the rest of the world, acknowledges. The

[19] The use of the figure Eros in the play might suggest more specific relevance to *The Symposium*.

unifying "action" of the play is not simply the conflict between Rome and Egypt and their representative values. Antony vacillates between these two empires, and the plot is woven around the inner conflict he suffers in attempting to choose between them. But the process of choosing is not a purely intellectual one: it is a question of his locating some emotional ground upon which to rebuild his old heroic sense of himself. His soldier's past stands behind him, a constant rebuke to the general who has assumed the role of "strumpet's fool," and it is this heroic image, Rosen suggests, which is "the only unquestioned ideal in the play."[20] Rosen comes very close to the truth, but the ideal, it might be noted, is incomplete if we set it against Cleopatra's final encomium of Antony. There soldier and lover are fused into one grand monumental form: the complete man, conqueror of territories and of hearts too. Yet it remains clear that insofar as Antony's aims are concerned, his soldierly past is what he seeks and what he cannot, at least in the first part of the play, reconcile with his sensuality. Indeed, it is none other than Caesar who presents most effectively the picture of the young, resolute, and self-controlled warrior of the past (in contrast to the pleasure-loving paramour of the present). Discussing Antony with Lepidus before Antony's return from Egypt, Caesar praises the conduct of the "triple pillar of the world" at the battle of Modena (where incidentally, Caesar defeated him). Addressing the absent Antony he recounts wondrous accomplishments:

[20] Rosen, p. 112. Rosen (p. 108) says: "I suggest that the play is not concerned primarily with the clash between the values of Egypt and Rome but with Antony, his divided allegiance, and most important, his fulfillment as man, which demands that he recapture his heroic past."

> Thou didst drink
> The stale of horses and the gilded puddle
> Which beasts would cough at; thy palate then did
>   deign
> The roughest berry on the rudest hedge;
> Yea, like the stag, when snow the pasture sheets,
> The barks of trees thou [browsed'st]; on the Alps
> It is reported thou didst eat strange flesh,
> Which some did die to look on; and all this—
> It wounds thine honour that I speak it now—
> Was borne so like a soldier, that thy cheek
> So much as lank'd not.   (I.iv.61-71)

Interestingly, to stress his point, Shakespeare has Caesar use an imagery of eating which evokes a reaction precisely opposite to that which Cleopatra's delight in feasting evokes. The rudest berry, the horse's stale, and the ghastly flesh Caesar uses to indicate Antony's former stoicism may be contrasted with the rich viands and wines that life with Cleopatra offers and the sensual connotations, shrewdly pointed out by Leo Kirschbaum, that accompany her imagery:[21]

> Now I feed myself
> With most delicious poison. . . .
>   (I.v.26-27)

> Give me some music; music, moody food
> Of us that trade in love.   (II.v.1-2)

The importance of the soldierly role to Antony is also emphasized by Ventidius, who brings to the foreground

---

[21] Leo Kirschbaum, "Shakespeare's Cleopatra," *SAB*, XIX (October 1944), 164-166. Kirschbaum's discussion of Cleopatra appears in a modified form in *Character and Characterization in Shakespeare*, pp. 99-110.

the subject of military accomplishment, and who notes
how Antony's desire for such accomplishment is connected
with his ambition to be once again the world's "foremost
man." In Act III Ventidius, after having routed the
Parthians, refuses to pursue them through Media and
Mesopotamia because he does not wish to offend Antony:

> *Ven.*   O Silius, Silius,
>   I have done enough; a lower place, note well,
>   May make too great an act. For learn this, Silius:
>   Better to leave undone, than by our deed
>   Acquire too high a fame when him we serve's
>   away.
>   Caesar and Antony have ever won
>   More in their officer than person. Sossius,
>   One of my place in Syria, his lieutenant,
>   For quick accumulation of renown,
>   Which he achiev'd by th' minute, lost his favour.
>   Who does i' th' wars more than his captain can
>   Becomes his captain's captain; and ambition,
>   The soldier's virtue, rather makes choice of loss,
>   Than gain which darkens him.
>   I could do more to do Antonius good,
>   But 'twould offend him; and in his offence
>   Should my performance perish.   (III.i.11-27)

If we accept Ventidius' criticism of his general, it would
seem that "reputation" plays an important part in motivating Antony. The end of military conquest for him
is not empire, as it is for Caesar, but "renown." This is
borne out also by the play's action. Antony's return to
Rome at the beginning of the drama is stimulated as
much by Pompey's sudden public recognition (Pompey
". . . stands up/For the main soldier") as by the "strong

necessity of the time" (the impending civil war between Caesar and Pompey). Antony's subsequent return to Egypt is prompted by similar considerations. In Rome, his interview with Caesar is successful enough. The most he will apologize for is having "neglected" lending arms to Caesar when Caesar required them, and reluctantly, for Fulvia's wars, of which he was "the ignorant motive." During the interview Antony speaks diplomatically, but with a sense of integrity, and the discussion ends with arrangements for a political marriage with Octavia.[22] But the brief exchange with the soothsayer which follows reveals that Antony has come to appreciate how much his celestial stock has depreciated. Antony asks the soothsayer:

> Say to me,
> Whose fortunes shall rise higher, Caesar's or mine?
> (II.iii.15-16)

The soothsayer's response is informative, for he speaks not of imperial conquest for the sake of territory or power, but simply of personal glory. Antony's "demon" is "noble, courageous, high, unmatchable,/Where Caesar's not"; but when Antony is near Caesar that spirit "becomes a fear, as being o'er power'd." Antony's "lustre thickens when he shines by." According to the soothsayer, in order for Antony's spirit to gain its full nobility once more, he must leave Caesar, and Antony's conclusion that his "better cunning faints" under Caesar's "chance" prompts the decision to return to Egypt, where his "pleasure lies." Having made peace with Caesar, Antony is willing for the time being to leave the empire in his capable hands rather than risk playing a subordinate

22 Stirling, *Unity in Shakespearean Tragedy*, pp. 161-164, 166-167.

role. Now, it might be said that the soothsayer, who is actually in Cleopatra's employ, has every reason to give the prognostication and advice he does. Furthermore, Stoll may very well be correct when he suggests that the soothsayer's injunction "serves as the excuse"[23] for Antony's return to sensual Egypt. Nevertheless, Shakespearean soothsayers are notoriously accurate in their predictions, and the sense we get from history (which surely does play a part in the drama) and the action itself that Caesar's star is in the ascendant may give some force to the soothsayer's oracular words. As to Antony's using the prediction as an "excuse" to return to his pleasure—there is certainly an element of rationalization in the decision he makes. On the other hand, his great sensitivity throughout the play to the question of his status in the world's eyes makes it conceivable that he envisions all men as potential competitors and that his true aim is always a heightening of his self-conception on grounds having little to do with "morality." Hence it is possible that the man who can return to Egypt for his pleasure can also return to preserve what he has regained in the way of self-esteem—and to wait.

Ultimately, however, he finds ample justification for his departure when in Athens he learns that Caesar has broken the pact arranged with Pompey before the famous party on Pompey's galley, and when he finds that Caesar has spoken "scantly" of him and has seized and imprisoned Lepidus. Antony announces his intentions to his new wife Octavia in the following language:

> *Ant.*   Gentle Octavia,
>   Let your best love draw to that point which
>   seeks

[23] Stoll, *Art and Artifice*, p. 145.

> Best to preserve it. If I lose mine honour,
> I lose myself; better I were not yours
> Than yours so branchless. But, as you requested,
> Yourself shall go between 's. The meantime, lady,
> I'll raise the preparation of a war
> Shall stain your brother. Make your soonest haste;
> So your desires are yours.   (III.iv.20-28)

Antony concludes that if he is to find his "honour," it will be by opposing Caesar, not by remaining subordinate to him or by permitting him to act in a high-handed manner. And it will be seen too that if opposition to Caesar means destruction for Antony, alignment with Cleopatra can at least offer him the opportunity for one last glorious blaze. To his own mind, combat for whatever purpose, and even in Cleopatra's name, can lead to the reestablishment of his soldier's reputation.

Cleopatra's role in all this is, of course, ambiguous enough. In a play containing "reiterated paradoxes" in language and action, as Benjamin T. Spencer puts it, she remains the chief paradox of all.[24] Her influence upon Antony has been understood by some critics as strictly pernicious, and these critics have good reason for their opinions.[25] Having subdued Antony's "captain's

[24] Benjamin T. Spencer, "*Antony and Cleopatra* and the Paradoxical Metaphor," *SQ*, IX (Summer 1959), 375.

[25] For instance, F. N. Dickey, *Not Wisely But Too Well* (San Marino, Calif., 1957), pp. 144-202; Daniel Stempel, "The Transmigration of the Crocodile," *SQ*, VII (Winter 1956), 59-72; and J. Leeds Barroll, "Antony and Pleasure," *JEGP*, LVII (October 1958), 708-720. For opposing views, see G. Wilson Knight, *The Imperial Theme*, pp. 247-250; Mark Van Doren, *Shakespeare* (Garden City, N.Y., 1939), p. 230; S. L. Bethell, *Shakespeare and the Popular Dramatic Tradition* (Durham, N.C., 1944), pp. 149-169. See also Willard Farnham, *Shakespeare's Tragic Frontier*, pp. 139-205, for a discussion of Macbeth, Timon, Coriolanus, and Antony as "deeply flawed" characters.

heart" and converted him into "the bellows and the fan/ To cool a gypsy's lust," her power over him is a mixture of physical attraction and a complex of the most dynamic feminine wiles and ways. The extent of her power is felt from the moment she opens her mouth—for her language, whether satirical or eloquent, seldom fails to distract our attention from Antony. As a creator and manipulator of scenes, she is little less than a genius; as an actress, she is the Duse of the Shakespearean world. Indeed, her success can be measured even in those scenes where she fails to accomplish her ends, and it is in these scenes that her attitude toward Antony appears the most ambiguous and paradoxical. But always her power, for better or worse, is felt—by ourselves and by Antony, whom she all but reduces to speechless frustration. In such scenes we also become aware of comedy as a qualifying point of view; but this lack of tragic tone is not limited merely to the earlier part of the play, as Bradley proposes.[26] Nor should the comic perspective be construed as a lapse of the imagination on the part of the dramatist. Comedy in *Antony and Cleopatra* is a calculated device which questions the entire issue of heroic possibility only in turn to be questioned itself, and by Cleopatra. The result of this dialog between the heroic, grandiloquent, and super-rational elements in the play and the comic, the satirical, and the realistic, is a widening of the perceptions effectively supported by the "spatial" structure of the drama.

A scene which illustrates the comic motif in *Antony and Cleopatra* and which also demonstrates some of the devices Cleopatra uses to subjugate Antony can be found directly after Antony has made his decision to return to

[26] A. C. Bradley, "Antony and Cleopatra," *Oxford Lectures* (London, 1909), p. 284.

Rome. Here we find Cleopatra at her most difficult and her most entertaining. Of course, it is Antony who is subjected to her jibes, her interruptions, and her flights of curiously exalted language. We can recognize so much more clearly than he how the interview provides her with an opportunity for assays at queenly self-demonstration. For the conquest of the male is her métier and her histrionics are a fine method for bewildering the enemy, for sounding him out, and for ascertaining whether losing the current skirmish is not the best tactic for winning the entire battle.

The scene commences with Cleopatra ordering Alexas to find Antony. She issues the following instructions:

> See where he is, who's with him, what he does.
> I did not send you. If you find him sad,
> Say I am dancing; if in mirth, report
> I am sudden sick. Quick, and return.
>
> (I.iii.2-5)

Long adept at love's subterfuges, Cleopatra issues her clipped and precise orders. Her man-eating instincts tell her precisely the strategy most likely to undermine her opponent's morale. Her announcement that she is "sick and sullen" upon Antony's entrance is greeted by his determination to announce imminent departure for Rome: "I am sorry to give breathing to my purpose,—"

But Cleopatra will not permit him to finish what he has apparently planned to say. She counters his earnestness with lines that seem straight out of Verdi:

> *Cleo.* Help me away, dear Charmian; I shall fall.
>   It cannot be thus long, the sides of nature
>   Will not sustain it.   (I.iii.15-17)

However, the "sides of nature" incapable of sustaining an unbearable strain might be more accurately identified as Antony's, not her own. His attempts to state his case with the dignity and forthrightness commensurate with his rank and the memory of what he once was are reduced during the first forty lines to a series of almost monosyllabic importunities and protestations, all engulfed in the unceasing flow of Cleopatra's rhetoric: her dismissals, threats, and satire. Thus Antony throughout the greater part of the scene sounds like an uxorious husband unable to make headway against his harridan wife: "Now, my dearest queen,—"; "What's the matter?"; "The gods best know,—"; "Cleopatra,—"; "Most sweet queen,—"; "How now, lady!" The impression we receive of Antony here, particularly when his ejaculations are telescoped in this way, is both humorous and pathetic. He suggests a frustrated actor whose lines are suddenly and bewilderingly cut short by an actress who refuses to wait for her cues.

Cleopatra on her part claims she has been betrayed, that she "saw the treasons planted" from the first. With incredible audacity, she accuses Antony of having been false to Fulvia, menaces him with threats of physical violence had she only Antony's "inches," and upon hearing of Fulvia's death, uses Antony's undemonstrative reaction to that sad event as a premonition of his reception of her own. Finally she caps all by crying, "Cut my lace, Charmian, come!" and hardly a moment later announces that she is "quickly ill and well,/So Antony loves." To Antony's pleas for forbearance and "true evidence to his love, which stands/An honourable trial," Cleopatra, merciless still, retorts, "So Fulvia told me" and demands "one scene of excellent dissembling; and let it look/Like perfect honour." With this remark, she of course hits home. Antony, all the while attempting to preserve his dignity and heroic demeanor, warns, "You'll heat my blood. No more." Honor now having become explicitly the question at issue, Cleopatra realizes she has struck Antony's most sensitive psychic and moral area. She advances boldly, her words a demolition crew, to directly attack the seat of his identity:

> *Cleo.* You can do better yet; but this is meetly.
> *Ant.* Now, by [my] sword,—
> *Cleo.*   And target.—Still he mends;
>   But this is not the best. Look, prithee, Charmian,
>   How this Herculean Roman does become
>   The carriage of his chafe.   (I.iii.81-85)

At this point Antony's reaction warns her that she has gone quite far enough; that, in fact, Antony is fully resolved upon departure. To humiliate him further might be to effect irreparable damage. Cleopatra has recourse to only one other strategy for the time being: she must give in as gracefully as possible, managing if she can to maintain the ties that bind him to her. Yet she can derive some satisfaction from having anticipated the pretexts of his arguments and having squelched relentlessly any pretensions he might have brought with him into her chamber.

As to Antony, it is difficult to say whether or to what extent he may be "posing" in this scene. Clearly, if he had intended to, unconsciously or not, he gets little enough chance. His bearing and the requirements of the situation would indicate that he had planned some sort of prepared address of departure for Cleopatra; but the queen's sallies curtail his rhetorical powers (powers he amply illustrates in other portions of the play) and prohibit him from discharging the volley of stalwart pronouncements we might expect from a man in his circumstances. His longest speech is fundamentally a factual account of the current state of affairs in the Roman Empire, during which he advances his reasons for having to leave Egypt. He includes as well several fairly cursory statements of love and loyalty to Cleopatra:

> *Ant.*   Hear me, Queen.
>   The strong necessity of time commands
>   Our services a while; but my full heart
>   Remains in use with you. . . .   (I.iii.41-44ff.)

and

>   By the fire
>   That quickens Nilus' slime, I go from hence
>   Thy soldier, servant; making peace or war
>   As thou [affect'st].   (I.iii.68-71)

Cleopatra, however, sees through the list of events and implied responsibilities preceding these statements to the image of past glory and the desire to reattain it which have helped influence Antony's decision to leave. Having mocked "this Herculean Roman" she nevertheless understands that his honor as the foremost soldier in the world is the prime factor motivating him, and that against such an adversary theatrics and satire are weapons with a double edge. She dismisses him with the language of a graceful loser who is apparently willing to surrender and bide *her* time:

>   But, sir, forgive me,
>   Since my becomings kill me when they do not
>   Eye well to you. Your honour calls you hence;
>   Therefore be deaf to my unpitied folly,

And all the gods go with you! Upon your sword
Sit laurell'd victory, and smooth success
Be strew'd before your feet!   (I.iii.95-101)

But if, as the description of this scene seems to indicate, Cleopatra functions as one of Antony's most efficient satirists, she is also his greatest idolator. She, who is so implicitly involved in his destruction, both by word and deed, is also the great protectress of his heroic image. Even as Antony is in Rome arranging his marriage with Octavia, Cleopatra is speaking in the following vein:

> O Charmian,
> Where think'st thou he is now? Stands he, or sits he?
> Or does he walk? Or is he on his horse?
> O happy horse, to bear the weight of Antony!
> Do bravely, horse! for wot'st thou whom thou mov'st?
> The demi-Atlas of the earth, the arm
> And burgonet of men. . . .   (I.v.18-24)

Yet Cleopatra's passion for Antony is so tightly interlocked with her own self-esteem that it may seem her hero is nothing more to her than another jewel in her crown of conquests—conquests not of territories but of those giants who conquer territories. Such giants are Julius Caesar and Pompey the Great, and from this point of view Antony would be their heir. Her love, therefore, appears to derive in part from those very self-admiring instincts that impel the remarkable theatrics she delivers during the course of the play. She draws status from the rank of those she conquers; and love for her is therefore always a battleground—sensual and enthralling—where, ironically, she herself is the prize and booty. And if winning can accomplish certain practical aims, all the better:

> He's speaking now,
> Or murmuring, "Where's my serpent of Old Nile?"
> For so he calls me. Now I feed myself
> With most delicious poison. Think on me,
> That am with Phoebus' amorous pinches black
> And wrinkled deep in time? Broad-fronted Caesar,
> When thou wast here above the ground, I was
> A morsel for a monarch; and great Pompey
> Would stand and make his eyes grow in my brow;
> There would he anchor his aspect and die
> With looking on his life.   (I.v.24-34)

In these lines Cleopatra's self-praise is expressed not
in anthems to her beauty, but in language that denies her
physical attractiveness for the sake of an internal force
of personality derived, it would appear, from the primitive nature of femininity itself. Her description of herself
as black with "Phoebus' amorous pinches" is a calculated
self-mockery;[27] yet the words draw attention to those
fascinating qualities which make the sun love her—
qualities reflected in the language she uses: a delight in
herself that permits mockery at her own expense and a
freshness of perception which can admit at least a modicum of truth in the face of her own self-love. After all,
she is no Juliet. "Wrinkled deep in time," her attractions
emanate not from the dewiness of youth and innocence,
but from the whole experience of her feminine sex. In
short, she charms. She is the supreme mistress, and perhaps it would be foolish of us to expect her to love with
the generosity of a Desdemona. Where she is generous,

[27] Irving Ribner, *Patterns in Shakespearian Tragedy*, p. 171,
however, notes that black is the "traditional color of lechery" (as
in *Titus* and *Othello*) and that the line identifies Cleopatra as a
symbol of lechery.

one assumes, is with her person, and *that* is miraculously conveyed to us through her style, her style of speaking and her style of acting. We are free, one supposes, to reject her on moral grounds, as Antony does several times in the play. But if we do, we must reject her gift as well, which is herself. That this gift is impelled by the self-esteem of the donor detracts not one jot from the pleasure we may take in it; and having taken that pleasure, as does Antony, as indeed does Shakespeare, we surely will not be hypocritical enough to make believe we can return it unused.

Nevertheless, Shakespeare is not reluctant to examine Cleopatra's charms in their most doubtful light. If in the last act she manages to remain queen over the empire of flesh and dreams, and thus achieve a kind of godhead, Antony can take the old affairs with Caesar and Pompey upon which she prides herself (whatever she may say of her "salad days") and adroitly expose her promiscuous and self-aggrandizing heart. In the scene after Actium, for instance, when Antony discovers Cleopatra interviewing Caesar's messenger Thyreus, he uses Cleopatra's imagery of eating against her: he pictures her not as the digester but the digested, and in none too flattering terms:

> *Ant.* I found you as a morsel cold upon
>   Dead Caesar's trencher; nay, you were a fragment
>   Of Cneius Pompey's; besides what hotter hours,
>   Unregist'red in vulgar fame, you have
>   Luxuriously pick'd out; for I am sure,
>   Though you can guess what temperance should
>   be,
>   You know not what it is.   (III.xiii.116-122)

Here the repetition of the very word Cleopatra has used in describing her delicious attributes—she calls herself a "morsel for a monarch"—[28] but from quite another perspective, sets in contrast the two competing Cleopatras we have in the play, those of strumpet and "goddess," the latter of which does not achieve its full realization until the death scene in the monument.

This pattern of two Cleopatras is repeated not only in the queen's ability to undermine Antony through mockery and reclaim him through poetry, or in the contrast between Cleopatra's self-admiring visions and the more critical portraits delivered by the play's various commentators (such as Enobarbus); the pattern is repeated in the action as well. Indeed, so ambiguous is Cleopatra that even Enobarbus, who sees through her histrionics with brilliant clarity, can be caught by the spell she casts. In Act I, after Antony has received the messengers from Rome and begins to determine upon leaving Egypt, Enobarbus, in fine satirical form, gives the following description of Antony's queen:

> *Ant.* She is cunning past man's thought.
> *Eno.* Alack, sir, no; her passions are made of nothing but the finest part of pure love. We cannot call her winds and waters sighs and tears. They are greater storms and tempests than almanacs can report. This cannot be cunning in her; if it be, she makes a shower of rain as well as Jove.

> (I.ii.150-157)

Nevertheless, in Rome, after Antony's interview with Caesar, Enobarbus delivers his superlative account of

---

[28] Charney (*Shakespeare's Roman Plays*, pp. 103-104) makes a similar point about this food imagery.

Cleopatra on her barge, and few critics have questioned
his praise in these lines:[29]

> For her own person,
> It beggar'd all description: she did lie
> In her pavilion—cloth-of-gold of tissue—
> O'er-picturing that Venus where we see
> The fancy outwork nature. On each side her
> Stood pretty dimpled boys, like smiling Cupids,
> With divers-color'd fans, whose wind did seem
> To [glow] the delicate cheeks which they did cool,
> And what they undid did.   (II.ii.202-210)

Once again, as in Cleopatra's encomium of Antony,
where "t' imagine/An Antony were nature's piece 'gainst
fancy" Enobarbus presents the queen as "O'er-picturing
that Venus where we see/The fancy outwork nature."
Her presence, in short, according to Enobarbus' estimation, surpasses in its natural reality what the imagination
can conceive.[30] It is as if Enobarbus had suddenly en-
countered the essential splendor of life itself, a splendor
not any the less rich for its baroque ornamentation, its
manifold and colorful contradictions, its "various light."
As the speech continues, interrupted only by Agrippa's
appreciative exclamations, the temperature of admiration
rises to that of awe, and Cleopatra is transformed into a
sister of the gracious elements themselves:

> The city cast
> Her people out upon her; and Antony

[29] See J. Leeds Barroll, "Enobarbus' Description of Cleopatra,"
TSLL, XXXVII (1958), 61-78, for an alternative interpretation of
this speech which relates Cleopatra to the medieval *Voluptas*.

[30] Charney (*Shakespeare's Roman Plays*, p. 118) says the speech
witnesses "the triumph of art over nature." Actually Enobarbus
perhaps goes further: here "nature" becomes an artistry higher than
art.

Enthron'd i' th' market-place, did sit alone,
Whistling to th' air, which, but for vacancy,
Had gone to gaze on Cleopatra too
And made a gap in nature.   (II.ii.218-223)

In her guise as Venus, whose love is as natural as the
human body, and as capricious, Cleopatra serves as the
potent subject of Enobarbus' and our imaginations. His
language rises to capture her "natural" reality, although
he claims she "beggar'd all description." Nature and
imagination merge, and Enobarbus can accept the creature who so puzzlingly makes "defect perfection." His,
the rational man's gesture of acquiescence, is Cleopatra's
greatest praise and one of the factors which ought to
remind us that "reason" is not the uncontended standard
in *Antony and Cleopatra*. It is, after all, Enobarbus who
dies from his own sense of disloyalty after leaving Antony
in the name of reason. Moreover, it is he too who provides the most compelling description of Cleopatra's commanding power, and in doing so, reveals that he is capable of giving the devil her due:

Age cannot wither her, nor custom stale
Her infinite variety. Other women cloy
The appetites they feed, but she makes hungry
Where most she satisfies; for vilest things
Become themselves in her, that the holy priests
Bless her when she is riggish.   (II.ii.240-245)

By means of her identification with nature, with Venus
(the force of nature which creates through love) and
with the fruits of the earth (via her own and Enobarbus'
eating imagery), Cleopatra in all her diversity, her many
shapes and forms, mirrors finally the magical potency

of life itself—life, which also makes men hungry where most it satisfies.

In the realm of action, the pattern of Cleopatra's influence works in much the same manner as her speeches. Under her aegis Antony acts both passionately and foolishly; however, as Cleopatra's general he demonstrates some of his most admirable traits as well. Antony's military folly in demanding that the first battle with Caesar take place by sea (a decision Cleopatra supports him in and has probably led him in); his following Cleopatra when she deserts the battle at Actium; the ease with which he forgives her ("Fall not a tear, I say; one of them rates/All that is won and lost"); his violent rage in ordering the whipping of Caesar's messenger Thyreus: all are instances of the "diminution in our captain's brain" too well rehearsed by this time to require more than cursory mention. On the other hand, Antony's military defense of Cleopatra and his function as soldier of Egypt deliver him a striking opportunity to confront the new master of the world, and to reclaim, at least momentarily, the part of himself he thought was lost forever. As Michael Lloyd says, Cleopatra's purpose is "to dominate and control Antony; but if the method is destructive, the purpose is creative. At Actium Cleopatra destroys the Roman Antony for whom love and war (or, in his own words, business and pleasure) stood in contrast, to remake him after her own kind. In military respects Shakespeare vindicates her. When next Antony goes to war the soldier and lover are no longer separate. Cleopatra is the armourer of his heart (IV.iv.7), and he makes 'these wars for Egypt.' In them he achieves an unprecedented stature as a soldier."[31] In brief, Antony

[31] Michael Lloyd, "Cleopatra as Isis," *SS*, XII (1959), 89. During

becomes the complete image of the hero: the images of soldier and lover coalesce in his mind and our own.

The scene in Act IV during which Cleopatra literally becomes Antony's "armourer" (and there is very likely a pun on the word) is another of the instances where the queen "allows" Antony, indeed prompts him, to demonstrate his virtues, in this case a gallantry and warmth that alter the bad impression he has made upon the audience in the previous scenes. Having captured his allegiance entirely, Cleopatra now permits him the luxury of a little self-glorification, because, of course, he is now defending her and her kingdom. But the sense of Antony's old identity makes itself felt here, and out of the scene emerges the flower of a royal intimacy, the marriage of Venus and Mars, framed in humor and irony. Cleopatra is helping Antony to put on his armor. The woman who earlier spoke of how she wore his "sword Philipan" now buckles her warrior into battle dress, and she is at her most engaging as she enacts the incompetent female doing her best at a man's job. The contrast between her femininity and Antony's generous manly responses set the two off in an effective montage. Cleopatra's role of squire here might be construed as strictly emasculating, but despite the symbolical ambiguity of the action, she works so beautifully with Antony that the feeling of harmony they create together is inescapable. The sensation that at long last Antony has found his true calling is like that of a dislocated bone settling into place:

his discussion of the goddess Isis and her relationship to Cleopatra, Lloyd points out a "martial element" in Cleopatra. Noting "Bellona is the servant of Venus," Lloyd mentions how the "Roman contrast between love and war is in Cleopatra a synthesis."

Cleo. Is not this buckled well?
Ant.   Rarely, rarely:
  He that unbuckles this, till we do please
  To daff't for our repose, shall hear a storm.
  Thou fumblest, Eros, and my queen's a squire
  More tight at this than thou. Dispatch. O love,
  That thou couldst see my wars today, and knew'st
  The royal occupation! Then shouldst see
  A workman in't.   (IV.iv.11-18)

Even more persuasive in demonstrating Antony's great
spirit and manly conduct is the scene which takes place
under the walls of Alexandria after Antony has beaten
back Caesar's army. Antony returns triumphantly to
Cleopatra, carrying with him the first victory he has had
in years. Having momentarily recaptured his lost heroism,
he generously praises his soldiers for their accomplishments. We see before us a great leader who in addition
to having waged a great battle, has managed to capture
the hearts and imaginations of his men:

                  I thank you all;
  For doughty-handed are you, and have fought
  Not as you serv'd the cause, but as 't had been
  Each man's like mine; you have shown all Hectors.
  Enter the city, clip your wives, your friends,
  Tell them your feats; whilst they with joyful tears
  Wash the congealment from your wounds, and kiss
  The honour'd gashes whole.   (IV.viii.4-11)

As for himself, he has proved, at least for the moment,
that he can still be the man he once was: not merely
a competitor of the boy, Caesar, but his conqueror and
thus the foremost of men. To Cleopatra, who has just

addressed him as "lord of lords!" and "infinite virtue,"
he replies:

> My nightingale,
> We have beat them to their beds. What girl! though
> grey
> Do something mingle with our younger brown, yet
> ha' we
> A brain that nourishes our nerves, and can
> Get goal for goal of youth. . . .   (IV.viii.18-22)

The Antony displayed in these passages is surely the sympathetic one critics have affectionately praised. In the speech to his men Antony exhibits the same magnanimity which causes him to loyally return the defected Enobarbus' treasure. His language is truly bounteous, and from it we can see why Arnold Stein rates magnanimity as the chief of Antony's virtues. It is evident, too, that if this magnanimity appears a symptom of his restored self-confidence, it is neither calculated nor in any sense artificial. As Stein observes, "Looked at narrowly, the generous feelings he can express and create derive from an image he has of himself. But the effects cannot be limited to, or explained away by, any simple exposure of source. In spite of all the play unsparingly reveals, Antony is the inscrutable master of a spontaneous and generous honesty."[32]

Yet Antony's triumph is short-lived and Cleopatra's function as destroyer is restored with the desertion of her fleet at the second sea battle. The queen on the barge who made her way along the Nile into Antony's arms, turns out once again to be a sea-serpent indeed. Water has magnified as well as reflected her manifold attrac-

[32] Arnold Stein, "The Image of Antony: Lyric and Tragic Imagination," *KR*, XXI (Autumn 1959), 594.

tions, and has become an apt metaphor for her instability. Like Dame Fortune, she reverses the ascending wheel, and Antony's reclaimed heroic image dissolves with his faith in Cleopatra. He describes how his ". . . fleet hath yielded to the foe, and yonder/They cast their caps up and carouse together/Like friends long lost." To Eros, he says, likening himself to a cloud which does not hold its shape, but can appear many things:

> Here I am Antony;
> Yet cannot hold this visible shape, my knave.
> (IV.xiv.13-14)

However, Cleopatra's reality, it will be admitted, does remain somewhat ambiguous throughout this sequence. Arriving on the scene her only response to Antony's "Ah, thou spell! Avaunt!" is a rather disingenuous "Why is my lord enrag'd against his love?" Furthermore when Mardian comes to tell Antony of the queen's "death," he claims, "My mistress lov'd thee, and her fortunes mingled with thine entirely." There is at least a chance his words are literally accurate, although even as he speaks he is aiding Cleopatra in one of her typical subterfuges; for, of course, the queen is no more dead than Antony is. Yet surely the betrayal at sea must have been arranged beforehand, and Cleopatra's later conduct indicates that she has been trying to manipulate a private deal with Caesar in order to retain as much of her kingdom as possible. Shakespeare, nevertheless, in no way confirms these suspicions by either word or gesture when he has Caesar and Cleopatra meet. To the end, Cleopatra's conduct remains inscrutable, as if she had some unmentioned purpose beneath the layers of her obvious self-interest, some purpose only she, the author or the gods can divine.

For Antony, in any event, "All is lost!" The investment of his identity and reputation into Cleopatra's hands appears to have terminated with his glory "false-play'd . . ./Into an enemy's triumph." But his defeat is due not to any failure of physical prowess or his capabilities as a general. Rather, Rome and Egypt, "the world and the flesh," combines forces to destroy his treasured honor and nobility.[33] Policy and nature, it would seem, have chosen their victim, each for its own reasons. But the pattern of destruction (notably of an aging Antony) is that of life itself. If Cleopatra has come to represent through her attractions and cruelty the bewitching duplicity of the human experience—the wonder of nature and imagination which "tricks" us into dreaming—Antony in his failure to conquer life utterly may be seen as subject to the fluctuations of time and tide: he is the hero who in making his own fortune chooses the fate due him all along:

> All come to this? The hearts
> That [spaniel'd] me at heels, to whom I gave
> Their wishes, do discandy, melt their sweets
> On blossoming Caesar; and this pine is bark'd
> That overtopp'd them all. Betray'd I am.
> O this false soul of Egypt! This grave charm,—
> Whose eye beck'd forth my wars and call'd them home,
> Whose bosom was my crownet, my chief end,—
> Like a right gipsy, hath at fast and loose
> Beguil'd me to the very heart of loss.   (IV.xii.20-29)

The heart of loss proves, in fact, even more complete than Antony might have imagined. For the entire process

[33] Danby, *Poets on Fortune's Hill*, p. 150.

of emasculation is completed by a sequence of events perhaps unprecedented in the Shakespearean tragic canon. Any tragic hero certainly deserves a dignified and unmolested scene of death. Antony, to be sure, is provided with an opportunity for such a death upon receiving from Mardian the news that Cleopatra has taken her own life. Yet with the subsequent action returns the comic perspective so prevalent at the beginning of the play, a perspective which now pursues Antony relentlessly until practically his very last word has been spoken.

At first things are serious enough. "Robbed" of his sword by Cleopatra, conquered by Caesar, the two conflicting elements in his life have reduced honor and reputation to a pitiable state. Not only does his honor seem to him irretrievably lost, but there actually appears to be little left in life to sustain him but anger and the desire for retribution:

> The witch shall die.
> To the young Roman boy she hath sold me, and I fall
> Under this plot. She dies for 't. . . .   (IV.xii.47-49)

But when Mardian arrives with the announcement of Cleopatra's feigned death (Shakespeare appropriately having a eunuch deliver the news to the impotent Antony), Antony's response is a recognition of the emasculating process of life. He sees immediately what his last heroic gesture must be: "Unarm, Eros; the long day's task is done/And we must sleep." His occupation, like Othello's, is gone. "No more a soldier," he says, and his love for Cleopatra is restored with the belief that his name was the last word upon her lips. His rededication to her is apparently complete:

I will o'ertake thee, Cleopatra, and
Weep for my pardon. So it must be, for now
All length is torture; since the torch is out,
Lie down, and stray no farther. . . .

(IV.xiv.44-47)

Convinced that Cleopatra's supposed suicide indicates her lasting loyalty to him, there is only one possibility open—the honorable death of the soldier and lover who has borne all but the ultimate defeat. He must rise to the image of this last nobility in order to recoup everything in one pure and self-defining gesture:

I, that with my sword
Quarter'd the world, and o'er green Neptune's back
With ships made cities, condemn myself to lack
The courage of a woman; less noble mind
Than she which by her death our Caesar tells,
"I am conqueror of myself." (IV.xiv.57-62)

We have reached, then, once more, the crucial moment, *the* heroic moment each of our tragic heroes has faced. The last chance to become, to be, the image he has believed in all along confronts Antony. But in the background the intonations of mockery have returned, for, perversely, we recall Cleopatra's parting words to Mardian: "Say that the last I spoke was 'Antony,'/And word it, prithee, piteously. Hence, Mardian,/And bring me how he takes my death. . . ." The statement is reminiscent of another Cleopatra made when she was testing Antony's loyalty and attempting to exert her control over him:

I did not send you. If you find him sad,
Say I am dancing: if in mirth, report

That I am sudden sick. Quick and return.

(I.iii.3-5)

Her desire that Mardian "word it, prithee, piteously,"
displays the same feminine calculation and introduces its
own note of humor as well. In light of her remarks and
her evident vitality, Antony's assays at a heroic stance
begin to take on a peculiar comic resonance.[34] To begin
with, Antony, like Brutus in *Julius Caesar,* needs a friend
to help dispatch him; however, as things turn out, there
is no Strato willing to serve. Eros, whom Antony calls
upon for assistance, instead of killing him, kills himself;
and when Antony falls on his sword, ludicrously enough,
his aim is bad and he bungles the job. He calls upon
his guards, then upon Diomed, but no one will put an
end to him. Rather he is fated to encounter a less dignified departure. Having learned from Diomed that
Cleopatra still lives after all and is now locked in her
monument, he orders his guards to bear him where she
is: and at the monument occurs a remarkable scene.
The comic mockery of Acts I and II returns almost
vengefully. Instead of the sure blow that dispatches the
heroic life, Antony lingers on, forced to contend somewhat preposterously for the last remnants of his dignity.
Instead of a manly suicide and a few last poignant words,

---

[34] Brents Stirling ("Cleopatra's Scene with Seleucus," *SQ*, XV
[Spring 1964], 305) notes that "emulation is a ruling motive in the
death of Antony" (and in Cleopatra's death, too). "At the same
time he will learn that one of the deaths he tried to imitate in com-
pleting his own tragedy was the pseudo-death in a bad tragi-comedy
improvised by Cleopatra." Holloway (pp. 102-105) remarks upon
the element of "emulation" as well. However, he notices it throughout the play, explaining that the lovers increasingly find each other
"an incomparable model of nobility and spirit." It is the nobility
of Antony and Cleopatra's love Holloway wishes to emphasize,
however, not comic irony.

the hero is "heaved" up into the monument where the arms of women, not soldiers, await him, and it is in these arms he finally dies. For Cleopatra has refused to leave her refuge lest she be taken by Caesar and led through the streets of Rome. The exchange between Antony and the queen is, moreover, surely a curious one. Antony's speech is appropriately formal and vaguely operatic in tone, but whatever his speech may be, Cleopatra's response is hardly that of a great heroine who ought to be willing to risk all dangers for one last kiss. Antony is requesting Cleopatra to descend from the monument:

> *Ant.* I am dying, Egypt, dying; only
>   I here importune death a while, until
>   Of many thousand kisses the poor last
>   I lay upon thy lips.
> *Cleo.*   I dare not, dear,—
>   Dear my lord, pardon,—I dare not,
>   Lest I be taken. Not th' imperious show
>   Of the full-fortun'd Caesar ever shall
>   Be brooch'd with me; if knife, drugs, serpents, have
>   Edge, sting, or operation, I am safe.
>
>   (IV.xv.18-26)

Furthermore, as Antony is hoisted up into the monument, the queen, evidently not completely overcome by Antony's grave condition, cries, "Here's sport indeed! How heavy weighs my lord!" And the soldiers a few lines down, lament in chorus, "A heavy sight," with a rather obvious pun on "heavy."

Antony, finally in the monument after the discomfort of his arrival, now wishes to make his dying speech.

What comes out, however, is a repetition of the line "I am dying, Egypt, dying," and this repetition has a most untragic effect. It is as if Antony were trying to "cash in," rhetorically speaking, on his own sad demise. He may have failed to retain his great heroic self-image, his words seem to imply, but he knows the lines a dying hero ought to speak and is capable of acting the role out in a striking manner, a manner which can make his audience "onion-ey'd."[35] Of course, Antony is surely not quite as calculating as this description makes him; yet there is a sensation that consciously or not, Antony is "bleeding" the situation. Nevertheless, he has some information to impart as well. "Give me some wine, and let me speak a little," he adjures Cleopatra. This too seems parallel

---

[35] Scholars have found a knotty problem in this "monument scene." The repetitions in the scene have been explained in three major ways. Bernard Jenkins says in *"Antony and Cleopatra*: Some Suggestions on the Monument Scene," *RES*, XXI (January 1945), p. 14: "The reference to Caesar and Octavia in the 'I dare not' speech, seems out of place and callous. . . . Her next speech 'Heere's sport indeed!. . .' seems overdone and boisterous. Much that is said, up to this point, is too intimate to be shouted from stage to balcony; and Antony, poor man, is kept waiting below much too long before he is drawn up. . . ." Jenkins suggests that there were two versions of the beginning of the scene and that both have gotten into the first folio in a confused form (p. 2). Mary Olive Thomas notes Wilson's reaction to the problem in her "The Repetitions in Antony's Death Scene," *SQ*, IX (Spring 1958), 153-157. Dover Wilson says the disturbance is due to a "cutter's" hand. The cutter neglected a proposed cut from "Peace" to "assist good friends." Ridley suggests cutting, too, with deletions neglected. Thomas herself has the idea that interpolations were made in the scene for the purpose of increasing its manageability on the stage. However, David Galloway, in "I Am Dying, Egypt, Dying," *N&Q*, CIII (August 1958), 330-335, implies that all the scholars are working in the wrong direction. The scene indicates Cleopatra's habitual inconsistency and the habitual tenor of the lovers' relationship. Charney, finally, presents an alternative interpretation based on a demonstrated metaphor of "elevation" (*Shakespeare's Roman Plays*, p. 135).

to the earlier scene, where he wished to speak of another departure, that for Rome. But once again, Cleopatra does not want to let him speak, either to deliver his information, or to proclaim his final words of farewell. Instead, she interrupts him, giving vent to her own indignation. Furthermore, she is not at all reluctant to express her doubts about the advice Antony has for her:

> *Ant.* I am dying, Egypt, dying.
>   Give me some wine, and let me speak a little.
> *Cleo.* No, let me speak; and let me rail so high,
>   That the false housewife Fortune break her wheel,
>   Provok'd by my offence.
> *Ant.*   One word, sweet queen:
>   Of Caesar seek your honour, with your safety, O!
> *Cleo.* They do not go together.
> *Ant.*   Gentle, hear me:
>   None about Caesar trust but Proculeius.
> *Cleo.* My resolution and my hands I'll trust,
>   None about Caesar.   (IV.xv.41-50)

Later we come to surmise that Antony's advice is suspicious enough; for Proculeius visits Cleopatra in Caesar's name, and his mission is to convince Cleopatra that Caesar will not lead her captive through Rome. But a "Roman triumph" is exactly what Caesar has in mind.[36]

---

[36] Connected with the problem in the monument scene is the difficulty concerning the advice Antony gives to Cleopatra before he expires (IV.xv.46-48). David S. Berkeley ("On Oversimplifying Antony," *CE*, XVII [November 1955], 96-99) observes on Antony's part a possible double-dealing, for Antony knows that the one thing Cleopatra fears is to be led by Caesar through the streets of Rome. Surely Antony has no reason to trust Caesar, so why should he give Cleopatra the advice he does? Moreover, Proculeius, it turns out, is the person who, on Caesar's orders, attempts to make Cleopatra

Nevertheless, it is only after Cleopatra has clearly stated her position in regard to Antony's statements that she allows him to speak uninterrupted, to make his final speech. His words, we find, are about as conventional a speech of this kind as we could have anticipated. Lacking the full-bodied resonance of Othello's or the anguished madness of Lear's, they sum up the whole tragic predicament the typical Shakespearean hero suffers in one long platitude:[37]

---

believe she will not be led through Rome in triumph. Is Antony seeking revenge on Cleopatra? Or is his advice merely a sign of misjudgment of character, certainly one of his more prevalent traits? Berkeley feels that the former view is the more possible one. Cynthia Grill ("Antony, Cleopatra, and Proculeius," *N&Q*, New Series, VII [January 1960], 191) notices Berkeley's discussion and rejects the possibility that Antony is willfully trying to trick Cleopatra. To do so, according to Miss Grill, would be for Antony to act entirely out of character. She sees more potentiality in Berkeley's second suggestion—that Antony is "ignorant of the extent of Proculeius' personal commitment." To Miss Grill, Antony's advice appears another manifestation of how all his deeds and decisions have failed since his separation from Rome, since the moment he allowed his will to take over his reason.

[37] The basis of the speech is Plutarch, who writes: "And as for him selfe, that she should not lament nor sorrowe for the miserable chaunge of his fortune at the end of his dayes; but rather that she should thinke him the more fortunate, for the former triumphes and honors he had received, considering that while he lived he was the noblest and greatest prince of the world, and that now he was overcome, not cowardly, but valiantly, a Romane by another Romane." As can be seen, Shakespeare's redaction is little more than a versified form of Plutarch's statement. Nevertheless, it seems to me Shakespeare may very well have noticed an unconscious irony in the statement, considering the advice Antony has just given Cleopatra (derived from Plutarch, too) and the whole tenor of his life. The possibility is that Shakespeare did not point up the speech poetically for exactly this reason. On the other hand, he might have simply been following his source. In any event, the speech's "flatness" sets up the magnificent statement by Cleopatra which follows. Her speech does not appear in Plutarch, and clearly it outshines Antony's. Holloway, however, to refer to another opinion, presents Antony's speech as "simple and sincere" (p. 116).

> The miserable change now at my end
> Lament nor sorrow at; but please your thoughts
> In feeding them with those my former fortunes
> Wherein I liv'd, the greatest prince o' th' world,
> The noblest; and do now not basely die,
> Nor cowardly put off my helmet to
> My countryman,—a Roman by a Roman
> Valiantly vanquish'd. Now my spirit is going;
> I can no more.   (IV.xv.51-59)

Yet even at this crucial moment Cleopatra is not satisfied to leave Antony the last eloquent word. Her language rises, overtopping his, and oddly, we see again that the self he has attempted to project in his speech attains its fullest reality through *her* imagination. We can even forgive her for fainting ("Cut my lace Charmian, come!") immediately afterward:

> The crown o' th' earth doth melt. My lord!
> O, wither'd is the garland of the war,
> The soldier's pole is fall'n! Young boys and girls
> Are level now with men; the odds is gone,
> And there is nothing left remarkable
> Beneath the visiting moon.   [Faints.]
>
> (IV.xv.63-68)

Thus even Antony's great tragic exit is controlled by Cleopatra, whom Antony, ironically, himself chose as the ruling force in his life. Her language here ennobles him; but it also commands our attention away from Antony toward her. Her language "upstages" him, even as it delineates the immense and moving effect his death has apparently had upon her. The sequence of images she delivers are emblems for his stature (curiously mixed with the sexual innuendo in a phrase like "The soldier's pole is fall'n"); but this stature we must reluctantly admit is perhaps more complete in Cleopatra's projection of it than it was in the flesh. Still, Cleopatra is not averse to perfecting defect in more than language. If Antony has failed to achieve full nobility in his manner of dying; if this Roman general's death has lacked the purity of Brutus', Cleopatra can make that death for him,[38] or at least she can try:

> We'll bury him; and then, what's brave, what's noble,
> Let's do it after the high Roman fashion,
> And make Death proud to take us.   (IV.xv.86-88)

As Brents Stirling tells us, now follows "a galaxy of stock comment" upon tragic stature in reference to Antony. The comments are made by Octavius, Agrippa, and Maecenas in the first scene of Act V. Octavius, for instance, speaks on the "world-wide convulsion" theme:

> *Caes.* The breaking of so great a thing should make
> A greater crack. The round world
> Should have shook lions into civil streets,
> And citizens to their dens. The name of Antony
> Is not a single doom; in the name lay
> A moiety of the world.   (V.i.14-19)

Notably the sort of supernatural quaking which anticipates Julius Caesar's death is lacking in Antony's, although we may recall that before the last battle, Antony's god Hercules makes a musical departure. Maecenas, at any rate, goes on to speak of "taints and honors," that "wag'd equal" in Antony (V.i.30). Agrippa supplies the tragic flaw theory:

[38] See Stirling, *Unity in Shakespearean Tragedy*, p. 176 and "Cleopatra's Scene with Seleucus," p. 305.

> A rarer spirit never
> Did steer humanity; but you gods will give us
> Some faults to make us men. Caesar is touch'd.
>
> (V.i.31-33)

Maecenas returns with the "Mirror for Magistrates" explanation:

> When such a spacious mirror's set before him [Caesar]
> He needs must see himself.   (V.i.34-35)

All this is capped by a traditional choric speech by Caesar, complete with apostrophe, tears, reference to the stars, and a final statement to the effect that Caesar will tell the tale of his association with Antony "at some meeter season"   (V.i.35-49).[39]

It is possible, to be sure, that the use of these speeches is utterly straightforward, or that the speeches themselves are merely the conventional laudatory remarks which customarily follow a tragic hero's death. In either case, the words of Caesar, Agrippa, and Maecenas should be accepted, one supposes, with due seriousness. On the other hand, the abundance of these remarks in one place may indicate the extent to which *Antony and Cleopatra* is an exploration and gentle mockery of the idea and techniques of tragedy themselves. Possibly, as John Danby says, it is this "grappling with technique" that makes for the impression the play is "a *tour de force* which Shakespeare employed for its own sake."[40]

Still, if *Antony and Cleopatra* is such a *tour de force*, a testing of tragic plot, character, and language, to see

---

[39] Stirling, *Unity in Shakespearean Tragedy*, p. 177. The basis of the speech is Plutarch. But Shakespeare pushes the rhetorical effect much further.

[40] Danby, *Poets on Fortune's Hill*, p. 150.

just how much pressure they can bear,[41] this is not to say that whatever distance is created by the various techniques employed isolates us from the characters or prevents us from sympathizing with them and their tragedy. The technique of perspectives utilized by *Antony and Cleopatra* is different by virtue of its humor from that utilized by *Coriolanus* (a play in which it is difficult to "feel" for the major character). In *Antony and Cleopatra*, satire, if it can be called such, is modified by a wonderful affection for the hero and heroine, a sense of warm absurdity that precludes utter condemnation of them. By means of such affectionate mockery Shakespeare manages to brilliantly sustain a hero whose sufferings, after all, can be felt, even as his character is held up to comic scrutiny.

But comedy, like "policy" is not subsumed into the transcendent vision Cleopatra projects of herself at the end of the play. Rather, as we shall see, it keeps itself in view with a gentle assertiveness, an additional factor which helps to keep our vision as wide and comprehending as possible. Equally, the political realism of Caesar, itself examined by comedy (witness the scene on Pompey's galley), "wins," as Burckhardt has suggested, nothing more than the territory it set out to conquer: Egypt. Though we can credit Caesar with literally having the last word, it is Cleopatra's last words we remember. Antony's death and the subsequent failure of Cleopatra's attempts to make a satisfactory arrangement with Caesar release the queen from the bonds of the flesh and allow her to "translate" nature's empire into the empire of the

[41] See A. P. Rossiter, *Angel With Horns and Other Shakespeare Lectures*, p. 272. Stirling ("Cleopatra's Scene with Seleucus," p. 305), says: "In *Antony and Cleopatra* Shakespeare deliberately tests the tragic mode."

heart and mind. And if we are translated too, this is
not necessarily because we have surrendered witlessly
to her fine poetry. Instead, it may be that we have come,
through our intimacy with Cleopatra, and Antony as
well, to recognize the claims of their final empire. With
its play-acting, its fervor for poses and stances, its compulsion to present pictures of nobility, to savor them
on the tongue, and to rehearse them in action, we may be
reminded that this is the essential empire of the metaphorical and symbolistic human mind—the empire of
aspiration, of imagination, of poetry and dreams:

> *Cleo.* I dream'd there was an Emperor Antony.
>   O, such another sleep, that I might see
>   But such another man? (V.ii.76-78)

In the last act, then, Cleopatra's "dream" of Antony
(and herself) is pitted against those realistic and comic
actions which develop beside it, and against the rational
attitudes of such characters as Dolabella as well. However, in addition to the great speeches on Antony and
those terminal ones upon herself, we are treated to
a queen who is also trying to wrest what she can from
the debris of loss. Act V, scene ii commences, for instance,
with a Cleopatra who dismisses the value of Caesar's
conquests while applauding the suicide she had determined to make at the end of Act IV:

> *Cleo.* My desolation does begin to make
>   A better life. 'Tis paltry to be Caesar;
>   Not being Fortune, he's but Fortune's knave,
>   A minister of her will: and it is great
>   To do that thing that ends all other deeds;
>   Which shackles accidents and bolts up change;

Which sleeps, and never palates more the dung,
The beggar's nurse and Caesar's.   (V.ii.1-8)

Here is the noble Cleopatra who pictures herself as
unbound by fortune, the total mistress of her end. Her
resolution upon death has freed her from Caesar's petty
world. No sooner has she finished speaking, however,
than Proculeius enters, and Cleopatra, wary and practical, is probing to see what she can salvage from Caesar.
To Proculeius she says:

> Antony
> Did tell me of you, bade me trust you; but
> I do not greatly care to be deceiv'd,
> That have no use for trusting. If your master
> Would have a queen his beggar, you must tell him
> That majesty, to keep decorum, must
> No less beg than a kingdom. If he please
> To give me conquer'd Egypt for my son,
> He gives me so much of mine own as I
> Will kneel to him with thanks.   (V.ii.12-21)

Having, it would appear, determined upon death for
herself, the queen seeks to preserve what she can of her
lost kingdom for her heirs. Yet when Caesar arrives, just
after Dolabella has informed her that his master surely
will return with her to Rome, Cleopatra takes a great
deal of care to give the "sole sir o' th' world," a list of
all her "money, plate, and jewels," in short, the treasure
he has captured in conquering Egypt. The famous
"Seleucus incident" occurs at this point. Called upon
to substantiate the fact that Cleopatra has reserved nothing for herself, Seleucus instead announces the queen
has kept back "enough to purchase" what she has "made

known." Cleopatra, furious, all but attacks Seleucus physically, castigates him for breaking faith, and admits she has retained "some lady trifles," with which to induce the "mediation" of Livia and Octavia. Whatever Cleopatra's purpose for retaining the treasure, and there are several possibilities; whatever Seleucus' reasons for revealing Cleopatra's secret, one thing is clear: although the incident in itself is a puzzle, surely we can agree that Cleopatra has been attempting to trick Caesar in *some* way, and thus is still very much in and of this world. Whether she has reserved the treasure because she is planning to flee if she is able, or because she will need it if she manages to keep her kingdom; even if the incident, as some critics have suggested, is prearranged by Cleopatra and Seleucus in order to make Caesar believe she will not take her life (on the logic that dead queens have no need of treasure), the effect is to complicate our judgment of Cleopatra's conduct and to reveal her as calculating subterfuges until the very end.[42] The incident, both Cleopatra's hiding the truth and

[42] Stirling ("Cleopatra's Scene With Seleucus," pp. 299-311) presents a discussion of the Seleucus incident as it appears in Plutarch and in Daniel's *Cleopatra* as well as an interpretation of the scene in Shakespeare. Stirling feels the scene is prepared for by several parallel scenes (IV.xiv, IV.xv and V.ii) in which "Cleopatra has come through uncertainty, equivocation or relapse, to a resolving climax" (pp. 306-311). In the Seleucus incident Stirling finds Cleopatra's "ambiguity" complete. If she is playing a part, the part, like any part for Cleopatra, becomes the queen herself because we have learned to accept her protean ambivalence (p. 310). In an earlier article on the double exposition of Portia's death ("*Julius Caesar* in Revision," *SQ*, XIII [Spring 1962], 187-205) Stirling refers to Shakespeare's use of "lively irony" and "significant anomaly" at the expense of "logic" of motivation. It appears to me he would attribute similar techniques to the Seleucus incident, and it is precisely to the use of such techniques that I refer in my own way with my interpretation of *Antony and Cleopatra*'s final acts.

Seleucus' unfaithful revealing of it, appears to be part and parcel of a whole pattern of such tricks and betrayals which find their way into the last acts. Some of these are, once again, cruxes: the Seleucus incident, as has been noted, and Antony's advice to Cleopatra concerning Proculeius. But Caesar's use of Proculeius to mislead the queen into believing he will not take her to Rome is not a crux and we have no difficulty accepting such a politic Caesar because in the first scene of Act V, we hear him tell Proculeius his plans:

> Come hither, Proculeius. Go and say
> We purpose her no shame. Give her what comforts
> The quality of her passion shall require,
> Lest, in her greatness, by some mortal stroke
> She do defeat us; for her life in Rome
> Would be eternal in our triumph. . . .

> (V.i.61-66)

Curiously too, we must admit that Dolabella, who tells the truth concerning his master's intentions toward Cleopatra is, although we may view the act sympathetically, betraying Caesar's confidence in him. It can be seen, therefore, that in the last two acts of the play, there is a cross-hatching of subterfuge and deception complicating the action. According to this interpretation—given that we can draw no definite conclusions where the action remains ambiguous—Antony's advice to Cleopatra regarding Proculeius and Cleopatra's subterfuge regarding her treasure are parallels to Caesar's attempt to trick Cleopatra, Seleucus' apparent failure to keep faith with his mistress, and Dolabella's betrayal of Caesar's confidence. What we may have, finally, is a mounting exposure of the ways of the world which forms a dynamic contrast to the visionary empire Cleopatra projects in her descriptions of Antony and herself in the terminal speeches. The information received from Dolabella—that is, the truth that Caesar is about to take the queen to Rome, effects an emotional release on the part of Cleopatra. Backed against the wall, she liberates herself from the entanglements of policy and life—and this liberation allows her a self-delivery into an imagined world, and allows us to accept this world with a feeling of relief.

To further substantiate this interpretation, it might be remembered that deceptions and breaches of faith play a significant part in the lives of all the major characters during the earlier portion of the play. Caesar, for example, betrays Antony, Lepidus, and Pompey when he breaks the pact established before the party on Pompey's galley. However, before this, Antony breaks faith with Caesar by determining to leave Rome and desert Octavia before Caesar has given him tangible reason for doing so. The fact of the matter is that Antony's long presence in Egypt prior to his return to Rome is a breach of faith with Caesar and Fulvia. Of Cleopatra's betrayals, those at Actium and Alexandria are the most striking, but her conduct continually suggests that she has purposes quite unrecognized by Antony or anyone else. To note this pattern of deception and betrayal is to do nothing more than support an interpretation that sees the conflict between policy and poetic grandeur as essential thematic material in the play. We can go on to add that the last acts of *Antony and Cleopatra* look like a coda which intensifies and sets into even more vivid contrast a thematic scheme which has been implied throughout.

Yet the last acts do more than simply intensify the play's principal conflict. They reveal significant truths about human action as well. The subterfuges of Cleopatra, Caesar, and Proculeius are actions, but these actions are conceived and implemented by the use of language: the characters lie in order to gain their ends. These lies, moreover, force their tellers to assume certain roles: Cleopatra must enact the great queen humbled, although she has no intention of submitting to the humiliation Caesar plans for her. Caesar, on his part, must play the part of the benevolent victor, although he has no intention of treating the queen in the manner she wishes. Proculeius' role derives from the instructions he receives from Caesar. He is to play the earnest servant of a victorious but kindly master. The "betrayals" of Seleucus and Dolabella, conversely, are the result of their refusing to play the parts given to them, each for his own reasons. Interestingly, Cleopatra's dream of Antony, whose "voice was propertied as all the tuned spheres" is also a kind of a lie which involves her in a certain role: it is a manifest inflation of the truth in view of the facts. Hence the speech Cleopatra makes after Caesar leaves her in the monument, the very Caesar she has just acknowledged as "My master, and my lord!" becomes extremely suggestive. She says to her women:

He words me, girls, he words me, that I should not
Be noble to myself. . . .   (V.ii.191-192)

Caesar's political machinations and Cleopatra's imaginative dreams are connected by the use of words, words which in each case, "trick" in their own way. The difference between Caesar's "political" use of language and Cleopatra's imaginative use is that Caesar's words aim at practical ends, while Cleopatra's dream establishes its own atmosphere, one perhaps based on self-esteem, but alive in ideality as well. Such words as hers begin and end in the self that creates them, in the self which hears them and recreates them. Their effect may be to move the human heart, but they do not change the physical condition of things. They cannot give Cleopatra back her lost Egypt, although they can reclaim the heroic image of Antony, create the "divine" image of Cleopatra, and build an empire which transcends physical boundaries. Cleopatra's last great act, therefore, is more than the action which takes her life: it concerns the magnificent theatrics which raise an easy death (for "she hath pursu'd conclusions infinite/Of easy ways to die") to what has been taken for an immolation scene.

Hence we might surmise that not only is the poetic reality of Antony and Cleopatra's highest language under examination in their play, and not only the idea and techniques of tragedy, but the whole complex we call drama itself; and by extension the drama in action, action which makes for life. Cleopatra's description of her fate in Rome—to be "shown" to ". . . mechanic slaves/With greasy aprons, rules, and hammers . . . in their thick breaths/Rank of gross diet" is actually fulfilled by the "showing" of her play on stage in Jacobean England. As Rosen indicates,[43] the words with which Cleopatra continues her description from one perspective fairly well characterize what has been taking place on stage during the course of the play:

> The quick comedians
> Extemporally will stage us, and present
> Our Alexandrian revels; Antony

43 Rosen, p. 157.

> Shall be brought drunken forth, and I shall see
> Some squeaking Cleopatra boy my greatness
> I' th' posture of a whore.   (V.ii.216-221)

Cleopatra's language momentarily shatters the illusion the audience has helped create with its own imaginative powers. For at heart any audience knows that what has been taking place on the stage is not real in the conventional sense, that it is, when reduced to its literal plane, nothing more than a series of "posturings" meant to "imitate" life. Yet the statement implies something about the relationship between this kind of posturing and that which makes for life, civilized life at least. Human action, stimulated as it is by ideals, aspirations— by what men think they can be, or ought to be, would like to be, or were—may be understood as "theatrical" in its own right.[44] For men, when not acting instinctively, attempt to fulfill their self-conceptions after trying their "roles" in the theater of their minds. And this rehearsal leads to the performance itself, performance in both senses of the word. If this is true, where human action is concerned, reality is whatever can be conceived and "imitated," whether this imitation be in action pure and simple, or in art, drama, or poetry. Such conceptions to be "imitated" are, philosophically speaking, the measure of our own belief. If we believe nothing is real, then to the mind thinking in this vein, nothing is real and no human act is meaningful, except perhaps as a fulfillment of instinct. But if we can conceive of everything as real, we are free to accept our own "infinite variety," and Cleopatra's and to live in a world of ap-

---

[44] See Anne Righter, *Shakespeare and the Idea of the Play* (London, 1962), pp. 75-79, on the Elizabethan view of "the play-like nature of human life" and life's ability to "imitate the drama."

parent contradictions, all of which reflect aspects of the truth.

The final position Shakespeare seems to attain in *Antony and Cleopatra* is that of accepting all of life with its insoluble contradictions and complexities. Each major perspective in the play bids for its own reality. This is as true for Caesar's system of "policy," which does, after all, achieve its primary end, as it is for Cleopatra's "poetic" imagination, which surmounts the limitations of her own character; and it is true for the comic perspective as well. Indeed, comedy again asserts itself with almost farcical intensity at the crucial moment Cleopatra is about to pass through her "transformation." The queen, whose "briefest end" has taken a whole act to accomplish, calls at last for her "crown and all." She is ready to put on her ceremonial vestments, robes which are related to those she wore at Cydnus and in the public square when she dressed as Isis, goddess of earth and fertility. In these garments she translates herself into a kind of Isis, a role which Michael Lloyd feels Shakespeare may have consciously adapted for Cleopatra.[45] However, the announcement of her scene of apotheosis is followed by the entrance of a rural fellow carrying the death-bearing asps in a basket of figs. Here we see Shakespeare's virtuosity at its highest; for Cleopatra, about to "play" her finest role, a role which really is a kind of revelation, must first have her interview with the clown, whose every

[45] Lloyd (p. 94) concludes, after investigating parallels between Cleopatra and Isis that "Shakespeare was acquainted with the cult of Isis from Plutarch's essay, and from Apuleius. They are echoed in his portrait of Cleopatra and her values, but denied to Antony." Lloyd points out an impressive number of parallels, verbal and otherwise, between Cleopatra and the traditional Isis, especially in "the divine humanity which is common to Isis and Cleopatra," their roles as "'true wife, the tender mother, the beneficent queen of nature.'"

comic word seems an unconscious *double entendre* commenting on the "strumpet" Cleopatra we have known.

Indeed, the clown, with his basket of figs and asps, brings into view the sexual implications of Cleopatra's death act and translates them into the traditional symbols of snakes and fruits, but in their comic proportions.[46] His language and the queen's are full of puns that should undercut Cleopatra's striking pose—that pose being an etherealized version of Venus and the forces of propagation:[47] for now she is "marble-constant" and the "fleeting moon" with all its changes is no longer any "planet" of hers.[48] Yet, as Donald C. Baker says, the clown's speeches actually ". . . serve a transitional purpose not only for the action which follows but for the tone of the language itself. . . . As is so often the case, Shakespeare anticipates and turns to his own use the ironic and humorous implications of a scene which otherwise might thwart his purpose. . . ."[49] The exchange between clown and queen is like a short satyr play in-

[46] *Ibid.*, p. 91. Lloyd refers to Holland's *Moralia* on the fig leaf. The fig leaf there suggests "the member of generation." Lloyd adds that undoubtedly Charmian is playing with this idea when she says, "O excellent! I love long life better than figs" (I.ii.31). In connection with this idea, Isis, according to Lloyd, is the goddess of "intelligence and motion together." Her name means " 'motion animate and wise.' " It seems obvious that motion suggests sexual "motion" as well as other kinds of creative motion. I might add, referring to Cleopatra's encomium of Antony, that those "dolphin like" delights of his, which show "his back above/ The element they liv'd in" suggest precisely this sexual motion. Thus within Cleopatra's hyperbole lives a sexual innuendo one can be sure is meant to amuse and delight us.

[47] Donald C. Baker gives a related, if slightly different account in "The Purging of Cleopatra," *SNL*, X (February 1960), 9.

[48] Lloyd, p. 92, discusses the relation of the moon imagery to the imagery of sexuality, the Isis image, and the elements of femininity and masculinity in Cleopatra.

[49] Baker, p. 9.

cluded in the ritual of transmogrification. The clown's words make their comic claims, claims we are ready enough to acknowledge, while functionally they "purge" (Baker's word) our laughter so it will not interfere with the ritual to follow. They break the tension and achieve a comic plateau from which Cleopatra can leap to new heights. The clown discusses the "pretty worm of Nilus":

> *Cleo.* Remember'st thou any that have died on 't?
> *Clown.* Very many, men and women too. I heard of
> one of them no longer than yesterday; a very honest
> woman, but something given to lie, as a woman
> should not do but in the way of honesty; how she
> died of the biting of it, what pain she felt; truly,
> she makes a very good report o' th' worm. But he
> that will believe all that they say, shall never be
> saved by half what they do. But this is most falliable,
> the worm's an odd worm.   (V.ii.249-259)

Here Cleopatra's word "died" signals the sexual implications of what is to follow, and the clown's speech humorously expands upon the idea. The picture of the woman to whom he recently gave the worm, "a very honest woman, but something given to lie" is easily referable to Cleopatra herself. "Honesty," of course, has its own sexual suggestiveness, and the pain the worm gives the remarkable dead lady (and what is Cleopatra now, at least in one sense, but such a lady?) ties the experience of death and the sex act together through the pun on "dying."[50] This play on words suggests thematic material to be developed some lines later when Cleopatra observes Iras dying: "If thou and nature can so gently part,/The stroke of death is as a lover's pinch,/Which

[50] *Ibid.*

hurts, and is desired." There death becomes in its sharp ease a kind of sexual act, the grave's worm and the worm as phallus fusing symbolically. Thus the clown's parting words, "I wish you joy o' th' worm" are especially pertinent and comic. But the clown, like many of Shakespeare's fools, is no mere fool. He sees that at least half the time the "joy o' th' worm" is nothing more than illusion: "I know," says the clown, "that a woman is a dish for the gods, if the devil dress her not. But, truly, these same whoreson devils do the gods great harm in their women; for in every ten they make, the devils mar five."

It is immediately after these last remarks that Cleopatra divests herself of *her* devil's "dressings" and presents her person as a "dish for the gods":

> Give me my robe, put on my crown; I have
> Immortal longings in me. . . .   (V.ii.283-284)

It is notable, however, that even at her most sublime Cleopatra does not escape her sensual nature, but rather uses it to intensify the experience she projects before us. To Charney, "she is always both 'queen' (female monarch) and 'quean' (wench, whore), and in this covert pun lies the secret of her attraction."[51] Furthermore, Kirschbaum in his discussion of Cleopatra's sensual imagery shows that "the obvious harlot and queenly lover both draw their metaphors from the same storehouse—or bagnio."[52] Of examples there are sufficient illustration: "Now no more/The juice of Egypt's grape shall moist this lip," reevokes the imagery of eating (and

---

[51] Charney, "Shakespeare's Style," p. 366. Thus Charney claims, "Cleopatra is heightened, but not transcendentalized by her death, and her character and motives remain in a certain ambiguity even at the end."

[52] Kirschbaum, "Shakespeare's Cleopatra," p. 163.

sensuality) which penetrates Cleopatra's language. The lines addressed to Iras as she finishes clothing the queen are drenched in warm sensuality: "Come then, and take the last warmth of my lips." Her fear that Iras, who dies first, will receive Antony's kiss before her is another instance of the fleshly intonation which informs these last great speeches. And finally, Cleopatra's description of the poison filling her veins, putting her into the last sleep of dreams, is the epitome of painless death realized in the language of sensual pleasure: "As sweet as balm, as soft as air, as gentle—/O Antony!" We can almost sense Cleopatra physically dissolving. Her easy death proves to be little less than a lover's ecstasy.[53]

Thus Cleopatra is fully herself in the great transformation scene, and it is difficult to agree with Schucking that the Cleopatra in the last two acts, "inwardly and outwardly a queen, has but little in common with the harlot of the first part."[54] For the truth is that the sensuality in the "strumpet" Cleopatra is the same sensuality we observe now in the queen's final loyalty to Antony, but seen, let us say, in the light of eternity. Despite Cleopatra's statements to the contrary, her sensual bondage is not broken until practically her last word is spoken. At this point, however, such bondage looks like freedom: the revelation is that for her it has always been freedom. The sensual is and has been the root of her nature, the informant of her mind and the essence of her life. Even her ideality is permeated with it. When she claims to be "fire and air," giving her "other elements . . . to baser life," her words are like a publication of identity which glorifies her through an appeal to the senses and through

[53] *Ibid.*, p. 168.

[54] Levin L. Schucking, *Character Problems in Shakespeare's Plays* (New York, 1922), p. 132.

the senses to the amazed mind. We recognize that free she is and free she has been all along, her force having always been in fact an amoral one. In actuality her histrionic gestures and her vacillations have been unqualified by any true sense of guilt or remorse. Indeed, if her diviner elements *are* fire and air, her return is to the realm of nature in a literal as well as a metaphorical sense, but certainly not to the traditional Christian heaven.[55] Like Venus, she is (or so she presents herself) the sea's daughter; thus she speaks to her servant in seaman's language, "Yare, yare, good Iras, quick"; and with her barge and her sea battles it is appropriate that she do so. But like Isis she is a personification of the ripe earth itself, the worm of death her lover and child:

> Peace, peace!
> Dost thou not see my baby at my breast,
> That sucks the nurse asleep.   (V.ii.311-313)

So strong is the illusion that Cleopatra creates, with her regalia, her ministering servants, her ritualizing, and above all, her impressive language, that it comes with a shock to remember she is a human being who can die, who is dying; that the asp is not a suckling babe, but a venomous snake, that her crown, when she finally dies, is awry and needs "mending." Yet poetry here seems to supersede all considerations. Her theatrics attain a reality as fascinating, as compelling, as complete as the drama we have seen enacted on the stage before us. Our

---

[55] Dolora G. Cunningham ("The Characterization of Shakespeare's Cleopatra," *SQ*, VI [Winter 1955], 9-17) reads the play in terms of Christian morality. She attempts to refute Schucking's charge of inconsistency of characterization by showing Cleopatra's last scene is one of repentance. However, there seems no real evidence of repentance in Cleopatra. See Mills, pp. 161-162.

minds may acknowledge her human frailty, but our imaginations, broadened by the play itself, accept the illusion of her greatness. We lean against the boundaries of possibility and imagine her divine. For the sake of her language and her superb gestures, we confer godhead, even while knowing that doom is in her flesh.

This illusion is so effectively produced that in the midst of one of Cleopatra's greatest speeches, Shakespeare can afford to have the queen vent the delight of her triumph upon the absent Caesar:

> [*To an asp, which she applies to her breast*]
> With thy sharp teeth this knot intrinsicate
> Of life at once untie. Poor venomous fool,
> Be angry, and dispatch. O, couldst thou speak,
> That I might hear thee call great Caesar ass
> Unpolicied!   (V.ii.307-311)

The last portion of this speech, in addition to threatening the tone of the ritual, reminds us that even the marvelous display we have been watching, *could*, after all, be construed as a form of policy. For Cleopatra has outsmarted Caesar in her dying: there will be no triumphal march in Rome with Cleopatra as captive. Nevertheless, the sudden shift of perspective, the breaking of tension with its comic overtones, once again serves only to accentuate the brilliant death scene; while we notice that Cleopatra is still the same Cleopatra we have always known—egotistical, perverse, and even trivial.[56] Yet so

[56] See Benjamin Spencer, p. 377; Kirschbaum, "Shakespeare's Cleopatra," p. 166; and Arthur M. Z. Norman, "Daniel's *The Tragedie of Cleopatra* and *Antony and Cleopatra*," *SQ*, IX (Winter 1958), 18. All note the ambiguity in Cleopatra's language in the last scene, an ambiguity which makes her a "goddess" and a very human female at the same time.

secure is Shakespeare's control that he can restore the scene's vibrant tone with Charmian's three simple words, "O eastern star!" and Cleopatra can die, serenely ecstatic, into the arms of her lover, death, who is Antony, her symbol of eternal life.

After this triumphant demonstration, though Caesar gain the world and become in the years to follow a "god" in his own right, how can his conventional words at the play's conclusion hope to capture the queen and her man of men? Her complexity, vitality, and control are beyond the powers of choric commentary. If mind and imagination do grow out of "nature," the physical world which creates and sustains them, Cleopatra has returned to her own world: that of the inconstant earth and its reflecting waters—the earth, the model of her character, with its seasonal fluctuations, its humors, its endless cycles of destruction and regeneration: the earth, which must destroy in order to create. "The asp, wriggling its way from the basket to her breast, carries more than its mortal sting; it bears the salt and savour of all that natural life whose passionate child Cleopatra had been. The asp is very much more than a theatrical convenience: it is a symbol of nature reclaiming one part of its own."[57] Moreover, it is this same "nature," which through the human imagination (itself dependent upon natural existence) can create an Antony and give him imaginative life forever:

> *Cleo.*   Husband, I come!
> Now to that name my courage prove my title!
>   (V.ii.290-291)

[57] Speaight, p. 139, quoted in Mills, p. 159.

In death, Antony is raised above Cleopatra, a god in his own right. Finally she is true, and he is true to her—perhaps because all other choices were "impossible"—yet art "mends" nature and makes the final impossibility possible. Charmian proves the point when she adds the finishing touch to the image Cleopatra has meant to deliver: "Your crown's [awry];/I'll mend it, and then play."

And, we might add, in the words of another Shakespearean character who is describing another sort of art:

> This is an art
> Which does mend Nature, change it rather, but
> The art itself is Nature.
>
> (*The Winter's Tale*, IV.iv.95-97)

In these lines Polixenes, King of Bohemia, is describing the "art" of grafting flowers to Perdita. Art here "mends" nature "or changes it rather," much as Charmian's adjustment of the queen's crown "mends" Cleopatra's image in death and fixes it. Charmian, in fact, "perfects" our final image of Cleopatra just as Cleopatra's final descriptions of Antony perfected our image of him. Cleopatra illuminated the "excellence" in Antony's "excellent falsehoods" and "excellent dissembling." The Herculean quality Antony "mended" even "in the carriage of his chafe" was mended by Cleopatra. In her great death scene Cleopatra mends her own image. Death and Charmian's hand add the crowning perfection:

> . . . she looks like sleep,
> As she would catch another Antony
> In her strong toil of grace.   (V.ii.384-351)

Nor should we be surprised at such astonishing feats, for as Sir Philip Sidney—that most noble and magnanimous of Renaissance gentlemen—tells us: "Only the poet, disdaining to be tied to any . . . subjection, lifted up with the vigor of his own invention, doth grow in effect another nature, in making things either better than nature bringeth forth, or, quite anew, forms such as never were in nature" (*An Apology for Poetry*). In the Renaissance, if art imitated nature, it perfected it, too.

It might be said, then, that the transformation of Cleopatra is a direct appeal to the imaginative sensibilities in spite of, indeed, because of, what we realistically know of both the queen and her lover. It is a question of art's perfecting nature before our eyes. Or to put the matter another way, it is a question of our "realizing" Antony's and Cleopatra's failings in a new light, a light which reveals in Cleopatra's endless subterfuges and betrayals the transcendent variety and contradiction of nature herself, and in Antony's self-deluded loyalty to her, that impassioned devotion to life in its mystery which can make a man a hero. The final "order" in *Antony and Cleopatra* is not political; neither is it "spiritual" in the conventional sense. It is "natural" to the extent that politics and self-interest are embraced by dependable cycles of time and change; it is "aesthetic" to the degree that art is capable of embracing nature, of redefining it, and giving it transcendence.

Cleopatra's art, like Shakespeare's, *is* drama, *is* poetry, and *is* "nature," too. Caesar may win Egypt; comedy may criticize her. But as it turns out, Cleopatra's "artistry" makes her queen of policy and queen of comedy as well. Everything is in her. Just as she has always been capable of fabricating, whether for deceitful reasons or otherwise, we see that in the monument she is only being true to herself in the highest terms she can muster.[58] "Lies," stories, dreams, histrionics—her *milieu* is the enacted word.[59] Her aspiring dream of Antony and herself is displayed to us in the "posture" she assumes even in the act of death. Her life is a play within a play, whose theatricality probes the essential "theatricality" of all human action. The actor who "boys" her "greatness" may "ballad" her "out o' tune," but he sings, it would appear, the truth.

[58] Burckhardt, "The King's Language," pp. 386-387. Burckhardt's idea, from which my own derives, is put in slightly different terms. He does not understand Cleopatra's poetry as rooted in nature, although he does see it as having a truth of its own. For Burckhardt, poetry's "law" is its own law. I am, I think, merely extending his conception, or broadening it. Poetry's law is its own law, but it is "natural" to the degree that it is the product of a nature creature: man. Thus to my eyes, Shakespeare sees (as was traditional in the Renaissance) nature as an artist, one of whose creatures, man, imitates nature in order to perfect her. Thus art perfects nature by virtue of the very nature which is the root of art's existence. Art, therefore, is natural. It "obeys" nature's laws in obeying art's laws, although the two laws are different. Ultimately, then, Cleopatra is the queen of nature as well as the queen of artists, and vice versa.

[59] In her excellent discussion of the aesthetic relevance of the theatrical metaphor in Shakespearean and pre-Shakespearean theater, Miss Righter accentuates the idea of the theatricality in life, how it is mirrored on the stage, and how life mirrors the theatricality of the stage. However, in *Antony and Cleopatra* she feels that "shadows, dreams, the actor and the play . . . are all degraded in the tragedy" (p. 188). I think the final effect of the tragedy suggests that this is only partially true.

BIBLIOGRAPHY

Ayres, Harry Morgan. "Shakespeare's Julius Caesar," *PMLA*, XXV (June 1910), 183-227.

Baker, Donald C. "The Purging of Cleopatra," *SNL*, X (February 1960), 9.

Barroll, J. Leeds. "Antony and Pleasure," *JEGP*, LVII (October 1958), 708-720.

―――. "Enobarbus' Description of Cleopatra," *TSLL*, XXXVII (1958), 61-78.

Berkeley, David S. "On Oversimplifying Antony," *CE*, XVII (November 1955), 96-99.

Bethell, S. L. *Shakespeare and the Popular Dramatic Tradition*. Durham, N. C.: Duke University Press, 1944.

―――. "Shakespeare's Imagery: The Diabolic Images in *Othello*," *SS*, V (1952), 62-80.

Blisset, William. "The Secret'st Man of Blood. A Study of Dramatic Irony in *Macbeth*," *SQ*, X (Summer 1959), 397-408.

Bloom, Allan D. "A Restatement," *APSR*, LIV (June 1960), 471-473.

―――. "Cosmopolitan Man and the Political Community: An Interpretation of *Othello*," *APSR*, LIV (March 1960), 130-157.

―――. "Political Philosophy and Poetry," *APSR*, LIV (June 1960), 457-464.

Bonjour, Adrien. *The Structure of Julius Caesar*. Liverpool: Liverpool University Press, 1958.

Bradley, A. C. "Antony and Cleopatra," *Oxford Lectures*. London: Macmillan and Co., Ltd., 1909.

―――. *Coriolanus*. British Academy: Second Annual Shakespeare Lecture. London: Oxford University Press, 1912.

―――. *Shakespearean Tragedy*. London: Macmillan and Co., Ltd., 1932.

Breyer, Bernard R. "A New Look at *Julius Caesar*," *Essays in Honor of Walter Clyde Curry*: Vanderbilt Studies in the Humanities, II. Nashville, Tenn.: Vanderbilt University Press, 1954, pp. 161-180.

Brittin, Norman A. "Coriolanus, Alceste, and Dramatic Genres," *PMLA*, LXXI (September 1956), 799-807.

Burckhardt, Sigurd. "English Bards and *APSR* Reviewers," *APSR*, LIV (March 1960), 158-166.

——. "On Reading Ordinary Prose," *APSR*, LIV (June 1960), 465-470.

——. "The King's Language: Shakespeare's Drama as Social Discovery," *AR*, XXI (Fall 1961), 369-387.

Burke, Kenneth. *A Grammar of Motives*. New York: Prentice-Hall, Inc., 1945.

——. "*Othello*: An Essay to Illustrate a Method," *HR*, IV (Summer 1951), 165-203.

Campbell, Lily B. *Shakespeare's Tragic Heroes*. Cambridge: At the University Press, 1930.

Campbell, O. J. *Shakespeare's Satire*. London: Oxford University Press, 1943.

Charlton, H. B. *Shakespearean Tragedy*. Cambridge: At the University Press, 1952.

Charney, Maurice. *Shakespeare's Roman Plays*. Cambridge, Mass.: Harvard University Press, 1961.

——. "Shakespeare's Style in *Julius Caesar* and *Antony and Cleopatra*," *ELH*, XXVI (September 1959), 355-367.

Coleridge, Samuel Taylor. *Lectures and Notes on Shakespeare*. London: G. Bell & Sons, 1897.

Croce, Benedetto. "Aesthetics," *Encyclopaedia Britannica*. 14th edition. I, 263-272.

Cunningham, Dolora G. "The Characterization of Shakespeare's Cleopatra," *SQ*, VI (Winter 1955), 9-17.

——. "*Macbeth*: The Tragedy of the Hardened Heart," *SQ*, XIV (Winter 1963), 39-47.

Danby, John F. *Poets on Fortune's Hill*. London: Faber & Faber, 1952.

——. *Shakespeare's Doctrine of Nature: A Study of King Lear*. London: Faber & Faber, 1949.

Dickey, F. N. *Not Wisely But Too Well*. San Marino, Calif.: The Huntington Library, 1957.

Draper, John W. "Shakespeare's Coriolanus: A Study in Renaissance Psychology," *WVUB*, III (September 1939), 22-36.

Dyson, Peter. "The Structural Function of the Banquet Scene in *Macbeth*," *SQ*, XIV (Autumn 1963), 369-378.

Eliot, T. S. *Selected Essays*. New York: Harcourt, Brace & Co., 1932.

Elliot, G. R. *Flaming Minister*. Durham, N. C.: Duke University Press, 1953.

Ellis-Fermor, Una. "The Nature of Plot in Drama," English Association *Essays and Studies*, XIII (1960), 65-81.

————. General ed. *The New Arden Shakespeare*. 21 vols. London: Methuen and Co., Ltd.; Cambridge, Mass.: Harvard University Press, 1951-1962.

————. *Shakespeare the Dramatist*: Annual Shakespeare Lecture of the British Academy. London: Geoffrey Cumberlege, 1948.

Farnham, Willard. *Shakespeare's Tragic Frontier*. Berkeley: University of California Press, 1950.

Foakes, R. A. "An Approach to *Julius Caesar*," *SQ*, V (Fall 1954), 259-270.

Furness, H. H., ed. *A New Variorum Shakespeare*. 32 vols. Philadelphia: J. B. Lippincott & Co., 1871-1956.

Galloway, David. "I Am Dying, Egypt, Dying," *N&Q*, CIII (August 1958), 330-355.

Granville-Barker, Harley. *Prefaces to Shakespeare*. 2 vols. Princeton, N.J.: Princeton University Press, 1947 and 1951.

Grill, Cynthia. "Antony, Cleopatra, and Proculeius," *N&Q*, new series, VII (January 1960), 191.

Hazlitt, William. *Characters of Shakespeare's Plays*. London: Printed by C. H. Reynell for R. Hunter, 1817.

Heilman, Robert B. *Magic in the Web*. Lexington, Ky.: University of Kentucky Press, 1956.

Holloway, John. *The Story of the Night*. London: Routledge and Kegan Paul, 1961.

Honig, Edwin. "Sejanus and Coriolanus: A Study in Alienation," *MLQ*, XII (December 1951), 407-421.

Hudson, H. N. *Shakespeare: His Life, Art and Characters.* 2 vols. New York: Ginn & Co., 1872.

Jenkins, Bernard. *"Antony and Cleopatra:* Some Suggestions on the Monument Scenes," *RES,* XXI (January 1945), 1-14.

Jones, Eldred D. "The Machiavel and the Moor," *EIC,* X (April 1960), 234-238.

Jorgensen, P. A. " 'Perplex'd in the Extreme': The Role of Thought in *Othello,*" *SQ,* XV (Spring 1964), 265-275.

Kirschbaum, Leo. *Character and Characterization in Shakespeare.* Detroit: Wayne State University Press, 1962.

———. "Shakespeare's Cleopatra," *SAB,* XIX (October 1944), 161-171.

———. "Shakespeare's Stage Blood," *PMLA,* LXIV (June 1949), 517-529.

Knight, G. Wilson. *The Imperial Theme.* London: Oxford University Press, 1939.

———. *The Wheel of Fire.* London: Methuen & Co., Ltd., 1949.

Knights, L. C. "Shakespeare and Political Wisdom," *SR,* LXI (Winter 1953), 43-55.

———. *Shakespeare's Politics: With Some Reflections on the Nature of Tradition*: Annual Shakespeare Lecture of the British Academy. London: Oxford University Press, 1957. Pp. 115-132.

———. *Some Shakespearean Themes.* London: Chatto & Windus, 1959.

Langer, Susanne K. *Philosophy in a New Key.* Cambridge, Mass.: Harvard University Press, 1960.

Lawlor, John. *The Tragic Sense in Shakespeare.* London: Chatto & Windus, 1960.

Leavis, F. R. "Diabolic Intellect and the Noble Hero: A Note on Othello," *Scrutiny,* VI (December 1937), 259-283.

Lees, F. N. "Coriolanus, Aristotle, and Bacon," *RES,* new series, I (April 1950), 114-125.

Lerner, Laurence. "The Machiavel and the Moor," *EIC*, IX (October 1959), 339-360.

Lewis, Wyndham. *The Lion and the Fox*. New York: Harper & Bros., n.d.

Lloyd, Michael. "Cleopatra as Isis," *SS*, XII (1959), 88-94.

MacCallum, M. W. *Shakespeare's Roman Plays and Their Backgrounds*. London: Macmillan & Co. Ltd., 1925.

Mills, L. J. "Cleopatra's Tragedy," *SQ*, XI (Spring 1960), 147-162.

Neilson, W. A. and C. J. Hill, eds. *The Complete Plays and Poems of William Shakespeare*. Cambridge, Mass.: The Riverside Press of Houghton Mifflin Co., 1942.

Norman, Arthur M. Z. "Daniel's *Tragedie of Cleopatra* and *Antony and Cleopatra*," *SQ*, IX (Winter 1958), 11-18.

Nowottny, Winifred M. T. "Justice and Love in *Othello*," *UTQ*, XXI (July 1952), 330-344.

Palmer, John. *Political Characters of Shakespeare*. London: Macmillan & Co. Ltd., 1945.

Phillips, James E. Jr. *The State in Shakespeare's Greek and Roman Plays*. New York: Columbia University Press, 1940.

Prior, Moody. "Character in Relation to Action in *Othello*," *MP*, XLIV (February 1947), 225-237.

Raymond, William O. "Motivation and Character Portrayal in *Othello*," *UTQ*, XVII (October 1947), 80-96.

Raysor, Thomas M., ed. *Coleridge's Shakespearean Criticism*. 2 vols. Cambridge, Mass.: Harvard University Press, 1930.

Rees, Joan. " 'Julius Caesar'—An Earlier Play, and an Interpretation," *MLR*, L (April 1955), 135-141.

Ribner, Irving. *Patterns in Shakespearian Tragedy*. London: Methuen & Co., Ltd., 1960.

———. "Political Issues in *Julius Caesar*," *JEGP*, LVI (January 1957), 10-22.

Righter, Anne. *Shakespeare and the Idea of the Play*. London: Chatto & Windus, 1962.

BIBLIOGRAPHY

Rosen, William. *Shakespeare and the Craft of Tragedy.* Cambridge, Mass.: Harvard University Press, 1960.

Rosenberg, Marvin. *The Masks of Othello.* Berkeley and Los Angeles: University of California Press, 1961.

Rossetti, R. M. "A Crux and No Crux," *SQ,* XIII (Summer 1962), 299-303.

Rossiter, A. P. *Angel With Horns and Other Shakespeare Lectures,* ed. Graham Storey. London: Longman's, Green & Co., Ltd., 1961.

Schanzer, Ernest. "The Problem of *Julius Caesar,*" *SQ,* VI (Summer 1955), 297-308.

——. "The Tragedy of Shakespeare's Brutus," *ELH,* XXII (March 1955), 1-15.

Schucking, Levin L. *Character Problems in Shakespeare's Plays.* New York: Henry Holt & Co., 1922.

Sewell, Arthur. *Character and Society in Shakespeare.* Oxford: At the Clarendon Press, 1951.

Siegel, Paul N. *Shakespearean Tragedy and the Elizabethan Compromise.* New York: New York University Press, 1957.

Smith, Gordon R. "Brutus, Virtue, and Will," *SQ,* X (Summer 1959), 367-379.

Speaight, Robert. *Nature in Shakespearean Tragedy.* London: Hollis & Carter, 1955.

Spencer, Benjamin T. "*Antony and Cleopatra* and the Paradoxical Metaphor," *SQ,* IX (Summer 1958), 373-378.

Spencer, Hazelton. *The Art and Life of William Shakespeare.* New York: Harcourt, Brace & Co., 1940.

Spencer, Theodore. *Shakespeare and the Nature of Man.* New York: The Macmillan Co., 1942.

Stein, Arnold. "Macbeth and Word-Magic," *SR,* LIX (Spring 1951), 271-284.

——. "The Image of Antony: Lyric and Tragic Imagination," *KR,* XXI (Autumn 1959), 586-606.

Stempel, Daniel. "The Transmigration of the Crocodile," *SQ,* VII (Winter 1956), 59-72.

Stirling, Brents. "Cleopatra's Scene With Seleucus," *SQ,* XV (Spring 1964), 299-311.

———. "*Julius Caesar* in Revision," *SQ*, XIII (Spring 1962), 187-205.

———. *Unity in Shakespearean Tragedy*. New York: Columbia University Press, 1956.

Stoll, E. E. *Art and Artifice in Shakespeare*. New York: Barnes & Noble, 1933.

———. "*Othello*: An Historical and Comparative Study," *University of Minnesota Studies in Language and Literature*, No. 2 (March 1915), 1-70.

———. *Shakespeare and Other Masters*. Cambridge, Mass.: Harvard University Press, 1940.

Strauss, Anselm. *Mirrors and Masks*. Glencoe, Ill.: The Free Press of Glencoe, Ill., 1959.

Stroup, T. B. "The Structure of *Antony and Cleopatra*," *SQ*, XV (Spring 1964), 289-298.

Thomas, Mary Olive. "The Repetitions in Antony's Death Scene," *SQ*, IX (Spring 1958), 153-157.

Traversi, Derek. *An Approach to Shakespeare*. 2nd edition. New York: Doubleday & Co., 1956. Copyright: Sands & Company, Ltd.

———. "Coriolanus," *Scrutiny*, VI (June 1937), 43-58.

Uhler, J. E. "*Julius Caesar*—A Morality of Respublica," *Studies in Shakespeare*, eds. A. D. Matthews and C. M. Emery. Coral Gables, Fla.: University of Miami Press, 1953. Pp. 96-106.

Van Doren, Mark. *Shakespeare*. Garden City, N. Y.; Doubleday & Co., 1939.

Waith, Eugene M. "Manhood and Valor in Two Shakespearean Tragedies," *ELH*, XVII (December 1950), 262-273.

Whitaker, Virgil K. *Shakespeare's Use of Learning*. San Marino, Calif.: The Huntington Library, 1953.

Wilson, Dover, ed. *The Works of Shakespeare*. 33 vols. Cambridge: At the University Press, 1921-1960.

INDEX

"abstract words" in *Othello*, 115-18, 120, 126

"acting" and "action" in *Othello*, 135

"actor" or "theater" image in *Julius Caesar*, 11, 38

Agrippa, 198, 214-15

Alexas, 190

animal imagery: in *Coriolanus*, 136-37, 144, 152; in *Othello*, 123-25, 128, 134

Antony and Cleopatra, 171-235; art in, 8, 182, 233-35; as "test" of drama, 223-24; as "test" of heroic possibility, 189; as "test" of imagination, 223-24; as "test" of tragedy, 215-16, 223-24; "barge" speech, 175, 197-99; comedy in, 179, 189-92, 206, 208-9, 211, 216-17, 225-28, 234

    compared with *Coriolanus*, 169; compared with *Julius Caesar*, 175-76; compared with *Othello*, 172-73; "dreams," 178-81, 217, 222-24, 235; eating imagery, 184, 196-97, 199-200, 228-29; heroic image, 7, 182-84, 185-88, 194, 200-202, 204-14; "hyperbolical" style, 175-76; imagination, 6, 176, 177, 181-82, 205, 213-14, 216-17, 221-25, 230-35; lies, words, and role playing, 222-23, 235; nature, 182, 198-99, 205, 216-17, 232-35; perspective on reality, 224-25; perspectives on characters, 174; poetic magnification in, 7, 177-82, 194, 213-14, 217, 222-26, 230-35; poetry of, 171-72, 174-78; poetry versus character and action, 174-78, 181-82; poetry versus "prosaic" reality, 174-82; policy, 216-17, 221, 225, 234; policy and nature, 205;

political order, 7, 234; "prosaic" policy versus poetic imagination, 218, 221-23, 231-32, 234; reason, 199; "reduction," 7, 178, 182, 189-94, 200, 203-209, 211-12; Seleucus incident, 218-22; short review of critical attitudes, 171-76; "stock comment" on Antony's death, 214-15; structure, 171-74, 189; subterfuge and betrayal, 175, 217-22, 225, 231, 232, 234; "theatrics," 8, 189-94, 213, 217, 222-35; traditional views of conflict, 174-75; "transformation" scene, 225-35; unifying action, 183

Antony (*Antony and Cleopatra*): as Mars, 201; as "mocked" tragic hero, 206-13; compared with Brutus, 208; compared with Macbeth, 72; death and the element of supernatural foreshadowing as compared to Julius Caesar's, 214; decision to return to Egypt, 186-88, 221; denigration of Cleopatra, 196-97; emasculation, 206; heroic self-image, 7, 182-83, 185-88, 194, 200-202, 204-14; heroism, 234; honor, 188, 191-93; image of the lover, 200-202, 207, 209; image as soldier, 184-86, 188; last speech compared to Lear's, 212; last speech compared to Othello's, 212; marriage to Octavia, 186; military self-image, 200-202, 206-207. *See also* heroic self-image; poetic and prosaic elements, 175-79, 181-82; reduction (active) by Cleopatra, 200, 203-209, 211; reduction (verbal) by Cleopatra, 7, 178, 182, 189-94, 211-12; reputation, 185-88, 205; self-fulfill-